DEVELOPMENT OF

Muslim Theology, Jurisprudence and Constitutional Theory

BY

DUNCAN B. MACDONALD, M.A., B.D.

SOMETIME SCHOLAR AND FELLOW OF THE
UNIVERSITY OF GLASGOW;

PROFESSOR OF SEMITIC LANGUAGES IN HARTFORD
THEOLOGICAL SEMINARY

[1903]

Reprint

[2011]

ZuuBooks specialize in offering rare printed and ebooks for affordable prices. For more information on our products and services for authors please contact us at ilifeebooks@gmail.com

This has been a ZuuBooks.com Publication. For New and Classic titles in Audiobooks, ebooks, and Paperback please visit us at www.zuuBooks.com Authors who are interested in publishing and distributing their works can contact us at ilifeebooks@gmail.com

DEVELOPMENT OF

Muslim Theology, Jurisprudence and Constitutional Theory

BY

DUNCAN B. MACDONALD, M.A., B.D.

INTRODUCTION

PART I
CONSTITUTIONAL DEVELOPMENT

CHAPTER I
FROM DEATH OF MUHAMMAD TO RISE OF ABBASIDS

CHAPTER II
TO RISE OF AYYUBIDS

CHAPTER III
TO PRESENT SITUATION

PART II
DEVELOPMENT OF JURISPRUDENCE

CHAPTER I
TO CLOSE OF UMAYYAD PERIOD

CHAPTER II
TO PRESENT SITUATION

PART III
DEVELOPMENT OF THEOLOGY

CHAPTER I

TO CLOSE OF UMAYYAD PERIOD

CHAPTER II
TO FOUNDATION OF FATIMID KHALIFATE

CHAPTER III
TO TRIUMPH OF ASH'ARITES IN EAST

CONTENTS

ERRATA

Page 30, line 5, for al-Mukanna read al-Muqanna.

"86, l. 19, for first Khalifa read second Khalifa.

"201, l. 26, for tasalsal read tasalsal.

"237, for Mansell read Mansel.

"267, l. 30, for Haqqari read Hakkari.

"299, l. 10, for Mushriqs read Mushriks.

"300, l. 4, for kalimatan ash-shahada read kalimata-sh-shahada.

"325, l. 23, for wihdaniya read wahdaniya.

"339, I. 11, for ihtiyaz read ihtiyaj.

PREFACE

It is with very great diffidence that I send out this book. Of the lack and need of some text-book of the kind there can be little doubt. From the educated man who wishes to read with intelligence his "Arabian Nights" to the student of history or of law or of theology who wishes to know how it has gone in such matters with the great Muslim world, there is demand enough and to spare. Still graver is the difficulty for the growing body of young men who are taking up the study of Arabic. In English or German or French there is no book to which a teacher may send his pupils for brief guidance on the development of these institutions; on the development of law there are only scattered and fragmentary papers, and on the development of theology there is practically nothing. But of the difficulty of supplying this need there can be even less doubt. Goldziher could do it fully and completely; no other Arabist alive could approach the task other than with trepidation. The following pages therefore form a kind of forlorn attempt, a rushing in on the part of one who is sure he is not an angel and is in grave doubt on the question of folly, but who also sees a gap and no great alacrity on the part of his betters toward filling it. One thing, however, I would premise with emphasis. All the results given here have been reached or verified from the Arabic sources. These sources are seldom stated either in the text or in the bibliography, as the book is intended to be useful to non-Arabists, but, throughout, they lie behind it and are its basis. By this it is not meant that the results of this book are claimed as original. Every Arabist will recognize at once from whose wells I have drawn and who have been my masters. Among these I would do homage in the first instance to Goldziher; what Arabist is not deep in his debt? With Goldziher's influence through books I would join the kindred influence of the living voice of my teacher Sachau. To him I render thanks and reverence now for his kindly sympathy and guidance. Others in whose debt I am are Nöldeke, Snouck Hurgronje, von Kremer, Lane--many more. Those who are left of these will know their own in my pages and will be merciful to my attempts to tread in their steps and to develop their results. What is my own, too, they will know; into questions of priority I have no desire to enter. Foot-notes which might have given to each scholar his due have been left unwritten. For the readers of this book such references in so vast a subject would be use., less. Such references, too, would have in the end be made to Arabic sources.

More direct help I have to acknowledge on several sides. To the atmosphere and scholarly ideals of Hartford Seminary I am indebted for the possibility of writing such a book as this, so far from the ordinary theological ruts. Among my colleagues Professor Gillett has especially aided me with criticism and suggestions on the terminology of scholastic theology. Dr. Talcott Williams, of Philadelphia, illumined for me the Idrisid movement in North Africa. One

[6]

complete sentence on p. 85 I have conveyed from a kindly notice in The Nation of my inaugural lecture on the development of Muslim Jurisprudence. Finally, and above all, I am indebted to my wife for much patient labor in copying and for keen and luminous criticism in planning and correcting. With thanks to her this preface may fitly close.

DUNCAN B. MACDONALD.

HARTFORD, December, 1902.

*** As it has proved impracticable to give in the body of the book a full transliteration of names and technical terms, the learner is referred for such exact forms to the chronological table and the index. In these hamza and ayn, the long vowels and the emphatic consonants are uniformly represented, the last by italic.

DEVELOPMENT OF

MUSLIM THEOLOGY, JURISPRUDENCE,

AND CONSTITUTIONAL THEORY

INTRODUCTION

IN human progress unity and complexity are the two correlatives forming together the great paradox. Life is manifold, but it is also one. So it is seldom possible, and still more seldom advisable, to divide a civilization into departments and to attempt to trace their separate developments; life nowhere can be cut in two with a hatchet. And this is emphatically true of the civilization of Islam. Its intellectual unity, for good and for evil, is its outstanding quality. It may have solved the problem of faith and science, as some hold; it may have crushed all thought which is not of faith, as many others hold. However that may be, its life and thought are a unity.

So, also, with its institutions. It might be possible to trace the developments of the European states out of the dying Roman Empire, even to watch the patrimony of the Church grow and again vanish, and yet take but little if any account of the Catholic theology. It might be possible to deal adequately with the growth of that system of theology and yet never touch either the Roman or the civil law, even to leave out of our view the canon law itself. In Europe the State may rule the Church, or the Church may rule the State; or they may stand side by side in somewhat dubious amity, supposedly taking no account each of the other. But in Muslim countries, Church and State are one indissolubly, and until the very essence of Islam passes away, that unity cannot be relaxed. The law of the land, too, is, in theory, the law of the Church. In the earlier days at least, canon and civil law were one. Thus we can never say in Islam, "he is a great lawyer; he, a great theologian; he, a great statesman." One man may be all three, almost he must be all three, if he is to be any one. The statesman may not practice theology or law, but his training, in great part, will be that of a theologian and a legist. The theologian-legist may not be a man of action, but he will be a court of ultimate appeal on the theory of the state. He will pass upon treaties; decide disputed successions; assign to each his due rank and title. He will tell the Commander of the Faithful himself what he may do and what, by law, lies beyond his reach.

It was, then, under the pressure of necessity only that the following sketch of the development of Muslim thought was divided into three parts. By no possible arrangement did it seem feasible to treat .the whole at once. Intolerable confusions and unintelligible complications would, to all appearance, be the result. As the most concrete and simple side, the development of the state is taken first. Second, on account of the shortness of the course which it ran, comes the development of the legal ideas and schools. Third comes the long and thrice complicated thread of theological thought. It is for the student to hold firmly in mind that this division is purely mechanical and for convenience only; that it corresponds to little or nothing in the real nature of the case. This will undoubtedly become clear to him as he proceeds. He will meet with the same names in all three divisions; he will meet with the same technicalities and the same scholastic system. A treatise on canon law is certainly different from one on theology, but each touches the other at innumerable points; their authors may easily be the same; each will be in great part unintelligible without the other. He must then labor to merge these three sections again into one another. His principal helps in this, along with diligent parallel reading, will be the chronological table and the index. In the table he will watch the succession of men and events grouped from all the three sections; from the index he will trace the activities of each man in these different spheres. The index, too, will give him the technical terms and he will observe their recurrence in historical, legal, and theological theory. Further, it will serve him as a vocabulary when he comes to read technical texts.

But, again, another warning is necessary. The sketch given here is incomplete, not only in details but in the ground that it covers. Important phases of Muslim law, theology, and state theory are of necessity passed over entirely. Thus Babism is not touched at all and the Shi'ite theology and law hardly at all. The Ibadite systems have the merest mention and Turkish and Persian mysticism are equally neglected. For such weighty organizations the Darwish Fraternities are most inadequately dealt with, and Muslim missionary enterprise might well be treated at length. Guidance on these and other points the student will seek in the bibliography. It, too, makes no pretence to completeness and consists of selected titles only. But it will serve at least as an introduction and clew to an exceedingly wide field. And it may be well to state here, in so many words, that no work can be done in this field without a reading knowledge of French and German, and no satisfactory work without some knowledge of Arabic.

And, again, this sketch is incomplete because the development of Islam is not yet over. If, as some say, the faith of Muhammad is a cul-de-sac, it is certainly a very long one; off it many courts and doors open; down it many peoples are still wandering. It is a faith, too, which brings us into touching distance with the great controversies of our own day. We see in it, as in a somewhat distorted mirror, the history of our own past. But we do not yet see its end, even as the end of Christianity is not yet in sight. It is for the student, then, to remember that Islam is a present reality and the Muslim faith a living organism, knowledge of whose laws may be of life or death for us who are in another camp. For there can be little doubt that the three antagonistic and militant civilizations of the world are those of Christendom, Islam, and China. When these are unified, or come to a mutual understanding, then, and only then, will the cause of civilization be secure. To aid some little to the understanding of Islam among us is the object of this book.

PART I

Constitutional Development

CHAPTER I

The death of Muhammad and the problem of the succession; the parties; families of Hashimids, Umayyads and Abbasids; election of Abu Bakr; nomination of Umar; his constitution; election of Uthman; Umayyads in power; murder of Uthman; origin of Shi'ites; election of Ali; civil war; Mu'awiya first Umayyad; origin of Kharijites; their revolts; Ibadites; development of Shi'ites; al-Husayn at Karbala; different Shi'ite constitutional theories; doctrine of the hidden Imam; revolts against Umayyads; rise of Abbasids; Umayyads of Cordova.

WITH the death of Muhammad at al-Madina in the year 11 of the Hijra (A.D. 632), the community of Islam stood face to face with three great questions. Of the existence of one they were conscious, at least in its immediate form; the others lay still for their consciousness in the future. The necessity was upon them to choose a leader to take the place of the Prophet of God, and thus to fix for all time what was to be the nature of the Muslim state. Muhammad had appointed no Joshua; unlike Moses he had died and given no guidance as to the man who should take up and carry on his work. If we can imagine the people of Israel left thus helpless on the other side of the Jordan with the course of conquest that they must pursue opening before them, we shall have a tolerably exact idea of the situation in Islam when Muhammad dropped the reins. Certainly, the people of Islam had little conception of what was involved in the great precedent that they were about to establish, but, nevertheless, there lies here, in the first elective council which they called, the beginning of all the confusions, rivalries, and uncertainties that were to limit and finally to destroy the succession of the Commanders of the Faithful.

Muhammad had ruled as an absolute monarch--a Prophet of God in his own right. He had no son; though had he left such issue it is not probable that it would have affected the direct result. Of Moses's son we hear nothing till long afterward, and then under very suspicious circumstances. The old free spirit of the Arabs was too strong, and as in the Ignorance (al-jalailiya), as they called the pre-Muslim age, the tribes had chosen from time to time their chiefs, so it was now fixed that in Islam the leader was to be elected by the people. But wherever there is an election, there there are parties; and this was no exception. Of such parties we may reckon roughly four. There were the Early Believers, who had suffered with Muhammad at Mecca, accompanied him to al-Madina and had fought at his side through all the Muslim campaigns. These were called Muhajirs, because they had made with him the Hijra or migration to al-Madina. Then there was the party of the citizens of al-Madina, who had invited him to come to them and had promised him allegiance. These were called Ansar or Helpers. Eventually we shall find these two factions growing together and forming the one party of the old original believers and Companions of Muhammad (sahibs, i.e., all those who came in contact with the Prophet as believers and who died in Islam), but at the first they stood apart and there was much jealousy between them. Then, in the third place, there was the party of recent converts who had only embraced Islam at the latest moment when Mecca was captured by Muhammad, and no other way of escape for them was open. They were the aristocratic party of Mecca and had fought the new faith to the last. Thus they were but indifferent believers and were regarded by the others with more than suspicion. Their principal family was descended from a certain Umayya, and was therefore called Umayyad. There will be much about this family in the sequel. Then, fourth, there was growing up a party that might be best described as legitimists; their theory was that the leadership belonged to the leader, not because he was elected to it by the Muslim community, but because it was his right. He was appointed to it by God as

[10]

completely as Muhammad had been. This idea developed, it is true, somewhat later, but it developed very rapidly. The times were such as to force it on.

These, then, were the parties of which account must be taken, but before proceeding to individuals in these parties, it will be well to fix some genealogical relationships, so as to be able to trace the family and tribal jealousies and intrigues that were so soon to transfer themselves from the little circle of Mecca and al-Madina and to fight themselves out on the broad field of Muslim history. For, in truth, in the development of no other state have little causes produced such great effects as here. For example, it may be said, broadly and yet truly, that the seclusion of Muslim women, with all its disastrous effects at the present day for a population of two hundred millions, runs back to the fact that A'isha, the fourteen-year-old wife of Muhammad, once lost a necklace under what the gossips of the time thought were suspicious circumstances. As to the point now in hand, it is quite certain that Muslim history for several hundred years was conditioned and motived by the quarrels of Meccan families. The accompanying genealogy will give the necessary starting-point. The mythical ancestor is Quraysh; hence "the Quraysh," or "Quraysh" as a name for the tribe. Within the tribe, the two most important families are those of Hashim and Umayya; their rivalries for the succession of the Prophet fill the first century and a half of Muslim history, and the immediately pre-Islamic history of Mecca is similarly filled with a contest between them as to the guardianship of the Ka'ba and the care of the pilgrims to that sanctuary. Whether this earlier history is real, or a reflection from the later Muslim times, we need not here consider. The next important division is that between the families of al-Abbas and Abu Talib, the uncles of the Prophet. From the one were descended the Abbasids, as whose heir-at-law the Sultan of the Ottoman Empire now claims the Khalifate, and from

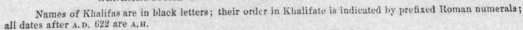
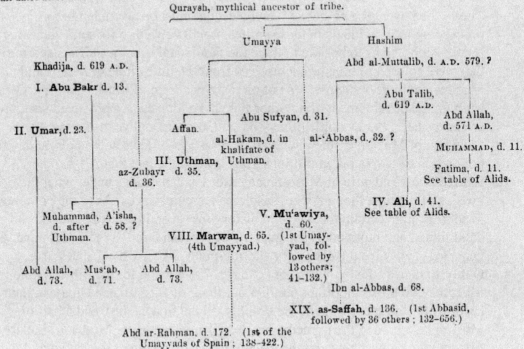

GENEALOGICAL CHART FOR EARLIEST HISTORY OF ISLAM

[12]

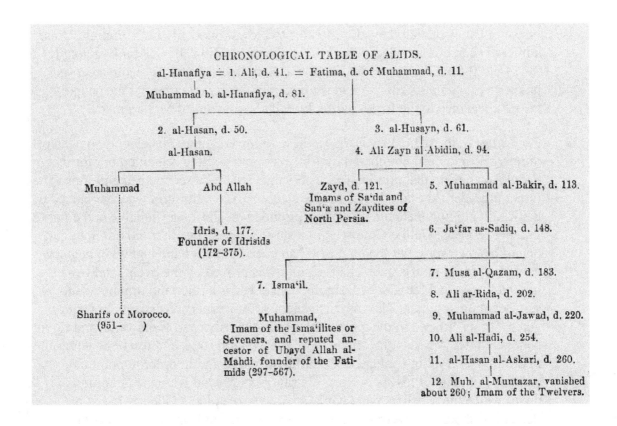

CHRONOLOGICAL TABLE OF ALIDS.

CHRONOLOGICAL CHART OF ALIDS

the other the different conflicting lines of Shi'ites, whose intricacies we shall soon have to face.

To return: in this first elective council the choice fell upon Abu Bakr. He was a man distinguished by his piety and his affection for and close intimacy with Muhammad. He was the father of Muhammad's favorite wife, A'isha, and was some two years younger than his son-in-law. He was, also, one of the earliest believers and it is evident that this, with his advanced age, always respected in Arabia, went far to secure his election. Yet his election did not pass off without a struggle in which the elements that later came to absolute schism and revolution are plainly visible. The scene, as it can be put together from Arabic historians, is curiously suggestive of the methods of modern politics. As soon as it was assured that the Prophet, the hand which had held together all those clashing interests, was really dead, a convention was called of the leaders of the people. There the strife ran so high between the Ansar, the Muhajirs and the Muslim aristocrats of the house of Umayya, that they almost came to blows. Suddenly in the tumult, Umar, a man of character and decision, "rushed the convention" by solemnly giving to Abu Bakr the hand-grasp of fealty. The accomplished fact was recognized--as it has always been in Islam--and on the next day the general mass of the people swore allegiance to the first Khalifa, literally Successor, of Muhammad.

On his death, in A.H. 13 (A.D. 634), there followed Umar. His election passed off quietly. He had been nominated by Abu Bakr and nothing remained but for the people to confirm that nomination. There thus entered a second principle--or rather precedent--beside that of simple election. A certain right was recognized in the Khalifa to nominate his successor, provided he chose one suitable and eligible in other respects. Unlike Cromwell in a similar case, Abu Bakr did not nominate one of his own sons, but the man who had been his right hand and who, he knew, could best build up the state. His foresight was proved by the event, and Umar proved the second founder of Islam by his genius as a ruler and organizer and his self-devotion as a man. Through his generals, Damascus and Jerusalem were taken, Persia crushed in the great battles of al-Qadisiya and Nahawand, and Egypt conquered. He was also the organizer of the Muslim state, and it will be advisable to describe part of his system, both for its own sake and in order to point the contrast with that of his successors. He saw clearly what were the conditions under which the Muslims must work, and devised a plan, evidently based on Persian methods of government, which, for the time at least, was perfect in its way.

The elements in the problem were simple. There was the flood of Arabs pouring out of Arabia and bearing everything down in their course. These must be retained as a conquering instrument if Islam were to exist. Thus they must be prevented from settling down on the rich lands they had seized,--from becoming agriculturists, merchants, and so on, and so losing their identity among other peoples. The whole Arab stock must be preserved as a warrior caste to fight the battles of God. This was secured by a regulation that no new lands should be held by a Muslim. When a country was conquered, the land was left to its previous possessors with the duty of paying a high rent to the Muslim state and, besides, of furnishing fodder and food, clothing and everything necessary to the Muslim camp that guarded them. These camps, or rather camp-cities, were scattered over the conquered countries and were practically settlements of Muslims in partibus infidelium. The duty of these Muslims was to be soldiers only. They were fed and clothed by the state, and the money raid into the public treasury, consisting of plunder or rents of conquered lands (kharaj), or the head-tax on all non-Muslims (jizya), was regularly divided among them and the other believers. If a non-Muslim embraced Islam, then he no longer paid the head-tax, but the land which he had previously held was divided among his former co-religionists, and they

[14]

became responsible to the state. He, on the other hand, received his share of the public moneys as regularly distributed. Within Arabia itself, no non-Muslim was permitted to live. It was preserved, if we may use the expression, as a breeding-ground for defenders of the faith and as a sacred soil not to be polluted by the foot of an unbeliever. It will readily be seen what the results of such a system must have been. The entire Muslim people was retained as a gigantic fighting machine, and the conquered peoples were machines again to furnish it with what was needed. The system was communistic, but in favor of one special caste. The others—the conquered peoples--were crushed to the ground beneath their burdens. Yet they could not sell their land and leave the country; there was no one to buy it. The Muslims would not, and their fellow-coreligionists could not, for with it went the land-tax.

Such was, in its essence, the constitution of Umar, forever famous in Muslim tradition. It stood for a short time, and could not have stood for a long time; but the cause of its overthrow was political and not social-economic. With the next Khalifa and the changes which came with him, it went, in great part, to the ground. The choice of Umar to the Khalifate had evidently been dictated by a consideration of his position as one of the earliest believers and as son-in-law of the Prophet. The party of Early Believers had thus succeeded twice in electing their candidate. But with the death of Umar in A.H. 23 (A.D. 644) the Meccan aristocratic party of the family of Umayya that had so long struggled against Muhammad and had only accepted Islam when their cause was hopelessly lost, had at last a chance. Umar left no directions as to his successor. He seems to have felt no certainty as to the man best fitted to take up the burden, and when his son sought to urge him to name a Khalifa, he is reported to have said, "If I appoint a Khalifa, Abu Bakr appointed a Khalifa; and if I leave the people without guidance, so did the Apostle of God." But there is also a story that after a vain attempt to persuade one of the Companions to permit himself to be nominated, he appointed an elective council of six to make the choice after his death under stringent conditions, which went all to wreck through the pressure of circumstances. The Umayyads succeeded in carrying the election of Uthman, one of their family, an old man and also a son-in-law of Muhammad, who by rare luck for them was an Early Believer. After his election it was soon evident that he was going to rule as an Umayyad and not as a Muslim. For generations back in Mecca, as has already been said, there had been, according to tradition, a continual struggle for pre-eminence between the families of Umayya and of Hashim. In the victory of Muhammad and the election of the first two Khalifas, the house of Hashim had conquered, but it had been the constant labor of the conquerors to remove all tribal and family distinctions and frictions and to bring the whole body of the Arabs to regard one another as brother Muslims. Now, with a Khalifa of the house of Umayya, all that was swept away, and it was evident that Uthman--a pious, weak man, in the hands of his energetic kinsfolk--was drifting to a point where the state would not exist for the Muslims but for the Umayyads. His evil spirit was his cousin Marwan ibn al-Hakam, whom he had appointed as his secretary and who eventually became fourth Umayyad Khalifa. The father of this man, al-Hakam ibn al-As, accepted Islam at the last moment when Mecca was captured, and, thereafter, was banished by Muhammad for treachery. Not till the reign of Uthman was he permitted to return, and his son, born after the Hijra, was the most active assertor of Umayyad claims. Under steady family pressure, Uthman removed the governors of provinces who had suffered with Muhammad and fought in the Path of God (sabil Allah), and put in their places his own relations, late embracers of the faith. He broke through the Constitution of Umar and gifted away great tracts of state lands. The feeling spread abroad that in the eyes of the Khalifa an Umayyad could do no wrong, and the Umayyads themselves were not backward in affording examples. To the Muhajirs and Ansar they were godless heathen, and probably the Muhajirs and Ansar were right. Finally, the indignation could no longer be restrained. Insurrections broke out in the camp-cities of al-Kufa and al-Basra, and in those of Egypt and at last in al-Madina itself. There, in A.H. 35 (A.D. 655), Uthman fell under the daggers of conspirators led by a Muhammad, a son of Abu Bakr, but a religious fanatic strangely different from his father, and the train was laid for a long civil war. In the confusion that followed the deed the chance of the legitimist party had come, and Ali, the cousin and son-in-law of the Prophet, was chosen.

Fortunately this is not a history of Islam, but of Muslim political institutions, and it is, therefore, unnecessary to go into the manifold and contradictory stories told of the events of this time. These have evidently been carefully redacted in the interests of later orthodoxy, and to protect the character of men whose descendants later came to power. The Alids built up in favor of Ali a highly ingenious but flatly fictitious narrative, embracing the whole early history and exhibiting him as the true Khalifa kept from his rights by one after the other of the first three, and suffering it all with angelic patience. This varies from the extreme Shi'ite position, which damns all the three at a sweep as usurpers, through a more moderate one which contents itself with cursing Umar and Uthman, to a rejection of Uthman only, and even, at the other extreme, satisfies itself with anathematizing the later Umayyads. At this point the Shi'ites join hands with the body of orthodox believers, who are all sectaries of Ali to a certain degree. Yet this tendency has been counteracted to some extent by a strongly catholic and irenic spirit which manifests itself in Islam. After a controversy is over and the figures in it have faded into the past, Islam casts a still deeper veil over the controversy itself and glorifies the actors on both sides into fathers and doctors of

[16]

the Church. An attempt is made to forget that they had fought one another so bitterly, and to hold to the fact only that they were brother Muslims. The Shi'ites well so-called, for Shi'a means sect, have never accepted this; but it is the usage of orthodox, commonly called Sunnite, Islam. A concrete expression of any result reached by the body of the believers then often takes the form of a tradition assigned to Muhammad. In this case, it is a saying of his that ten men, specified by name and prominent leaders in these early squabbles, were certain of Paradise. It has further become an article in Muslim creeds, that the Companions of the Prophet are not to be mentioned save with praise; and one school of theologians, in their zeal for the historic Khalifate, even forbade the cursing of Yazid, the slayer of al-Husayn (p. 28 below), and reckoned as the worst of all the Umayyads, because he had been a Khalifa in full and regular standing. This catholic recognition of the unity of Islam we shall meet again and again.

Abandoning, then, any attempt to trace the details and to adjust the rights and wrongs of this story, we return to the fixed fact of the election of Ali and the accession to power of the legitimist party. This legitimist party, or parties, had been gradually developing, and their peculiar and mutually discordant views deserve attention. Those views all glorified Ali, the full cousin of Muhammad and husband of his daughter Fatima, but upon very different grounds. There could not but exist the feeling that a descendant of the Prophet should be his successor, and the children of Ali, al-Hasan and al-Husayn were his only grandchildren and only surviving male descendants. This, of course, reflected a dignity upon Ali, their father, and gave him a claim to the Khalifate. Again, Ali himself seems to have made a great and hardly comprehensible impression upon his contemporaries. The proverb ran with the people, "There is no sword save Dhu-l-faqar, and no youth save Ali." He was not, perhaps, so great a general as one or two others of his time, but he stood alone as a warrior in single combat; he was a poet and an orator, but no statesman. As one of the earliest of the Early Believers, it might be expected that the Muhajirs would support him, and so they did; but the matter went much farther, and he seems to have excited a feeling of personal attachment and devotion different from that rendered to the preceding Khalifas. Strange and mystical doctrines were afloat as to his claim. The idea of election was thrown aside, and his adherents proclaimed his right by the will and appointment of God to the successorship of the Prophet. As God had appointed Muhammad as Prophet, so He had appointed Ali as his helper in life and his successor in death. This was preached in Egypt as early as the year 32.

It will easily be seen that with such a following, uniting so many elements, his election could be brought about. Thus it was; but an evil suspicion rested upon him. Men thought, and probably rightly, that he could have saved the aged Uthman if he had willed, and they even went the length of accusing him of being art and part in the murder itself. The ground was hollow beneath his feet. Further, there were two other old Companions of the Prophet, Talha and az-Zubayr, who thought they had a still better claim to the Khalifate; and they were joined by A'isha, the favorite wife of Muhammad, now, as a finished intrigante, the evil genius of Islam. Ali had reaped all the advantage of the conspiracy and murder, and it was easy to raise against him the cry of revenge for Uthman. Then the civil war began. In the struggle with Talha and az-Zubayr, Ali was victorious. Both fell at the battle of the Camel (A.H. 36), so called from the presence bf A'isha mounted on a camel like a chieftainess of the old days. But a new element was to enter. The governorship of Syria had been held for a long time by Mu'awiya, an Umayyad, and there the Umayyad influence was supreme. There, too, had grown up a spirit of religious indifference, combined with a preservation of all the forms of the faith. Mu'awiya was a statesman by nature, and had moulded his province into an almost independent kingdom. The Syrian army was devoted to him, and could be depended upon to have no other interests than his. From the beginning of Ali's reign, he had been biding his time; had not given his allegiance, but had waited for the hour to strike for revenge for Uthman and power for himself. The time came and Mu'awiya won. We here pass over lightly a long and contradictory story. It is enough to note how the irony of history wrought itself out, and a son of the Abu Sufyan who had done so much to persecute and oppose Muhammad in his early and dark days and had been the last to acknowledge his mission, became his successor and the ruler of his people. But with Ali ends the revered series of the four "Khalifas who followed a right course" (al-khulafa ar-rashidun), reverenced now by all orthodox Muslims, and there begins the division of Islam into sects, religious and political--it comes to the same thing.

The Umayyads themselves clearly recognized that with their accession to power a change had come in the nature of the Muslim state. Mu'awiya said openly that he was the first king in Islam, though he retained and used officially the title of Khalifa and Commander of the Faithful. Yet such a change could not be complete nor could it carry with it the whole people--that is clear of itself. For more than one hundred years the house of Umayya held its own. Syria was solid with it and it was supported by many statesmen and soldiers; but outside of Syria and north Arabia it could count on no part of the population. An anti-Khalifa, Abd Allah, son of the az-Zubayr of whom we have already heard, long held the sacred cities against them. Only in A.H. 75 (A.D. 692) was he killed after Mecca had been stormed and taken by their armies. Southern Arabia and Mesopotamia, with its camp-cities al-Kufa and al-Basra, Persia and Egypt, were, from time to time, more or less in revolt. These risings went in one or other of two directions. There were two great anti-Umayyad sects. At one time in Mu'awiya's contest with Ali, he trapped All into the fatal step of arbitrating his claim to the Khalifate. It was fatal,

[18]

for by it Ali alienated some of his own party and gained less than nothing on the other side. Part of Ali's army seceded in protest and rebellion, because he--the duly elected Khalifa--submitted his claim to any shadow of doubt. ` On the other hand, they could not accept Mu'awiya, for him they regarded as un-duly elected and a mere usurper. Thus they drifted and split into innumerable sub-sects. They were called Kharijites--goers out--because they went out from among the other Muslims, refused to regard them as Muslims and held themselves apart. For centuries they continued a thorn in the side of all established authority. Their principles were absolutely democratic. Their idea of the Khalifate was the old one of the time of Abu Bakr and Umar. The Khalifa was to be elected by the whole Muslim community and could be deposed again at need. He need be of no special family or tribe; he might be a slave, provided he was a good Muslim ruler. Some admitted that a woman might be Khalifa, and others denied the need of any Khalifa at all; the Muslim congregation could rule itself. Their religious views were of a similarly unyielding and antique cast, but with that we have nothing now to do.

It cannot be doubted that these men were the true representatives of the old Islam. They claimed for themselves the heirship to Abu Bakr and Umar, and their claim was just. Islam had been secularized; worldly ambition, fratricidal strife, luxury, and sin had destroyed the old bond of brotherhood. So they drew themselves apart and went their own way, a way which their descendants still follow in Uman, in east Africa, and in Algeria. To them the orthodox Muslims--meaning by that the general body of Muslims--were antipathetic more than even Christians or Jews. These were "people of a book" (ahl kitab), i.e., followers of a revealed religion, and kindly treatment of them was commanded in the Qur'an. They had never embraced Islam, and were to be judged and treated on their own merits. The non-Kharijite Muslims, on the other hand, were renegades (murtadds) and were to be killed at sight. It is easy to understand to what such a view as this led. Numberless revolts, assassinations, plunderings marked their history. Crushed to the ground again and again, again and again they recovered. They were Arabs of the desert; and the desert was always there as a refuge. It is probable, but as yet unproved, that mingled with the political reasons for their existence as a sect went tribal jealousies and frictions; of such there have ever been enough and to spare in Arabia. Naturally, under varying conditions, their views and attitudes varied. In the, wild mountains of Khuzistan, one of their centres and strongholds, the primitive barbarism of their faith had full sway. It drew its legitimate consequence, lived out its life, and vanished from the scene. The more moderate section of the Kharijites centred round al-Basra. Their leader there was Abd Allah ibn Ibad, and from about the year 60 on the schism between his followers and the more absolute of these "come-outers" can be traced. It is characteristic of the

[19]

latter that they aided for a time Abd Allah ibn az-Zubayr when he was besieged in Mecca by the Umayyads, but deserted him finally because he refused to join the names of Talha and his own father, az-Zubayr, with those of Uthman and Ali in a general commination. The Kharijites were all good at cursing, and the later history of this section of them shows a process of disintegration by successive secessions, each departing in protest and cursing those left behind as heathen and unbelievers. Characteristic, too, for the difference between the two sections, were their respective attitudes toward the children of their opponents. The more absolute party held that the children of unbelievers were to be killed with their parents; the followers of Abd Allah ibn Ibad, that they were to be allowed to grow up and then given their choice. Again, there was a difference of opinion as to the standing of those who held with the Kharijites but remained at home and did not actually fight in the Path of God. These the one party rejected and the other accepted. Again, were the non-Kharijites Muslims to the extent that the Kharijites might live amongst them and mix with them? This the severely logical party denied, but Abd Allah ibn Ibad affirmed.

From this it will be abundantly clear that the only party with a possible future was that of Ibn Ibad. His sect survives to the present day under the name of Ibadites. Very early it spread to Uman, and, according to their traditions, their first Imam, or president, was elected about A.H. 134. He was of a family which had reigned there before Islam,. and from the time of his election on, the Ibadites have succeeded in holding Uman against the rest of the Muslim world. Naturally, the election of the Imam by the community has turned into the rule of a series of dynasties; but the theory of election has always held fast. They were sailors, merchants, and colonizers already by the tenth century A.D., and carried their state with its theology and law to Zanzibar and the coast of East Africa generally. Still earlier Ibadite fugitives passed into North Africa, and there thcy still maintain the simplicity of their republican ideal and their primitive theological and legal views. Their home is in the Mzab in the south of Algeria, and, though as traders and capitalists they may travel far, yet they always return thither. Any mingling in marriage with other Muslims is forbidden them.

At the opposite extreme from these in political matters stands the sect that is called the Shi'a. It, as we have seen, is the name given to the party that glorifies Ali and his descendants and regards the Khalifate as belonging to them by right divine. How early this feeling arose we have already seen, but the extremes to which in time the idea was carried, the innumerable differing views that developed, the maze of conspiracies, tortuous and underground in their methods, some in good faith and some in bad, to which it gave rise, render the history of the Shi'a the most difficult side of a knowledge of the Muslim East. Yet some attempt at it must be made. If there was ever a romance in history, it is the story of the

[20]

founding of the Fatimid dynasty in Egypt; if there was ever the survival of a petrifaction in history, it is the survival to the present day of the Assassins and the Druses; if there was ever the persistence of an idea, it is in the present Shi'ite government in Persia and in the faith in that Mahdi for whom the whole world of Islam still looks to appear and bring in the reign of justice and the truth upon the earth. All these have sprung from the devotion to Ali and his children on the part of their followers twelve centuries ago.

In A.H. 40 (A.D. 660) Ali fell by the dagger of a Kharijite. These being at the opposite pole from the Shi'ites, are the only Muslim sect that curses and abhors Ali, his family and all their works. Orthodox Islam reveres Ali and accepts his Khalifate; his family it also reverences, but rejects their pretensions. The instinct of Islam is to respect the accomplished fact, and so even the Umayyads, one and all, stand in the list of the successors of the Prophet, much as Alexander VI and his immediate predecessors do in that of the Popes.

To Ali succeeded his son, al-Hasan, but his name does not stand on the roll of the Khalifate as usually reckoned. It shows some Shi'ite tinge when the historian says, "In the Khalifate of al-Hasan," and, thereafter, proceeds with, "In the days of Mu'awiya," the Umayyad Khalifa who followed him. Mu'awiya had received the allegiance of the Syrian Muslims and when he advanced on al-Kufa, where al-Hasan was, al-Hasan met him and gave over into his hands all his supposed rights. That was in A.H. 41; in A.H. 49 he was dead by poison. Twelve years later al-Husayn, his brother, and many of his house fell at Karbala in battle against hopeless odds. It is this last tragedy that has left the deepest mark of all on the Muslim imagination. Yearly when the fatal day, the day of Ashura, the tenth of the month Muharram, comes round, the story is rehearsed again at Karbala and throughout, indeed, all the Shi'ite world in what is a veritable Passion Play. No Muslim, especially no Persian, can read of the death of al-Husayn, or see it acted before his eyes, without quivering and invoking the curse of God upon all those who had aught to do with it or gained aught by it. That curse has clung fast through all the centuries to the name of Yazid, the Umayyad Khalifa of the time, and only the stiffest theologians of the traditional school have labored to save his memory through the merits of the historical Khalifate. But even after this tragedy it was not out with the blood of Muhammad. Many descendants were left and their party lived on in strange, half underground fashion, as sects do in the East, occasionally coming to the surface and bursting out in wild and, for long, useless rebellion.

In these revolts the Shi'a was worthy of its name, and split into many separate divisions, according to the individuals of the house of Ali to whom allegiance was rendered and who were regarded as leaders, titular or real. These subdivisions

[21]

differed, also, in the principle governing the choice of a leader and in the attitude of the people toward him. Shi'ism, from being a political question, became theological. The position of the Shi'ite was and is that there must be a law (nass) regulating the choice of the Imam, or leader of the Muslim community; that that law is one of the most important dogmas of the faith and cannot have been left by the Prophet to develop itself under the pressure of circumstances; that there is such an Imam clearly pointed out and that it is the duty of the Muslim to seek him out and follow him. Thus there was a party who regarded the leadership as belonging to Ali himself, and then to any of his descendants by any of his wives. These attached themselves especially to his son Muhammad, known from his mother as Muhammad ibn al-Hanafiya, who died in 81, and to his descendants and successors. It was in this sect that the most characteristic Shi'ite views first developed. This Muhammad seems to have been the first concerning whom it was taught, after his death, that he was being preserved by God alive in retirement and would come forth at his appointed time to bring in the rule of righteousness upon the earth. In some of the innumerable sub-sects the doctrine of the deity, even, of Ali was early held, in others a doctrine of metempsychosis, generally among men and especially from one Imam to his successor others, again, advanced the duty of seeking the rightful Imam and rendering allegiance to him till it covered the whole field of faith and morals--no more was required of the believer. To one of these sects, al-Mukanna, "the Veiled Prophet of Khorasan," adhered before he started on his own account.

We have seen already that so early as 32 the doctrine had been preached in Egypt that Ali was the God-appointed successor of the Prophet. Here we have its legitimate development, which was all the quicker as it had, or assumed, a theological basis, and did not simply urge the claims to leadership of the family of the Prophet after the fashion in which inheritance runs among earthly kings. That was the position at first of the other and far more important Shi'ite wing. It regarded the leadership as being in the blood of Muhammad and therefore limited to the children of Ali by his wife Fatima, the daughter of Muhammad. Again, the attitude toward the person of the leader varied, as we have already seen. One party held that the leadership was by the right of the appointment of God, but that the leader himself was simply a man as other men. These would add to "the two words" (al-kalimalani) of the creed, "There is no god but God, and Muhammad is the Apostle of God," a third clause, "and Ali is the representative of God." Others regarded him as an incarnation of divinity; a continuing divine revelation in human form. His soul passed, when he died, to his next successor. He was, therefore, infallible and sinless, and was to be treated with absolute, blind obedience Here there is a mingling of the most strangely varied ideas. In Persia the people had been too long accustomed to looking upon their rulers as divine for them to be capable of taking up any other position. A story is told of the governor of a Persian province who wrote to the Khalifa of his time that he was not able to prevent his people from giving him the style and treatment of a god; they did not understand any other kind of ruler; it was as much as his authority was worth to attempt to make them desist. From this attitude, combined with the idea of the transmigration of souls, the extreme Shi'ite doctrine was derived.

But though the party of Ali might regard the descendants of Ali as semi-divine, yet their conspiracies and revolts were uniformly unsuccessful, and it became a very dangerous thing to head one. The party was willing to get up a rising at any time, but the leader was apt to hang back. In fact, one of the most curious features of the whole movement was the uselessness of the family of Ali and the extent to which they were utilized by others. They have been, in a sense, the cat's-paws of history. Gradually they themselves drew back into retirement and vanished from the stage, and, with their vanishing, a new doctrine arose. It was that of the hidden Imam. We have already seen the case of Muhammad ibn al-Hanafiya, whom Muslims reckon as the first of these concealed ones. Another descendant of Ali, on another line of descent, vanished in the same way in the latter part of the second century of the Hijra, and another about A.H. 260. Their respective followers held that they were being kept in concealment by God and would be brought back at the appointed time to rule over the world and bring in a kind of Muslim millennium. This is the oriental version of the story of Arthur in Avalon and of Frederick Barbarossa in Kyffhaiiser.

But that has led us far away and we must go back to the fall of the Umayyads and the again disappointed hopes of the Alids. By the time of the last Khalifa of the Umayyad house, Marwan II, A.H. 127-132 (A.D. 744-750), the whole empire was more or less in rebellion, partly Shi'ite and partly Kharijite. The Shi'ites themselves had, as usual, no man strong enough to act as leader; that part was taken by as-Saffah, a descendant of al-Abbas, an uncle of Muhammad. The rebellion was ostensibly to bring again into power the family of the Prophet, but under that the Abbasids understood the family of Hashim, while the Alids took it in the more exact sense of themselves. They were made a cat's-paw, the Abbasid dynasty was founded, and they were thrown over. Thus, the Khalifate remained persistently in the hands of those who, up to the last, had been hostile to the Prophet. This al-Abbas had embraced the faith only when Mecca was taken by the Muslims. Later historians, jealous for the good name of the ancestor of the longest line of all the Successors, have labored to build up a legend that al-Abbas stayed in Mecca only because he could there be more useful in the cause of his nephew. This is one of the perversions of early history of which the Muslim chronicles are full. But the story of the Umayyads is not yet out. From the ruin that overwhelmed them, one escaped and fled to North Africa. There, he vainly tried to draw together a power. At last, seeing in Spain some better prospect of success, he crossed thither, and by courage, statesmanship, and patience, carved out a new Umayyad empire that lasted for 300 years. One of his descendants in A.H. 317 (A.D. 929) took the title of Khalifa and claimed the homage due to the Commander of the Faithful. There is story that al-Mansur, the second Abbasid, once asked his courtiers, "Who is the Falcon of Quraysh?" They named one after another of the great men of the tribe, beginning, naturally, with his majesty himself, but to no purpose. "No," he said, "the Falcon of Quraysh is Abd ar-Rahman, the Umayyad, who found his way over deserts and seas, flung himself alone into a strange country, and there, without any helper but himself, built up a realm. There has been none like him of the blood of Quraysh."

CHAPTER II

Shi'ite revolts against Abbasids; Idrisids; Zaydites; Imamites; the Twelvers; constitutional theory of modern Persia; origin of Fatimids; Maymun the oculist; plan of the conspiracy; the Seveners; the Qarmatians; Ubayd Allah al-Mahdi and founding of Fatimid dynasty in North Africa; their spread to Egypt and to Syria; al-Hakim Bi'amrillah; the Druses; the Assassins; Saladin and the Ayyubids.

IT is not in place here to deal with all the numberless little Shi'ite revolts against the Abbasids which now followed. Those only are of interest to us which had more or less permanent effect on the Muslim state and states. Earliest among such comes the revolt which founded the dynasty of the Idrisids. About the middle of the second century the Abbasids were hard pressed. The heavens themselves seemed to mingle in the conflict. The early years of their rule had been marked by great showers of shooting stars, and the end of the age was reckoned near by both parties. Messianic hope was alive, and a Mahdi, a Guided of God, was looked for. This had long been the attitude of the Alids, and the Abbasids began to feel a necessity to gain for their de facto rule the sanction of theocratic hopes. In 143 Halley's comet was visible for twenty days, and in 147 there were again showers of shooting stars. On the part of the Abbasids, homage was solemnly rendered to the eldest son of al-Mansur, the Khalifa of the time, as successor of his father, under the title al-Mahdi, and several sayings were forged and ascribed to the Prophet which told who and what manner of man the Mahdi would be, in terms which clearly pointed to this heir-apparent. The Alids, on their side, were urged on to fresh revolts. These risings were still political in character and hardly at all theological; they expressed the claims to sovereignty of the house of the Prophet. On the suppression of one of them at al-Madina in 169, Idris ibn Abd Allah, a grandson of al-Hasan, escaped to North Africa--that refuge of the politically disaffected--and there at the far-off Volubilis of the Romans, in the modern Morocco, founded a state. It lasted till 375, and planted firmly the authority of the family of Muhammad in the western half of North Africa. Other Alid states rose in its place, and in 961 the dynasty of the Sharifs of Morocco was established by a Muhammad, a descendant of a Muhammad, brother of the same Abd Allah, grandson of al-Hasan. This family still rules in Morocco and claims the title of Khalifa of the Prophet and Commander of the Faithful. Strictly, they are Shi'ites, but their sectarianism sits lightly upon them; it is political only and they have no touch of the violent religious antagonism to the Sunnite Muslims that is to be found in Persian Shi'ism. As adherents of the legal school of Malik ibn Anas, their Sunna is the same as that of orthodox Islam. The Sahih of al-Bukhari (see below, p. 79) is held in especially high reverence, and one division of the Moorish army always carries a copy of it as a talisman. They are really a bit of the second century of the Hijra crystallized and surviving into our time.

Another Shi'ite line which lasts more or less down to the present day, is that of the Zaydites of al-Yaman. They were so called from their adherence to Zayd, a grandson of al-Husayn, and their sect spread in north Persia and south Arabia. The north Persian branch is of little historic importance for our purpose. For some sixty-four years, from 250 on, it held Tabaristan, struck coins and exercised all sovereign rights; then it fell before the Samanids. The other branch has had a much longer history. It was founded about 280, at Sa'da in al-Yaman and there, and later at San'a, Zaydite Imams have ruled off and on till our day. The Turkish hold upon south Arabia has always been of the slightest. Sometimes they have been absolutely expelled from the country, and their control has never extended beyond the limits of their garrisoned posts. The position of these Zaydites was much less extreme than that of the other Shi'ites. They were strictly Fatimites, that is, they held that any descendant of Fatima could be Imam. Further, circumstances might justify the passing over, for a time, of such a legitimate Imam and the election as leader of someone who had no equally good claim. Thus, they reverenced Abu Bakr and Umar and regarded their Khalifate as just, even though Ali was there with a better claim. The election of these two Khalifas had been to the advantage of the Muslim state. Some of them even accepted the Khalifate of Uthman and only denounced his evil deeds. Further, they regarded it as possible that there might be two Imams at the same time, especially when they were in countries widely apart. This, apparently, sprang from the sect being divided between north Persia and south Arabia. Theologically, or philosophically--it is hard to hold the two apart in Islam--the Zaydites were accused of rationalism. Their founder, Zayd, the grandson of al-Husayn, had studied under the great Mu'tazilite, Wasil ibn Ata, of whom much more hereafter.

But if the Zaydites were lax both in their theology and in their theory of the state, that cannot be said of another division of the Shi'ites, called the Imamites on account of the stress which they laid on the doctrine of the person of the Imam.

For them the Imam of the time was explicitly and personally indicated, Ali by Muhammad and each of the others in turn by his predecessor. But it was hard to reconcile with this a priori position that an Imam must have been indicated, the fact that there was no agreement as to the Imam who had been indicated. Down all possible lines of descent the sacred succession was traced until, of the seventy-two sects that the Prophet had foretold for his people, seventy, at least, were occupied by the Imamites alone. Further, the number of Hidden Imams was constantly running up; with every generation, Alids found it convenient to withdraw into retirement and have reports given out of their own deaths. Then two sects would come into existence--one which stopped at the Alid in question, and said that he was being kept in concealment by God to be brought back at His pleasure; and another which passed the Imamship on to the next generation. Out of this chaos two sects, adhering to two series of Imams, stand clear through their historical importance. The one is that of the Twelvers (Ithua'ashariya); theirs is the official creed of modern Persia. About A.H. 260 a certain Muhammad ibn al-Hasan, twelfth in descent from Ali, vanished in the way just described. The sect which looked for his return increased and flourished until, at length, with the conquest of Persia in A.H. 907 (A.D. 1502) by the Safawids--a family of Alid descent which joined arms to sainthood--Persia became Shi'ite, and the series of the Shahs of Persia was begun. The position of the Shah is therefore essentially different from that of the Khalifa of the Sunnites. The Khalifa is the successor of Muhammad, with a dignity and authority which inheres in himself; he is both king and pontiff; the Shah is a mere locum tenens, and reigns only until God is pleased to restore to men the true Imam. That Imam is still in existence, though hidden from human eyes. The Shah, therefore, has strictly no legal authority; he is only a guardian of the public order. True legal authority lies, rather, with the learned doctors of religion and law. As a consequence of this, the Shi'ites still have Mujtahids, divines and legists who have a right to form opinions of their own, can expound the original sources at first hand, and can claim the unquestioning assent of their disciples. Such men have not existed among the Sunnites since the middle of the third century of the Hijra; from that time on all Sunnites have been compelled to swear to the words of some master or other, long dead.

This division of the Shi'ites is the only one that exists in great numbers down to the present day. The second of the two mentioned above came to power earlier, ran a shorter course, and has now vanished from the stage, leaving nothing but an historical mystery and two or three fossilized, half-secret sects--strange survivals which, like the survivals of geology, tell us what were the living and dominant forces in the older world. It will be worth while to enter upon some detail in reciting its history, both for its own romantic interest and as an example of the methods of Shi'ite propaganda. Its success shows how the Abbasid empire was

[26]

gradually undermined and brought to its fall. It itself was the most magnificent conspiracy, or rather fraud, in all history. To understand its possibility and its results, we must hold in mind the nature of the Persian race and the condition of that race at this time. Herodotus was told by his Persian friends that one of the three things Persian youth was taught was to tell the truth. That may have been the case in the time of Herodotus, but certainly this teaching has had no effect whatever on an innate tendency in the opposite direction; and it is just possible that Herodotus's friends, in giving him that information, were giving also an example of this tendency. Travellers have been told curious things before now, but certainly none more curious than this. As we know the Persian in history, he is a born liar. He is, therefore, a born conspirator. He has great quickness of mind, adaptability, and, apart from religious emotion, no conscience. In the third century of the Hijra (the ninth A.D.), the Persians were either devoted Shi'ites or simple unbelievers. The one class would do anything for the descendants of Ali; the other, anything for themselves. This second class, further, would by preference combine doing something for themselves with doing something against Islam and the Arabs, the conquerors of their country. So much by way of premise.

In the early part of this third century, there lived at Jerusalem a Persian oculist named Maymun. He was a man of high education, professional and otherwise; had no beliefs to speak of, and understood the times. He had a son, Abd Allah, and trained him carefully for a career. Abd Allah, however known as Abd Allah ibn Maymun--though he had thought of starting as a prophet himself, saw that the time was not ripe, and planned a larger and more magnificent scheme. This was to be no ordinary conspiracy to burst after a few years or months, but one requiring generations to develop. It was to bring universal dominion to his descendants, and overthrow Islam and the Arab rule. It succeeded in great part, very nearly absolutely.

His plan was to unite all classes and parties in a conspiracy under one head, promising to each individual the things which he considered most desirable. For the Shi'ites, it was to be a Shi'ite conspiracy; for the Kharijites, it took a Kharijite tinge; for Persian nationalists, it was anti-Arab; for free-thinkers, it was frankly nihilistic. Abd Allah himself seems to have been a sceptic of the most refined stamp. The working of this plan was achieved by a system of grades like those in freemasonry. His emissaries went out, settled each in a village and gradually won the confidence of its inhabitants. A marked characteristic of the time was unrest and general hostility to the government. Thus, there was an excellent field for work. To the enormous majority of those involved in it the conspiracy was Shi'ite only, and it has been regarded as such by many of its historians; but it is now tolerably plain how simply nihilistic were its ultimate principles. The first object of the missionary was to excite religious doubt in the mind of his subject, by pointing out curious difficulties and subtle questions in theology. At the same time he hinted that there were those who could answer these questions. If his subject proved tractable and desired to learn further, an oath of secrecy and absolute obedience and a fee were demanded--all quite after the modern fashion. Then he was led up through several grades, gradually shaking his faith in orthodox Islam and its teachers and bringing him to believe in the idea of an Imam, or guide in religious things, till the fourth grade was reached. There the theological system was developed, and Islam, for the first time, absolutely deserted. We have dealt already with the doctrine of the Hidden Imam and with the present-day creed of Persia, that the twelfth in descent from Ali is in hiding and will return when his time comes. But down the same line of descent seven Imams had been reckoned to a certain vanished Isma'il, and this Isma'il was adopted by Abd Allah ibn Maymun as his Imam and as titular head of his conspiracy. Hence, his followers are called Isma'ilians and Seveners (Sab'iya). The story which is told of the split between the Seveners and the Twelvers, which were to be, is characteristic of the whole movement and of the wider divergence of the Seveners from ordinary Islam and its laws. The sixth Imam was Ja'far as-Sadiq (d. A.H. 148); he appointed his son Isma'il as his successor. But Isma'il was found drunk on one occasion, and his father in wrath passed the Imamship on to his brother, Musa al-Qazam, who is accordingly reckoned as seventh Imam by the Twelvers. One party, however, refused to recognize this transfer. Isma'il's drunkenness, they held, was a proof of his greater spirituality of mind; he did not follow the face-value (zahr) of the law, but its hidden meaning (batn). This is an example of a tendency, strong in Shi'ism, to find a higher spiritual meaning lying within the external or verbal form of the law; and in proportion as a sect exalted Ali, so it diverged from literal acceptance of the Qur'an. The most extreme Shi'ites, who tended to deify their Imam, were known on that account as Batinites or Innerites. On this more hereafter.

But to return to the Seveners: in the fourth grade a further refinement was added. Everything went in sevens, the Prophets as well as the Imams. The Prophets had been Adam, Noah, Abraham, Moses, Jesus, Muhammad and Isma'il, or rather his son Muhammad, for Isma'il himself had died in his father's lifetime. Each of these Prophets had had a helper. The helper of Adam had been Seth; of Noah, Shem; and the helper of Muhammad, the son of Isma'il, was Abd Allah ibn Maymun himself. Between each pair of Prophets there came six Imams--it must be remembered that the world was never left without an Imam--but these Imams had had no revelation to make; were only guides to already revealed truth. Thus, we have a series of seven times seven Imams, the first, and thereafter each seventh, having the superior dignity of Prophet. The last of the forty-nine Imams, this Muhammad ibn Isma'il, is the greatest and last of the Prophets, and Abd Allah ibn

[28]

Maymun has to prepare the way for him and to aid him generally. It is at this point that the adherent of this system ceases to be a Muslim. The idea of a series of Prophets is genuinely Islamic, but Muhammad, in Muslim theology, is the last of the Prophets and the greatest, and after him there will come no more.

Such, then, was the system that those who passed the fourth degree learned and accepted. The great majority did not pass beyond; but those who were judged worthy were admitted to three further degrees. In these degrees, their respect for religious teaching of every kind, doctrinal, moral, ritual, was gradually undermined; the Prophets and their works were depreciated and philosophy and philosophers put in their place. The end was to lead the very few who were admitted to the inmost secrets of the conspiracy to the same position as its founder. It is clear what a tremendous weapon, or rather machine, was thus created. Each man was given the amount of light he could bear and which was suited to his prejudices, and he was made to believe that the end of the whole work would be the attaining of what he regarded as most desirable. The missionaries were all things to all men, in the broadest sense, and could work with a Kharijite fanatic, who longed for the days of Umar; a Bedawi Arab, whose only idea was plunder; a Persian driven to wild cries and tears by the thought of the fate of Ali, the well-beloved, and of his sons; a peasant, who did not care for any family or religion but only wished to live in peace and be let alone by the tax-gatherers; a Syrian mystic, who did not know very well what he thought, but lived in a world of dreams; or a materialist, whose desire was to clear all religions out of the way and give humanity a chance. All was fish that came to their net. So the long seed-planting went on. Abd Allah ibn Maymun had to flee to Salamiya in Syria, died there and went to his own place--if he got his deserts, no desirable one--and Ahmad, his son or grandson, took up the work in his stead. With him the movement tends to the surface, and we begin to touch hard facts and dates. In southern Mesopotamia--what is called the Arab Iraq--we find a sect appearing, nicknamed Qarmatians, from one of their leaders. In A.H. 277 (A.D. 890-1) they were sufficiently numerous and knew their strength enough to hold a fortress and thus enter upon open rebellion. They were peasants, we must remember, Nabateans and no Arabs, only Muslims by compulsion, and thus what we have here is really a Jacquerie, or Peasants' War. But a disturbance of any kind suited the Isma'ilians. From there the rising spread into Bahrayn and on to south Arabia, varying in its character with the character of the people.

But there was another still more important development in progress. A missionary had gone to North Africa and there worked with success among the Berber tribes about Constantine, in what is now Algeria. These have always been ready for any change. He gave himself out as forerunner of the Mahdi, promised them the good of both worlds, and called them to arms. The actual rising was in A.H. 269 (A.D.

one of the greatest mysteries that are to be met with in history. In many ways he reminds us curiously of the madness of the Julian house; and, in truth, such a secret movement as that of which he was a part, carried on through generations from father to son, could not but leave a trace on the brain. We must remember that the Khalifa of the time was not always of necessity the head of the conspiracy, or even fully initiated into it. In the latter part of the Fatimid rule we find distinct traces of such a power behind the throne, consisting, as we may imagine, of descendants and pupils of those who had been fully initiated from the first and had passed through all the grades. In the case of al-Hakim, it is possible, even, to trace to a certain extent, the development of his initiation. During the first part of his reign he was fanatically Muslim and Shi'ite. He persecuted alternately the Christians and the Jews, and then the orthodox and the Shi'ites. In the latter part, there was a change. He had, apparently, reached a point of philosophical indifference, for the persecutions of Christians and Jews ceased, and those who had been forced to embrace Islam were permitted to relapse. This last was without parallel, till in 1844 Lord Stratford de Redcliffe wrung from the Porte the concession that a Muslim who apostatized to Christianity should not be put to death. But, mingled with this indifference, there appeared a strange but regular development of Shi'ite doctrine. Some of his followers began to proclaim openly that the deity was incarnate in him, and it was evident that he himself accepted and believed this. But the Egyptian populace would have none of it, and the too rash innovators had to flee. Some went to the Lebanon and there preached to the native mountain tribes. The results of their labors are the Druses of to-day, who worship al-Hakim still and expect his return to introduce the end of all things. Finally, al-Hakim vanished on the night of February 12, A.D. 1021, and left a mystery unread to this day. Whether he was murdered, and if so why, or vanished of free-will, and if so again why, we have no means of telling. Our guess will depend upon our reading of his character. So much is certain, that he was a ruler of the autocratic type, who introduced many reforms, most of which the people of his time could not in the least understand and therefore misrepresented as the mere whims of a tyrant, and many of which, from our ignorance, are still obscure to us. If we can imagine such a man of strong personality and desire for the good of his people but with a touch of madness in the brain, cast thus in the midst between his orthodox subjects and a wholly unbelieving inner government, we shall perhaps have the clew to the strange stories told of him.

Another product of this conspiracy, and the last to which we shall refer, is the sect known as the Assassins, whose Grand Master was a name of terror to the Crusaders as the Old Man of the Mountain. It, too, was founded, and apparently for a purpose of personal vengeance, by a Persian who began as a Shi'ite and ended as nothing. He came to Egypt, studied under the Fatimids--they had

[31]

established at Cairo a great school of science--and returned to Persia as their agent to carry on their propaganda. His methods were the same as theirs, with a difference. That was the reduction of assassination to a fine art. From his eagle's nest of Alamut--such is the meaning of the name--and later from Masyaf in the Lebanon and other mountain fortresses, he and his successors spread terror through Persia and Syria and were only finally stamped out by the Mongol flood under Hulagu in the middle of the seventh century of the Hijra (the 13th A.D.). Of the sect there are still scattered remnants in Syria and India, and as late as 1866 an English judge at Bombay had to decide a case of disputed succession according to the law of the Assassins. Finally, the Fatimid dynasty itself fell before the Kurd, Salah ad-Din, the Saladin of our annals, and Egypt was again orthodox.

CHAPTER III

The problem of the Abbasids; the House of Barmak; the crumbling of the empire; the Prætorians of Baghdad; the Buwayhids; the situation of the Khalifa under them; the Saljuqs; the possibilities of development under them; the Mongols and the Abbasid end; the Egyptian Abbasids; the Ottoman Sultans, their heirs; theory of the Khalifate; the modern situation; the signs of sovereignty for Muslims; five grounds of the claim of the Ottoman Sultan; the consequences for the Sultan; other Muslim constitutions; the Shi'ites; the Ibadites; the Wahhabites; the Brotherhood of as-Sanusi.

WE must now return to the Abbasids, whose empire we left crumbling away. It was a shrewd stroke of policy on the part of its founder to put the new capital, Baghdad, on the Tigris, right between Persia, Syria and Arabia. For the only hope of permanence to the empire lay in welding these into a unity. For a short time, in the hands of the first vigorous rulers, and, especially, during fifty years of guidance by the House of Barmak--Persians who flung in their lot with the Abbasids and were their stay till the madness of Harun ar-Rashid cast them down- -this seemed to be succeeding; but, just as the empire of Charlemagne melted under his sons, so did the empire of al-Mansur and al-Ma'mun. The Bedawi tribes fell back into the desert and to the free chaos of the old pre-Islamic life. As the great philosophical historian, Ibn Khaldun, has remarked, the Arabs by their nature are incapable of founding an empire except when united by religious enthusiasm, and are of all peoples least capable of governing an empire when founded. After the first Abbasids, it is a fatal error to view the Muslim dynasties as Arab or to speak of the Muslim civilization as Arabian. The conquered peoples overcame their conquerors. Persian nationalism reasserted itself and in native independent dynasties flung off the Arab yoke. These dynasties were mostly Shi'ite; Shi'ism, in great part, is the revolt of the Aryan against Semitic monotheism. The process in all this was gradual but certain. Governors of

[32]

provinces revolted and became semi-independent. Sometimes they acknowledged a shadowy sovereignty of the Khalifa, by having his name on their coins and in the Friday prayers; sometimes they did not. At other times they were, or claimed to be, Alids, and when Alids revolted, they revolted absolutely. With them, it was a question of conscience. At last, not even in his own City of Peace or in his own palace was the Khalifa master. As in Rome, so in Baghdad, a body-guard of mercenaries assumed control and their leader was de facto ruler. Later, from A.H. 320 to 447 (A.D. 932-1055), the Sunnite Khalifa found himself the ward and puppet of the Shi'ite Buwayhids. Baghdad itself they held from 334. But still, a curious spiritual value--we cannot call it authority--was left to the shadowy successors of Muhammad. Muslim princes even in far-off India did not feel quite safe upon their thrones unless they had been solemnly in-vested by the Khalifa and given their fitting title. Those very rulers in whose power the Khalifa's life lay sought sanction from him for their rule. At one time there seemed to be some hope that the fatal unity of theocratical Islam would be broken and that a dualism with promise of development through conflict--such as the rivalry between Pope and Emperor which kept Europe alive and prevented both State and Church from falling into decrepit decay--might grow up; that the Khalifa might become a purely spiritual ruler with functions of his own, ruling with mutual subordination and co-ordinate jurisdiction beside a temporal Sultan. The Buwayhids were Shi'ites and merely tolerated, for state reasons, the impieties of the Sunnite Khalifas. But in 447 (A.D. 1055), Tughril Beg, the Saljuq, entered Baghdad, was proclaimed Sultan of the Muslims and freed the Khalifa from the Shi'ite yoke. By 470, all western Asia, from the borders of Afghanistan to those of Egypt and the Greek Empire, were Saljuq. With the Saljuq Sultan as Emperor and the Khalifa as Pope, there was a chance that the Muslim State might enter on a stage of healthy growth through conflict. But that was not to be. Neither State nor Church rose to the great opportunity and the experiment was finally and forever cut off by the Mongol flood. When the next great Sultanate that of the Ottoman Turks--arose, it gathered into its hands the reins of the Khalifate as well. This is what might have been in Islam, built on actual history in Europe. The situation that did arise in Islam may become more clear to us if we can imagine that in Europe the vast plans of Gregory VII. had been carried out and the Pope had become the temporal as well as the spiritual head of the Christian world. Such a situation would have been similar to that in the world of Islam at its earliest time during some few years under the dynasty of the Umayyads, when the one temporal and spiritual sovereign ruled from Samarqand to Spain. Then we can imagine how the vast fabric of such an imperial system broke down by its own weight. Under conflicting claims of legitimacy, an anti-Pope arose and the great schism began. Thereafter the process of disintegration was still more rapid. Provinces rose in insurrection and dropped away from each rival Pope. Kingdoms grew up and the

[33]

sovereigns over them professed themselves to be the lieutenants of the supreme Pontiff and sought investiture from him. Last, the States of the Church itself--all that was left to it--came under the rule of some one of these princes and the Pope was, to all intents, a prisoner in his own palace. Yet the sovereignty of the Khalifa was not simply a legal fiction, any more than that of the Pope would have been in the parallel just sketched. The Muslim princes thought it well to seek spiritual recognition from him, just as Napoleon I. found it prudent to have himself crowned by Pius VII.

But a wave was soon to break in and sweep away all these forms. It came with the Mongols under Hulagu, who passed from the destruction of the Assassins to the destruction of Baghdad and the Khalifate. In A.H. 656 (A.D. 1258), the city was taken and the end of the Abbasids had come. An uncle of the reigning Khalifa escaped and fled to Egypt, where the Mamluk Sultan received him and gave him a spiritual court and ecclesiastical recognition. He found it good to have a Khalifa of his own to use in any question of legitimacy. The name had yet so much value. Finally, in 1517, the Mamluk rule went down before the Ottoman Turks, and the story told by them is that the last Abbasid, when he died in 1538, gave over his rights to their Sultan, Sulayman the Great. Since then, the Ottoman Sultan of Constantinople has claimed to be the Khalifa of Muhammad and the spiritual head of the Muslim world.

Such were the fates of the Commanders of the Faithful. We have traced them through a long and devious course, full of confusions and complications. Leaving aside the legitimist party, the whole may be summed in a word. The theoretical position was that the Imam, or leader, must be elected by the Muslim community, and that position has never, theoretically, been abandoned. Each new Ottoman sovereign is solemnly elected by the Ulama, or canon lawyers and divines of Constantinople. His temporal sovereignty comes by blood; in bestowing this spiritual sovereignty the Ulama act as representatives of the People of Muhammad. Thus the theoretical position was liable to much modification in practice. The Muslim community resolves itself into the people of the capital; still further, into the body-guard of the dead Khalifa; and, finally, as now, into the peculiar custodians of the Faith. Among the Ibadites the position from the first seems to have been that only those learned in the law should act as electors. Along with this, the doctrine developed that it was the duty of the people to recognize un fait accompli and to do homage to a successful usurper--until another more successful should appear. They had learned that it was better to have a bad ruler than no ruler at all. This was the end of the democracy of Islam.

Finally, it may be well to give some account of the constitutional question as it exists at the present day. The greatest of the Sultans of Islam is undoubtedly the

[34]

Emperor of India. Under his rule are far more Muslims than fall to any other. But the theory of the Muslim State never contemplated the possibility of Muslims living under the rule of an unbeliever. For them, the world is divided into two parts, the one is Dar al-Islam, abode of Islam; and the other is Dar al-harb, abode of war. In the end, Dar al-harb must disappear into Dar al-Islam and the whole world be Muslim. These names indicate with sufficient clearness what the Muslim attitude is toward non-Muslims. It is still a moot point among canon lawyers, however, whether Jihad, or holy war, may be made, unprovoked, upon any Dar al-harb. One thing is certain, there must be a reasonable prospect of success to justify any such movement; the lives of Muslims must not be thrown away. Further, the necessity of the case--in India, especially--has brought up the doctrine that any country in which the peculiar usages of Islam are protected and its injunctions--even some of them--followed, must be regarded as Dar al-Islam and that Jihad within its borders is forbidden. We may doubt, however, if this doctrine would hold back the Indian Muslims to any extent if a good opportunity for a Jihad really presented itself. The Shi'ites, it may be remarked, cannot enter upon a Jihad at all until the Hidden Imam returns and leads their armies.

Again the two signs of sovereignty for Muslims are that the name of the sovereign should be on the coinage and that he should be prayed for in the Friday sermon (khutba). In India, the custom seems to be to pray for "the ruler of the age" without name.; then each worshipper can apply it as he chooses. But there has crept in a custom in a few mosques of praying for the Ottoman Sultan as the Khalifa; the English government busies itself little with these things until compelled, and the custom will doubtless spread. The Ottoman Sultan is certainly next greatest to the Emperor of India and would seem, as a Muslim ruling Muslims, to have an unassailable position. But in his case also difficult and ambiguous constitutional questions can be raised. He has claimed the Khalifate, as we have seen, since 1538, but the claim is a shaky one and brings awkward responsibilities. As stated at the present day, it has five grounds. First, de facto right; the Ottoman Sultan won his title by the sword and holds it by the sword. Second, election; this form has been already described. Third, nomination by the last Abbasid Khalifa of Egypt; so Abu Bakr nominated Umar to succeed him, and precedent is everything in Islam. Fourth, possession and guardianship of the two Harams, or Sacred Cities, Mecca and al Madina. Fifth, possession of some relies of the Prophet saved from the sack of Baghdad and delivered to Sultan Salim, on his conquest of Egypt, by the last Abbasid. But these all shatter against the fixed fact that absolutely accepted traditions from the Prophet assert that the Khalifa must be of the family of Quraysh; so long as there are two left of that tribe, one must be Khalifa and the other his helper. Still, here, as everywhere, the principal of Ijma, Agreement of the Muslim people, (see p. 105) comes in and must be

[35]

reckoned with. These very traditions are probably an expression in concrete form of popular agreement. The Khalifate itself is confessedly based upon agreement. The canon lawyers state the case thus: The Imamites and Isma'ilians hold that the appointment of a leader is incumbent upon God. There is only the difference that the Imamites say that a leader is necessary in order to maintain the laws unimpaired, while the Isma'ilians regard him as essential in order to give instruction about God. The Kharijites, on the other hand, recognize no fundamental need of an Imam; he is only allowable. Some of them held that he should be appointed in time of public trouble to do away with the trouble, thus a kind of dictator; others, in time of peace, because only then can the people agree. The Mu'tazilites and the Zaydites held that it was for man to appoint, but that the necessity was based on reason; men needed such a leader. Yet some Mu'tazilites taught that the basis was partly reason and partly obedience to tradition. On the other hand, the Sunnites hold that the appointment of an Imam is incumbent upon men and that the basis is obedience to the tradition of the Agreement of the Muslim world from the earliest times. The community of Islam may have disputed over the individual to be appointed, but they never doubted that the maintenance of the faith in its purity required a leader, and that it was, therefore, incumbent on men to appoint one. The basis is Ijma, Agreement, not Scripture or tradition from Muhammad or analogy based on these two.

It will be seen from this that the de facto ground to the claim of the Ottoman Sultan is the best. The Muslim community must have a leader; this is the greatest Muslim ruling Muslims; he claims the leadership and holds it. If the English rule were to become Muslim, the Muslims would rally to it. The ground of election amounts to nothing, the nomination to little more, except for antiquarians; the possession of the Prophetic relics is a sentiment that would have weight with the crowd only; no canon lawyer would seriously urge it. The guardianship of the two Harams is precarious. A Turkish reverse in Syria would withdraw every Turkish soldier from Arabia and the great Sharif families of Mecca, all of the blood of the Prophet, would proclaim a Khalifa from among themselves. At present, only the Turkish garrison holds them in check.

But a Khalifa has responsibilities. He absolutely cannot become a constitutional monarch in our sense. He rules under law--divine law--and the people can depose him if he breaks it; but he cannot set up beside himself a constitutional assembly and give it rights against himself. He is the successor of Muhammad and must rule, within limitations, as an absolute monarch. So impossible is the modern Khalifate, and so gigantic are its responsibilities. The millions of Chinese Muslims look to him and all Muslims of central Asia; the Muslims of India who are not Shi'ite also look to him. So, too, in Africa and wherever in the world the People of Muhammad have gone, their eyes turn to the Bosphorus and the Great

Sultan. This is what has been called the modern Pan-Islamic movement; it is a modern fact.

The position of the other Muslim sects we have already seen. Of Shi'ite rulers, there are the Imamites in Persia; scattered Zaydites still in south Arabia and fugitive in Africa; strange secret bodies of Isma'ilians--Druses, Nusayrites, Assassins--still holding their own in mountain recesses, forgotten by the world; oldest of all, the Sharifs of Morocco, who are Sunnites and antedate all theological differences, holding only by the blood of the Prophet. At Zanzibar, Uman and the Mzab in Algeria are the descendants of the Kharijites. Probably, somewhere or other, there are some fossilized descendants of every sect that has ever arisen, either to trouble the peace of Islam or to save it from scholastic decrepitude and death. Insurrections and heresies have their own uses.

It only remains to make mention of two modern movements which have deeply affected the Islam of to-day. The Pan-Islamic movement, noticed above, strives as much as anything to bring the Muslim world into closer touch with the science and thought of the Christian world, rallying all the Muslim peoples at the same time round the Ottoman Sultan as their spiritual head and holding fast by the kernel of Islam. It is a reform movement whose trend is forward. The other two, to which we now come, are reform movements also, but their trend is backward. They look to the good old days of early Islam and try to restore them.

The first is that of the Wahhabites, so called from Muhammad ibn Abd al-Wahhab (Slave of the Bountiful), its founder, a native of Najd in central Arabia, who died in 1787. His aim was to bring Islam back to its primitive purity and to do away with all the usages and beliefs which had arisen to cloud its absolute monotheism. But attempts at reformation in Islam have never led to anything but the founding of new dynasties. They may begin with a saintly reformer, but in the first or the second generation there s sure to come the conquering disciple; religion and rule go together, and he who meddles with the one must next grasp at the other. The third stage is the extinction of the new dynasty and the vanishing of its party into a more or less secret sect, the vitality of which is again directed into religious channels. The Wahhabites were no exception. Their rule extended from the Persian Gulf to the Red Sea, touched al-Yaman and Hadramawt and included some districts of the Pashalik of Baghdad. That was early in the nineteenth century; but now, after many dynastic changes, the rule of the Wahhabites proper has almost ceased, although the Turks have not gained any new footing in Najd. There, a native Arab dynasty has sprung up which is free from Turkish control in every respect, and has its seat in Ha'il. But the zeal of the Wahhabites gave an impulse to reform in the general body of Muslims which is not yet, by any. means, extinct. Especially in India, their views have been widely spread by missionaries, and at one time there was grave fear of a Wahhabite insurrection. But dead parties in Islam seldom rise again, and the life of Wahhabism has passed into the Muslim Church as a whole. Politically it has failed, but the spirit of reform remains and has undoubtedly influenced the second reform movement to which we now come.

That is the Brotherhood of as-Sanusi, founded in 1837 by Muhammad ibn Ali as-Sanusi in order to reform and spread the faith. The tendency to organize has always been strong among Orientals, and in Islam itself there have risen, as we have seen, from the earliest times, secret societies for conspiracy and insurrection. But apart from these dubious organizations, religious feeling has also expressed itself in brotherhoods closely corresponding to the monastic orders of Europe, except that they were, and are, self-governing and under no relations but those of sentiment to the head of the Muslim Faith. Rather, these orders of darwishes have been inclined toward heresies of a mystical and pantheistic type more than toward the development and support of the severely scholastic theology of orthodox Islam. This is a side of Muhammadanism with which we shall have to deal in some detail hereafter. In the meantime, it is enough to say that the Brotherhood of as-Sanusi is one of the orders of darwishes, but distinguished from all its predecessors in its severely reforming and puritanic character. It has taken up the task of the Wahhabites and is working out the same problem in a rather different way. Its principles are of the strictest monotheism; all usages and ideas that do not accord with their views of the exact letter of the Qur'an are prohibited. The present head of the Brotherhood, the son of the founder, who himself died in 1859, claims to be the Mahdi and has established a theocratic state at Jarabub, in the eastern Sahara, between Egypt and Tripolis. The mother house of the order is there, and from it missionaries have gone out and established other houses throughout all north Africa and Morocco and far into the interior. The Head himself has of late retreated farther into the desert. There is also an important centre at Mecca, where the pilgrims and the Bedawis are vitiated into the order in great numbers. From Mecca these brethren return to their homes all over the Muslim world, and the order is said to be especially popular in the Malay Archipelago. So there has sprung up in Islam, in tremendous ramifications, an imperium in imperio. All the brethren in all the degrees--for, just as in the monastic orders of Europe, there are active members and lay members--reverence and pay blind obedience to the Head in his inaccessible oasis in the African desert. There he works toward the end, and there can be little doubt what that end will be. Sooner or later Europe--in the first instance, England in Egypt and France in Algeria--will have to face the bursting of this storm. For this Mahdi is different from him of Khartum and the southern Sudan in that he knows how to rule and wait; for years he has gathered arms and munitions, and trained men for the great

[38]

Jihad. When his plans are ready and his time is come, a new chapter will be opened in the history of Islam, a chapter which will cast into forgetfulness even the recent volcanic outburst in China. It will then be for the Ottoman Sultan of the time to show what he and his Khalifate are worth. He will have to decide whether he will throw in his lot with a Mahdi of the old Islam and the dream of a Muslim millennium, or boldly turn to new things and carry the Successorship and the People of Muhammad to join the civilized world.

PART II

Development of Jurisprudence

CHAPTER I

The scope of jurisprudence among Muslims; the earliest elements in it, Arab custom, Jewish law, personality of Muhammad; his attitude toward law; elements after death of Muhammad; Qur'an, Usage of the Prophet, common law of al-Madina; conception of Sunna before Muhammad and after; traditions and their transmission; traditions in book form; influence of Umayyads; forgery of traditions; the Muwatta of Malik ibn Anas; the Musnad of Ahmad ibn Hanbal; the musannafs; al-Bukhari; Muslim; Ibn Maja; at-Tirmidhi; an-Nasa'i; al-Baghawi; the problem of the Muslim lawyers; their sources; Roman law; the influence of the doctrine of the Responsa prudentium; Opinion in Islam; the Law of Nature or Equity in Islam; istihsan; istislah; Analogy; the patriarchal period in Islam; the Umayyad period; the growth of the canon law.

IN tracing the development of Muslim jurisprudence few of the difficulties are encountered which surrounded Sir Henry Maine when he first examined the origins and history of European law. We do not need to push our researches back to the primitive family, nor to work our way through periods of centuries guided by the merest fragments of documents and hints of usage. Our subject was born in the light of history; it ran its course in a couple of hundred years and has left at every important point authoritative evidences of its whence, its how, and its whither. Our difficulties are different, but sufficiently great. Shortly, they are two. The mass of material is overpowering; the strangeness of the ideas involved is perplexing. The wealth of material will become plain, to some extent at least, as the history is traced; but for the strangeness of the contents, of the arrangement and the atmosphere of these codes some preparation must be given from the outset. How, indeed, can we meet a legal code which knows no distinction of personal or public, of civil or criminal law; which prescribes and describes the use of the toothpick and decides when a wedding invitation may be declined, which enters into the minutest and most unsavory details of family life and lays own

[39]

rules of religious retreat? Is it by some subtle connection of thought that the chapter on oaths and vows follows immediately that on horse-racing, and a section on the building line on a street is inserted in a chapter on bankruptcy and composition? One thing, at least, is abundantly clear. Muslim law, in the most absolute sense, fits the old definition, and is the science of all things, human and divine. It tells what we must render to Cæsar and what to God, what to ourselves, and what to our fellows. The bounds of the Platonic definition of rendering to each man his due it utterly shatters. While Muslim theology defines everything that a man shall believe of things in heaven and in earth and beneath the earth--and this is no flat rhetoric--Muslim law prescribes everything that a man shall do to God, to his neighbor, and to himself. It takes all duty for its portion and defines all action in terms of duty. Nothing can escape the narrow meshes of its net. One of the greatest legists of Islam never ate a watermelon because he could not find that the usage of the Prophet had laid down and sanctioned a canonical method of doing so.

It will, therefore, be well for the student to work through the sketch of a code of Muslim law which is inserted in Appendix I. One has been chosen which belongs to the school of ash-Shafi‘i because of its general accessibility. It should be remembered that what is given is the merest table of contents. The standard Arabic commentary on the book extends to eight hundred and eleven closely printed quarto pages. Even a mere reading of this table of contents, however, will show in how different a sphere of thought from ours Muslim law moves and lives. But we must return to the beginning of things, to the egg from which this tremendous system was hatched.

The mother-city of Islam was the little town of Yathrib, called Madinat an-Nabi, the City of the Prophet, or, shortly, al-Madina, ever since the Hijra or Migration of Muhammad to it in the year 622 of the Christian era. Here the first Muslim state was founded, and the germinal principles of Muslim jurisprudence fixed. Both state and jurisprudence were the result of the inter-working of the same highly complicated causes. The ferments in the case may be classified and described as follows: First, in the town itself before the appearance of Muhammad on its little stage little, but so momentous for the future--there were two parties, often at war, oftener at peace. There was a genuine Arab element and there was a large settlement of Jews. To the Arabs any conception of law was utterly foreign. An Arab tribe has no constitution; its system is one of individualism; the single man is a sovereign and no writ can lie against him; the tribe can cast him forth from its midst; it cannot otherwise coerce him. So stands the case now in the desert, and so it was then. Some slight hold there might be on the tribe through the fear of the tribal God, but on the individual Arab, always a somewhat cynical sceptic, that hold was of the slightest. Further, the avenging of a broken oath was left to the God that had witnessed the oath; if he did not care to right his client, no one else would interfere. There was customary law, undoubtedly, but it was protected by no sanction and enforced by no authority. If both parties chose to invoke it, well; if not, neither had anything o fear but the anger of his opponent. That law o custom we shall find again appearing in the system o Islam, but there it will be backed by the sanction of the wrath of God working through the authority of the state. The Jewish element was in a different case. They may have been Jewish immigrants, they may have been Jewish proselytes--many Arab tribes, we know, had gone over bodily to Judaism--but their lives were ruled and guided by Jewish law. To the primitive and divine legislation on Sinai there was an immense accretion by legal fiction and by usage; the Roman codes had left their mark and the customary law of the desert as well. All this was working in the life of the town when Muhammad and his little band of fugitives from Mecca entered it. Being Meccans, they must have brought with them the more developed legal ideas of that trading centre; but these were of comparatively little account in the scale. The new and dominating element was the personality of Muhammad himself. His contribution was legislation pure and simple, the only legislation that has ever been in Islam. Till his death, ten years later, he ruled his community as an absolute monarch, as a prophet in his own right. He sat in the gate and judged the people. He had no need of a code, for his own will was enough. He followed the customary law of the town, as it has been described above, when it suited him, and when he judged that it was best. If not, he left it and there was a revelation. So the legislative part of the Qur'an grew out of such scraps sent down out of heaven to meet the needs of the squabbles and questions of the townsfolk of al-Madina. The system was one of pure opportunism; but of what body of legislation can that not be said? Of course, on the one hand, not all decisions were backed by a revelation, and Muhammad seems, on the other, to have made a few attempts to deal systematically with certain standing and constantly recur-ring problems--such, for example, as the conflicting claims of heirs in an estate, and the whole complicated question of divorce--but in general, the position holds that Muhammad as a lawyer lived from hand to mouth. He did not draw up any twelve tables or ten commandments, or code, or digest; he was there and the people could come and ask him questions when they chose, and that was enough. The conception of a rounded and complete system which will meet any case and to which all cases must be adjusted by legal fiction or equity, the conception which we owe to the genius and experience of the Roman lawyers, was foreign to his thought. From time to time he got into difficulties. A revelation proved too wide or too narrow, or left out some important possibility. Then there came another to supplement or correct, or even to set the first quite aside--Muhammad had no scruples about progressive revelation as applied to himself. Thus, through these

[41]

interpretive acts, as we may call them, many flat contradictions have come into the Qur'an and have proved the delight of generations of Muslim jurisconsults.

Such, then, was the state of things legal in al-Madina during the ten years of Muhammad's rule there until his death in A.D. 632. Of law there was, strictly speaking, none. In his decisions, Muhammad could follow certainly the customary law of the town; but to do so there was no necessity upon him other than prudence, for his authority was absolute. Yet even with such authority and such freedom, his task was a hard one. The Jews, the native Arabs of al-Madina, and his fellow fugitives from Mecca lived in more or less of friction. He had to see to it that his decisions did not bring that friction to the point of throwing the whole community into a flame. The Jews, it is true, were soon eliminated, but the influence of their law lasted in the customary law of the town long after they themselves had become insignificant. Still, with all this, the suitor before Muhammad had no certainty on what basis his claims would be judged; whether it would be the old law of the town, or a rough equity based on Muhammad's own ideas, or a special revelation ad hoc. So far, then, we may be said to have the three elements--common law, equity, legislation. Legal fiction we shall meet later; Muhammad had no need of it.

But with the death of Muhammad in A.D. 632 the situation was completely changed. We can now speak of Muslim law; legislation plays no longer any part; the process of collecting, arranging, correlating, and developing has begun. Consider the situation as it must have presented itself to one of the immediate successors of Muhammad, as he sat in his place and judged the people. When a case came up for decision, there were several sources from which a law in point might be drawn. First among them was the Qur'an. It had been collected from the fragmentary state in which Muhammad had left it by Abu Bakr, his first Khalifa, some two years after his death. Again, some ten years later, it was revised and given forth in a final public recension by Uthman, the third Khalifa. This was the absolute word of God--thoughts and language--and stood and, in theory, still stands first of all sources for theology and law. If it contained a law clearly applying to the case in hand, there was no more to be said; divine legislation had settled the matter. If not, recourse was next had to the decisions of the Prophet. Had a similar one come before him, and how had he ruled? If the memories of the Companions of the Prophet, the Sahibs, could adduce nothing similar from one of his decisions, then the judge had to look further for an authority. But the decisions of Muhammad had been many, the memories of his Companions were capacious, and possessed further, as we must recognize with regret, a constructive power that helped the early judges of Islam out of many close corners. But if tradition even-- true or false--finally failed, then the judge fell back on the common law of al-Madina, that customary law already mentioned. When that, too, failed, the last

[42]

recourse was had to the common-sense of the judge--roughly, what we would call equity. At the beginning, therefore, of Muslim law, it had the following sources-- legislation, the usage of Muhammad, the usage of al-Madina, equity. Naturally, as time went on and the figure of the founder drew back and became more obscure and more venerated, equity gradually into disuse; a closer search was m de for decisions of that founder which could in any way be pressed into service; a method of analog closely allied to legal fiction, was built up to assist in this, and the development of Muslim jurisprudence as a system and a science was fairly begun. Further, in later times, the decisions of the first four Khalifas and the agreement (ijma) of the immediate Companions of Muhammad came to assume an importance only second to that of Muhammad himself. Later still, as a result of this, the opinion grew up that a general agreement of the jurisconsults of any particular time was to be regarded as a legitimate source of law. But we must return to consider our subject more broadly and in another field.

The fact has already been brought out that the sphere of law is much wider in Islam than it has ever been with us. By it all the minutest acts of a Muslim are guarded. Europe, also, passed through a stage similar to this in its sumptuary laws; and the tendency toward inquisitorial legislation still exists in America, but not even the most mediævally minded American Western State has ventured to put upon its statute-book regulations as to the use of the toothpick and the wash-cloth. Thus, the Muslim conception of law is so wide as to reach essential difference. A Muslim is told by his code not only what is required under penalty, but also what is either recommended or disliked though without reward or penalty being involved. He may certainly consult his lawyer, to learn how near the wind he can sail without unpleasant consequences; but he may also consult him as his spiritual director with regard to the relative praiseworthiness or blameworthiness of classes of actions of which our law takes no cognizance. In consequence, actions are divided by Muslim canon lawyers (faqihs) into five classes. First, necessary (fard or wajib); a duty the omission of which is punished, the doing rewarded. Secondly, recommended (mandub or mustahabb); the doing is rewarded, but the omission is not punished. Thirdly, permitted (ja'iz or mubah); legally indifferent. Fourthly, disliked (makruh); disapproved by the law, but not under penalty. Fifthly, forbidden (haram); an action punishable by law. All this being so, it will be easily understood that the record of the manners and customs of the Prophet, of the little details of his life and conversation, came to assume a high importance. Much of that was too petty ever to reach expression in the great digests of law; not even the most zealous fixer of life by rule and line would condemn his fellow-religionist because he preferred to carry a different kind of walking-stick from that approved by the Prophet, or found it fitting to arrange his hair in a different way. But still, all pious Muslims paid attention to such things,

[43]

and fenced their lives about with the strictest Prophetic precedent. In consequence of this, there early arose in Islam a class of students who made it their business to investigate and hand down the minutest details as to the habits of Muhammad. This was a separate thing from the study of law, although fated to be eventually connected with it. Even in the time of the Jahiliya--the period before Islam, variously explained as the ignorance or as the rudeness, uncivilizedness--it had been a fixed trait of the Arab mind to hold closely to old paths. An inherent conservatism canonized the sunna--custom, usage--of the ancients; any stepping aside from it was a bid'a--innovation--and had to win its way by its merits, in the teeth of strong prejudice. With the coming of Muhammad and the preaching of Islam, this ancestral sunna had in great part to yield. But the temper of the Arab mind remained firm, and the sunna of Muhammad took its place. Pious Muslims did not say, "Such was the usage of our fathers, and it is mine;" but, "I follow the usage of the Prophet of God." Then, just as the old sunna of the heathen times had expressed itself through the stories of great warriors, of their battles and loves; through anecdotes of wise men, and their keen and eloquent words; so it was with the sunna of the one man, Muhammad. What he said, and what he did; what he refrained from doing; what he gave quasi-approval to by silence; all was passed on in rapidly increasing, pregnant little narratives. First, his immediate Companions would note, either by committing to memory or to a written record, his utterances and table-talk generally. We have evidence of several such Boswells, who fixed his words as they fell. Later, probably, would come notes of his doings and his customs, and of all the little and great happenings of the town. Above all, a record was being gathered of all the cases judged by him, and of his decisions; of all the answers which he gave to formal questions on religious life and faith. All this was jotted down by the Companions on sahifas--odd sheets-- just as they had done in the Ignorance with the proverbs of the wise and their dark sayings. The records of sayings were called hadiths; the rest, as a whole, sunna-- custom, for its details was used the plural, sunan--customs. At first, each man had his own collection in memory or in writing. Then, after the death of the Prophet and when his first Companions were dropping off, these collections were passed on to others of the second generation. And so the chain ran on and in time a tradition came to consist formally of two things--the text or matter (matn) so handed on, and the succession (isnad) over whose lips it had passed. A said, "There narrated to me B, saying, 'There narrated to me C, saying,'" so far the isnad, until the last link came, and the matn, the Prophet of God said, "Some of my injunctions abrogate others," or "The Jann were created of a smokeless flame," or whatever it might be. What has just been said suggests that it was at first indifferent whether traditions were preserved orally or in writing. That is true of the first generation; but it must be remembered at the sane time, that the actual passing on was oral; the writing merely aided the memory to hold that which was

[44]

already learned. But with time, and certainly by the middle of the second century of the Hijra, two opposing tendencies in this respect had developed. Many continued to put their trust in the written Word, and even came to pass traditions on without any oral communication. But for others there lay grave dangers in this. One was evidently real. The unhappy character of the Arabic script, especially when written without diacritical points, often made it hard, if not practically impossible, to understand such short, contextless texts as the traditions. A guide was necessary to show how the word should be read, and how understood. At the present time a European scholar will sometimes be helpless before even a fully vocalized text, and must take refuge in native commentaries or in that oral tradition, if it still exists and he has access to it, which supplies at least a third of the meaning of an Arabic book. Strengthening this came theological reasons. The words of the Prophet would be profaned if they were in a book. Or, again, they would be too much honored and the Qur'an itself might be neglected. This last fear has been justified to a certain extent by the event. On these grounds, and many more, the writing and transmitting in writing of traditions came to be fiercely opposed; and the opposition continued, as a theological exercise, long after many books of traditions were in existence, and after the oral transmission had become the merest farce and had even frankly dropped out.

It is to the formation of these books of traditions, or, as we night say, traditions in literature, that we must now turn. For long, the fragmentary sahifas and private collections made by separate scholars for their own use sufficed. Books dealing with law (fiqh) were written before there were any in that department of literature called hadith. The cause of this is tolerably plain. Law and treatises of law were a necessity for the public and thus were encouraged by the state. The study of traditions, on the other hand, was less essential and of a more personal and private nature. Further, under the dynasty of the Umayyads, who reigned from A.D. 41 to A.H. 132, theological literature was little encouraged. They were simple heathen in all but name, and belonged, and recognized that they belonged, not to Islam but to the Jahiliya. For reasons of state, they encouraged and spread--also freely forged and encouraged others to forge--such traditions as were favorable to their plans and to their rule generally. This was necessary if they were to carry the body of the people with them. But they regarded themselves as kings and not as the heads of the Muslim people. This same device has been used after them by all the contending factions of Islam. Each party has sought sanction for its views by representing them in traditions from the Prophet, and the thing has gone so far that on almost every disputed point there are absolutely conflicting prophetic utterances in circulation. It has even been held, and with some justification, that the entire body of normative tradition at present in existence was forged for a purpose. With this attitude of the Umayyads we shall have to deal at greater

[45]

length later. It is sufficient now to note that the first real appearance of hadith in literature was in the Muwatta of Malik ibn Anas who died in A.H. 179.

Yet even this appearance is not so much of hadith for its own sake, as of usages bearing upon law and of the law that can be drawn from these usages. The book is a corpus iuris not a corpus traditionum. Its object was not so much to separate from the mass of traditions in circulation those which could be regarded as sound of origin and to unite them in a formal collection, as to build up a system of law based partly on tradition. The previous works dealing with law proper had been of a speculative character, had shown much subjective reliance on their own opinion on the part of the writers and had drawn little from the sacred usage of the Prophet and quoted few of his traditional sayings. Against that the book of Malik was a protest and formed a link between such law books pure and the collections of traditions pure with which we now come to deal.

To Malik the matn, or text, of a tradition had been the only thing of importance. To the isnad, or chain of authority running back to the Prophet, he had paid little attention. He, as we have seen, was a lawyer and gathered traditions, not for their own sake but to use them in law. To others, the tradition was the thing, and too much care could not be given to its details and its authenticity. And the care was really called for. With the course of time and the growing demand, the supply of traditions had also grown until there was no doubt in the mind of anyone that an enormous proportion were simple forgeries. To weed out the sound ones, attention had to be given to the isnad; the names upon it had to be examined; the fact of their having been in intercourse to be determined; the possibility of the case in general to be tested. Thus there were formed real collections of supposedly sound traditions, which were called Musnads, because each tradition was musnad--propped; supported--against the Companions from whom it proceeded. In accordance with this also they were arranged according to the Companions. After the name of the Companion were given all the traditions leading back to him. One of the earliest and greatest of these books was the Musnad of Ahmad ibn Hanbal, who died A.H. 241; of him more hereafter. This book has been printed recently at Cairo in six quarto volumes of 2,885 pages and is said to contain about thirty thousand traditions going back to seven hundred Companions.

But another type of tradition-book was growing up, less mechanical in arrangement. It is the Musannaf, the arranged, classified--and in it the traditions are arranged in chapters according to their subject matter. The first Musannaf to make a permanent mark was the Sahih--sound--of al-Bukhari, who died in A. H. 257. It is still extant and is the most respected of all the collections of traditions. The principle of arrangement in it is legal; that is, the traditions are classified in these chapters so as to afford bases for a complete system of jurisprudence. Al-

Bukhari was a strong opponent of speculative law and his book was thus a protest against a tendency which, as we shall see later, was strong in his time. Another point in which al-Bukhari made his influence felt and with greater effect, was increased severity in the testing of tractions. He established very strict laws, though of a somewhat mechanical kind, and was most scrupulous in applying them. His book contains about seven thousand traditions, and he chose those, so at least runs the story, out of six hundred thousand which he found in circulation. The rest were rejected as failing to meet his tests. How far the forgery of traditions had gone may be seen from the example of Ibn Abi Awja, who was executed in A.H. 155, and who confessed that he had himself put into circulation four thousand that were false. Another and a similar Sahih is that of Muslim, who died in A.H. 261. He was not so markedly juristic as al-Bukhari. His object was rather to purify the mass of existing tradition from illegitimate accretions than to construct a basis for a complete law code. He has prefixed a valuable introduction on the science of tradition generally. In some slight details his principle of criticism differed from that of al-Bukhari.

These two collections, called the two Sahihs--as-Sahihan--are technically jami's, i.e. they contain all the different classes of traditions, historical, ethical, dogmatic and legal. They have also come to be, by common agreement, the two most honored authorities in the Muslim world. A believer finds it hard, if not impossible, to reject a tradition that is found in both.

But there are four other collections which are called Sunan--Usages--and which stand only second to the two Sahihs. These are by Ibn Maja (d. 303), Abu Da'ud as-Sijistani (d. 275), at-Tirmidhi (d. 279) and an-Nasa'i (d. 303). They deal almost entirely with legal traditions, those that tell what is permitted and what is forbidden, and do not convey information on religious and theological subjects. They are also much more lenient in their criticisms of dubious traditions. To work exclusion with them, the rejection needed to be tolerably unanimous. This was required by their standpoint and endeavor, which was to find a basis for all the minutest developments and details of jurisprudence, civil and religious.

These six books, the two Sahihs and the four Sunans, came to be regarded in time as the principal and all-important sources for traditional science. This had already come about by the end of the fifth century, although even after that voices of uncertainty continued to make themselves heard. Ibn Maja seems to have been the last to secure firm footing, but even he is included by al-Baghawi (d. 516) in his Masabih as-sunna, an attempted epitome into one book of what was valuable in all. Still, long after that, Ibn Khaldun, the great historian (d. 808), speaks of five fundamental works; and others speak of seven, adding the Muwatta of Malik to the six above. Others, again, especially in the West, extended the number of canonical works to ten, though with varying members; but all these must be regarded as more or less local, temporary, and individual eccentricities. The position of the six stands tolerably firm.

So much it has been necessary to interpolate and anticipate with regard to the students of tradition whose interest lay in gathering up and preserving, not in using and applying. From the earliest time, then, there existed these two classes in the bosom of Islam, students of tradition proper and of law proper. For long they did not clash; but a collision was inevitable sooner or later.

Yet, if the circle of the Muslim horizon had not widened beyond the little market-town of al-Madina, that collision might have been long in coining. Its immediate causes were from without, and are to be found in the wave of conquest that carried Islam, within the century, to Samarqand beyond the Oxus and to Tours in central France. Consider what that wave of conquest was and meant. Within fourteen years of the Hijra, Damascus was taken, and within seventeen years, all Syria and Mesopotamia. By the year 21, the Muslims held Persia; in 41 they were at Herat, and in 56 they reached Samarqand. In the West, Egypt was taken in the year 20; but the way through northern Africa was long and hard. Carthage did not fall till 74, but Spain was conquered with the fall of Toledo in 93. It was in A.D. 732, the year of the Hijra 114, that the wave at last was turned and the mercy of Tours was wrought by Charles the Hammer; but the Muslims still held Narbonne and raided in Burgundy and the Dauphiné. The wealth that flowed into Arabia from these expeditions was enormous; money and slaves and luxuries of every kind went far to transform the old life of hardness and simplicity. Great estates grew up: fortunes were made and lost; the intricacies of the Syrian and Persian civilizations overcame their conquerors. All this meant new legal conditions and problems. The system that had sufficed to guard the right to a few sheep or camels had to be transformed before it would suffice to adjust the rights and claims of a tribe of millionnaires. But it must not be thought that these expeditions were only campaigns of plunder. With the Muslim armies everywhere went law and justice, such as it was. Jurists accompanied each army and were settled in the great camp cities which were built to hold the conquered lands. Al-Basra and al-Kufa and Fustat, the parent of Cairo, owe their origin to this, and it was in these new seats of militant Islam that speculative jurisprudence arose and moulded the Muslim system.

The early lawyers had much to do and much to learn, and it is to their credit that they recognized both necessities. Muslim law is no product of the desert or of the mind of Muhammad, as some have said; but rather of the labor of these men, struggling with a gigantic problem. They might have taken their task much more easily than they did; they might have lived as Muhammad had done, from hand to

[48]

mouth, and have concealed their own sloth by force and free invention of authorities. But they recognized their responsibility to God and man and the necessity of building up a stable and complete means of rendering justice. These armies of Muslims, we must remember, were not like the hordes of Attila or Chingis Khan, destroyers only. The lands they conquered were put to hard tribute, but it was under a reign of law. They recognized frankly that it was for them that this mighty empire existed; but they recognized also that it could continue to exist only with order and duty imposed upon all. They saw, too, how deficient was their own knowledge and learned willingly of the people among loin they had come. And here, a second time, Roman law--the parent-law of the world--made itself felt. There were schools of that law in Syria at Cæsarea and Beyrout, but we need not imagine that the Muslim jurists studied there. Rather, it was the practical school of the courts as they actually existed which they attended. These courts were permitted to continue in existence till Islam had learned from them all that was needed. We can still recognize certain principles that were so carried over. That the duty of proof lies upon the plaintiff, and the right of defending himself with an oath upon the defendant; the doctrine of invariable custom and that of the different kinds of legal presumption. These, as expressed in Arabic, are almost verbal renderings of the pregnant utterances of Latin law.

But most important of all was a liberty suggested by that system to the Muslim jurisconsults. This was through the part played in the older school by the Responsa Prudentium, answers by prominent lawyers to questions put to them by their clients, in which the older law of the Twelve Tables was expounded, expanded, and often practically set aside by their comments. Sir Henry Maine thus states the situation: "The authors of the new jurisprudence, during the whole progress of its formation, professed the most sedulous respect for the letter of the code. They were merely explaining it, deciphering it, bringing out its full meaning; but then, in the result, by placing texts together, by adjusting the law to states of fact which actually presented themselves, and by speculating on its possible application to others which might occur, by introducing principles of interpretation derived from the exegesis of other written documents which fell under their observation, they educed a vast variety of canons which had never been dreamt of by the compilers of the Twelve Tables, and which were in truth rarely or never to be found there." All this precisely applies to the development of law in Islam. The part of the Twelve Tables was taken by the statute law of the Qur'an and the case law derived from the Usage of Muhammad; that of the Roman Iurisprudentes by those speculative jurists who worked mostly outside of al-Madina in the camp cities of Mesopotamia and Syria--the very name for lawyer in Arabic, faqih, plural fuaqha, is a translation of prudens, prudentes; and that of the Responsa, the answers, by the "Opinion" which they claimed as a legitimate

[49]

legal method and source. Further, the validity of a general agreement of jurisconsults "reminds us of the rescript of Hadrian, which ordains that, if the opinions of the licensed prudentes all agreed, such common opinion had the force of statute; but if they disagreed, the judge might follow which he chose." The Arabic term, ra'y, here rendered Opinion, has passed through marked vicissitudes of usage. In old Arabic, before it, in the view of some, began to keep bad company, it meant an opinion that was thoughtful, weighed and reasonable, as opposed to a hasty dictate of ill-regulated passion. In that sense it is used in a tradition--probably forged--handed down from Muhammad. He was sending a judge to take charge of legal affairs in al-Yaman, and asked him on what he would base his legal decisions. "On the Qur'an," he replied. "But if that contains nothing to the purpose?" "Then upon your usage." "But if that also fails you?" "Then I will follow my own opinion." And the Prophet approved his purpose. A similar tradition goes back to Umar, the first Khalifa, and it, too, is probably a later forgery, written to defend this source of law. But, with the revolt against the use of Opinion, to which we shall soon come, the term itself fell into grave disrepute and came to signify an unfounded conclusion. In its extremest development it went beyond the Responsa, which professed always to be in exact accord with the letter of the older law, and attained to be Equity in the strict sense; that is, the rejection of the letter of the law for a view supposed to be more in accordance with the spirit of justice itself. Thus, Equity, in the English sense, is the law administered by the Court of Chancery and claims, in the words again of Sir Henry Maine, to "override the older jurisprudence of the country on the strength of an intrinsic ethical superiority." In Roman law, as introduced by the edict of the Prætor, it was the law of Nature, "the part of law 'which natural reason appoints for all mankind.'" This is represented in Islam under two forms, covered by two technical terms. The one is that the legist, in spite of the fact that the analogy of the fixed code clearly points to one course, "considers it better" (istihsan) to follow a different one; and the other is that, under the same conditions, he chooses a free course "for the sake of general benefit to the community" (istislah). Further scope of Equity Muslim law never reached, and the legitimacy of these two developments was, as we shall see, bitterly contested. The freedom of opinion, with its possibility of a system of Equity, had eventually to be given up, and all that was left in its place was a permissibility of analogical deduction (qiyas), the nearest thing to which in Western law is Legal Fiction. In a word, the possibility of development by Equity was lost, and Legal Fiction entered in its place. But this anticipates, and we must return to the strictly historical movement.

During the first thirty years after the death of Muhammad--the period covered by the reigns of the four theocratic rulers whom Islam still calls "the Four Just, or

Rightly Guided Khalifas" (al-Khulafa ar-rashidun)--the two twin studies of tradition (hadith) and of law (fiqh) were fostered and encouraged by the state. The centre of that state was still in al-Madina, on ground sacred with the memories of the Prophet, amid the scenes where he had himself been lord and judge, and under the conditions in which his life as ruler had been cast. All the sources, except that of divine revelation, which had been open to him, were open to his successors and they made full use of all. Round that mother-hearth of Islam was still gathered the great body of the immediate Companions of Muhammad, and they formed a deliberative or consulting council to aid the Khalifa in his task. The gathering of tradition and the developing of law were vital functions; they were the basis of the public life of the state. This patriarchal period in Muslim history is the golden age of Islam. It ended with the death of Ali, in the year 40 of the Hijra, and the succession of Mu'awiya in the following year. "For thirty years," runs a tradition from the Prophet, "my People will tread in my Path (sunna); then will come kings and princes."

And so it was Mu'awiya was the first of the Umayyad dynasty and with him and them Islam, in all but the name, was at an end. He and they were Arab kings of the old type that had reigned before Muhammad at al-Hira and Ghassan, whose will had been their law. The capital of the new kingdom was Damascus; al-Madina became a place of refuge, a Cave of Adullam, for the old Muslim party. There they might spin theories of state and of law, and lament the good old days; so long as there was no rebellion, the Umayyads cared little for those things or for the men who dreamt them. Once, the Umayyads were driven to capture and sack the holy city, a horror in Islam to this day. After that there was peace, the peace of the accomplished fact. This is the genuinely Arab period in the history of Islam. It is a period fall of color and light and life; of love and song, battle and feasting. Thought was free and conduct too. The great theologian of the Greek Church, John of Damascus, held high office at the Umayyad court, and al-Akhtal, a Christian at least in name, was their poet laureate. It is true that the stated services of religion were kept up and on every Friday the Khalifa had to entertain the people by a display of eloquence and wit in the weekly sermon. But the old world was dead and the days of its unity would never come again. So all knew, except the irreconcilable party, the last of the true Muslims who still haunted the sacred soil of al-Madina and labored in the old paths. They gathered the traditions of the Prophet; they regulated their lives more and more strictly by his usage; they gave ghostly council to the pious who sought their help; they labored to build up elaborate systems of law. But it was all elaboration and hypothetical purely. There was in it no vitalizing force from practical life.

From this time on Muslim law has been more or less in the position held by the canon law of the Roman Church in a country that will not recognize it yet dares

[51]

not utterly reject it. The Umayyads were statesmen and opportunists; they lived, in legal things, as much from hand to mouth as Muhammad had done, He cut all knots with divine legislation; they cut them with the edge of their will. Under them, as under him, a system of law was impossible. But at the same time, in quiet and in secret, this canon law of Islam was slowly growing up, slowly rounding into full perfection of detailed correlation. It was governing absolutely the private lives of all the good Muslims that were left, and even the godless Umayyads, as they had to preach on Fridays to the People of Muhammad, so they had to deal with it cautiously and respectfully. Of the names and lives of these obscure jurists little has reached us and it is needless to give that little here. Only with the final fall of the Umayyads, in the year of the Hijra 132, do we come into the light and see the different schools forming under clear and definite leaders.

CHAPTER II

The Abbasid revolution; the compromise; the problem of the Abbasids; the two classes of canon lawyers and theologians; the rise of legal schools; Abu Hanifa; his application of Legal Fiction; istihsan: the Qadi Abu Yusuf; Muhammad ibn al-Hasan; Sufyan ath-Thawri; al-Awza'i; Malik ibn Anas; the Usage of al-Madina; istislah; the doctrine of Agreement; the beginning of controversy; traditionalists or historical lawyers versus rationalists or philosophical lawyers; ash-Shafi'i, a mediator and systematizer; the Agreement of the Muslim people a formal source; "My People will never agree in an error;" the resultant four sources, Qur'an, Usage, Analogy, Agreement; the traditionalist revolt; Da'ud az-Zahiri and literalism; Ahmad ibn Hanbal; the four abiding schools; the Agreement of Islam; the Disagreement of Islam; iurare in verba magistri; the degrees of authority; the canon and the civil codes in Islam; their respective spheres; distribution of schools at present day; Shi'ite law; Ibadite law.

THAT great revolution which brought the Abbasid dynasty to power seemed at first to the pious theologians and lawyers to be a return of the old days. They dreamt of entering again into their rights; that the canon law would be the full law of the land. It was only slowly that their eyes were opened, and many gave up the vain contest and contented themselves with compromise. This had been rare under the Umayyads; the one or two canon lawyers who had thrown in their lot with them had been marked men. Az-Zuhri (d. 124), a man of the highest moral and theological reputation who played a very important part in the first codifying of traditions, was one of these, and the later pious historians have had hard work to smooth over his connection with the impious Umayyads. Probably--it may be well to say here---the stories against the Umayyads have been much heightened in color by their later tellers and also az-Zuhri, being a man of insight and statesmanship, may have recognized that their rule was the best chance for peace

[52]

in the country. Muslims have come generally to accept the position that unbelief on the part of the government, if the government is strong and just, is better than true belief and anarchy. This has found expression, as all such things do, in traditions put in the mouth of the Prophet.

But while only a few canonists had taken the part of the Umayyads, far more accepted the favors of the Abbasids, took office under them and worked in their cause. The Abbasids, too, had need of such men. It was practically the religious sentiment of the people that had overthrown the Umayyads and raised them to power; and that religious sentiment, though it could never be fully satisfied, must yet be respected and, more important still, used. There is a striking parallel between the situation then, and that of Scotland at the Revolution Settlement of 1688. The power of the Stuarts--that is, of the worldly Umayyads--had been overthrown. The oppressed Church of the Covenant--that is, the old Muslim party--had been freed. The state was to be settled upon a new basis. What was that basis to be? The Covenanting party demanded the, recognition of the Headship of Christ--that the Kirk should rule the state, or should be the state, and that all other religious views should be put under penalty. The old Muslim party looked for similar things. That religious life should be purified; that the canon law should be again the law of the state; that the constitution of Umar should be restored. How the Covenanters were disappointed, how much they got and how much they failed to get, needs no telling here.

Exactly in the same way it befell the old Muslims. The theological reformation was sweeping and complete. The first Abbasids were pious, at least outwardly; the state was put upon a pious footing. The canon law also was formally restored, but with large practical modifications. Canon lawyers were received into the service of the state, provided they were adaptable enough. Impossible men had no place under the Abbasids; their officials must be pliable and dexterous, for a new modus vivendi was to be found. The rough and ready Umayyad cutting of the knot had failed; the turn had now come for piety and dexterity in twisting law. The court lawyers learned to drive a coach and four through any of the old statutes, and found their fortunes in their brains. So the issue was bridged. But a large party of malcontents was left, and from this time on in Islam the lawyers and the theologians have divided into two classes, the one admitting, as a matter of expediency, the authority of the powers of the time and aiding them in their task as rulers; the other, irreconcilable and unreconciled, denouncing the state as sunk in unbelief and deadly sin and its lawyers as traitors to the cause of religion. To pursue our parallel, they are represented in Scotland by a handful of Covenanting congregations and in America by the much more numerous and powerful Reformed Presbyterian Church.

[53]

It is a significant fact that with the lifting of the Umayyad pressure and the encouragement of legal studies--such as it was--by the Abbasids, definite and recognized schools of law began to form. What had so long been in process in secret became public, and its results crystallized under certain prominent teachers. We will now take up these schools in the order of the death dates of their founders; we will establish their principles and trace their histories. We shall find the same conceptions recurring again and again which have already been brought out, Qur'an, tradition (hadith), agreement (ijma), opinion (ra'y), analogy (qiyas), local usage (urf), preference (istihsan), in the teeth of the written law--till at length, when the battle is over, the sources will have limited themselves to the four which ha e survived to the present day--Qur'an, tradition, agreement, analogy. And, similarly, of the six schools to be mentioned, four only will remain to the present time, but these of equal rank and validity in the eyes of the Believers.

The Abbasids came to power in the year of the Hijra 132, and in 150 died Abu Hanifa, the first student and teacher to leave behind him a systematic body of teaching and a missionary school of pupils. He was a Persian by race, and perhaps the most distinguished example of the rule that Muslim scientists and thinkers might write in Arabic but were seldom of Arab blood. He does not seem to have held office as a judge or to have, practised law at all. He was, rather, an academic student, a speculative or philosophical jurist we might call him. His system of law; therefore, was not based upon the exigencies of experience; it did not arise from an attempt to meet actual cases. We might say of it, rather, but in a good sense, that it was a system of casuistry, an attempt to build up on scientific principles a set of rules which would answer every conceivable question of law. In the hands of some of his pupils, when applied to actual facts, it tended to develop into casuistry in a bad sense; but no charge of perverting justice for his own advantage seems to have been brought against Abu Hanifa himself. His chief instruments in constructing his system were opinion and analogy. He leaned little upon traditions of the usage of Muhammad, but preferred to take the Qur'anic texts and develop from them his details. But the doing of this compelled him to modify simple opinion--equivalent to equity as we have seen--and limit it to analogy of some written statute (nass). He could hardly forsake a plain res iudicata of Muhammad, and follow his own otherwise unsupported views. but he might choose to do so if he could base it on analogy from the Qur'an. Thus, he came to use what was practically legal fiction. It is the application of an old law in some sense or way that was never dreamt of by the first imposer of the law, and which may, in fact, run directly counter to the purpose of the law. The fiction is that it is the original law that is being observed, while, as a matter of fact, there has come in its place an entirely different law. So Abu Hanifa would contend that

[54]

he was following the divine legislation of the Qur'an, while his adversaries contended that he was only following his own opinion.

But if, on the one hand, he was thus limited from equity to legal fiction, on another he developed a new principle of even greater freedom. Reference has already been made to the changes which were of necessity involved in the new conditions of the countries conquered by the Muslims. Often the law of the desert not only failed to apply to town and agricultural life; it was even directly mischievous. On account of this, a consideration of local conditions was early accepted as a principle, but in general terms. These were reduced to definiteness by Abu Hanifa under the formula of "holding for better" (istihsan). He would say, "The analogy in the case points to such and such a rule but under the circumstances I hold it for better to rule thus and thus."

This method, as we shall see later, was vehemently attacked by his opponents, as wads his system in general. Yet that system by its philosophical perfection--due to its theoretical origin--and perfection in detail--due to generations of practical workers--has survived all attack and can now be said to be the leading one of the four existing schools. No legal writings of Abu Hanifa have reached us, nor does he seem to have, himself, cast his system into a finished code. That was done by his immediate pupils, and especially by two, the Qadi Abu Yusuf, who died in 182, and Muhammad ibn al-Hasan, who died in 189. The first was consulting lawyer and chief Qadi to the great Khalifa Harun ar-Rashid, and, if stories can be believed, proved himself as complaisant of conscience as a court casuist need be. Innumerable are the tales afloat of his minute knowledge of legal subtleties and his fertility of device in applying them to meet the whims of his master, Harun. Some of them have found a resting place in that great mirror of mediæval Muslim life, The Thousand and One Nights; reference may be made to Night 296. Through his influence, the school of Abu Hanifa gained an official importance which it never thereafter lost. He wrote for Harun a book which we have still, on the canon law as applied to the revenues of the state, a thorny and almost impossible subject, for the canon law makes really no provision for the necessary funds of even a simple form of government and much less for such an array of palaces and officials as had grown up around the Abbasids. His book is marked by great piety in expression and by ability of the highest kind in reconciling the irreconcilable.

But all the canon lawyers did not fall in so easily with the new ways. Many found that only in asceticism, in renunciation of the world and engaging in pious exercises was there any chance of their maintaining the old standards in a state that was for them based on oppression and robbery. One of these was Sufyan ath-Thawri, a lawyer of high repute, who narrowly missed founding a separate school

[55]

of law and who died in 161. There has come down to us a correspondence between him and Harun, which, though it cannot possibly be genuine, throws much light on the disappointment of the sincerely religious section. Harun writes on his accession to the Khalifate (170), complaining that Sufyan had not visited him, in spite of their bond of brotherhood, and offering him wealth from the public treasury. Sufyan replied, denouncing such use of public funds and all the other uses of them by Harun--many enough--except those precisely laid down in the codes. On the basis of these, Harun would have had to work for his own living. There are also other denunciations for crimes in the ruler which he punished in others. Harun is said to have kept the letter and wept over it at intervals, but no change of life on his part is recorded. Apparently, with the accession of the Abbasids ascetic and mystical Islam made a great development. It became plain to the pious that no man could inherit both this world and the next.

While Abu Hanifa was developing his system in Mesopotamia, al-Awza'i was working similarly in Syria. He was born at Baalbec, lived at Damascus, and at Beyrout where he died in 157. Of him and his teaching we know comparatively little. But so far it is clear that he was not a speculative jurist of the same type as Abu Hanifa, but paid especial attention to traditions. At one time is school was followed by the Muslims of Syria and the entire West to Morocco and Spain. But its day was a short one. The school of Abu Hanifa, championed by Abu Yusuf with his tremendous influence as chief Qadi of the Abbasid empire, pushed it aside, and at the present day it has no place except in history. For us, its interest is that of another witness to the early rise and spread of systems of jurisprudence outside of Arabia.

In A.H. 179, three years before the death of Abu Yusuf and twenty-nine after that of Abu Hanifa, there died at al-Madina the founder and head of an independent school of a very different type. This was Malik ibn Anas, under whose hands what we may call, for distinction, the historical school of al-Madina took form. Al-Madina, it will be remembered, was the mother-city of Muslim law. It was the special home of the traditions of the Prophet and the scene of his legislative and judicial life. Its pre-Islamic customary law had been sanctioned, in a sense, by his use. It had been the capital of the state in its purest days. From the height of all these privileges its traditionists and lawyers looked down upon the outsiders and parvenus who had begun to intermeddle in sacred things.

But it must not be thought that this school was of a rigid traditionism. The case was quite the reverse, and in many respects it is hard to make a distinction between it and that of Abu Hanifa. Its first source was, of necessity, the Qur'an. Then came the usage of the Prophet. This merged into the usage of the Successors of the Prophet and the unwritten custom of the town. It will be seen that here the historical weight of the place came to bear. No other place, no other community, could furnish that later tradition with anything like the same authority. Further, Malik ibn Anas was a practical jurist, a working judge. He was occupied in meeting real cases from day to day. When he sat in public and judged the people, or with his pupils around him and expounded and developed the law, he could look back upon a line of canon lawyers who had sat, in his place and done as he was doing. In that lies the great difference. He was in practical touch with actual life; that was one point; and, secondly, he was in the direct line of the apostolic succession, and in the precise environment of the Prophet. So when he went beyond Qur'an, prophetic usage, agreement, and gave out decisions on simple opinion, the feeling of the community justified him. It was a different thing for Malik ibn Anas, sitting there in state in al-Madina, to use his judgment, than for some quick-brained vagabond of a Persian or Syrian proselyte, some pauvre diable with neither kith nor kin in the country, to lay down principles of law. So the pride of the city of the Prophet distinguished between him and Abu Hanifa.

But though the speculative element in the school of Malik, apart from its local and historical environment, which gave it unifying weight, was essentially the same as in the school of Abu Hanifa, yet it is true that at al-Madina it played a less important part. Malik used tradition more copiously and took refuge in opinion less frequently. Without opinion, he could not have built his system; but for him it was not so much a primary principle as a means of escape. Yet one principle of great freedom he did derive from it and lay down with clearness; it is the conception of the public advantage (istislah). When a rule would work general injury it is to be set aside even in the teeth of a valid analogy. This, it will be seen, is nearly the same as the preference of Abu Hanifa. The technical term istislah, chosen by Malik to express his idea, was probably intended to distinguish it from that of Abu Hanifa, and also to suggest in the public advantage (maslaha) a more valid basis than the mere preference of the legist.

Another conception which Malik and his school developed into greater exactitude and force was that of the agreement (ijma). It will be remembered that from the death of Muhammad all the surviving Companions resident in al-Madina formed a kind of consultive council to aid the Khalifa with their store of tradition and experience. Their agreement on any point was final; it was the voice of the Church. This doctrine of the infallibility of the body of the believers developed in Islam until at its widest it was practically the same as the canon of catholic truth formulated by Vincent of Lerins, Quod ubique, quod semper, quod ab omnibus. But Malik, according to the usual view, had no intention of granting any such deciding power to the outside world. The world for him was al-Madina and the agreement of al-Madina established catholic verity. Yet there are narratives which

[57]

suggest that he approved the agreement and local usage of al-Madina for al-Madina because they suited al-Madina. Other places might also have their local usages which suited them better.

In the next school we shall find the principle of agreement put upon a broader basis and granted greater weight. Finally, Malik is the first founder of a system from whom a law book, the Muwatta mentioned above, has come down to us. It is not in the exact sense, a manual or code; rather a collection of materials for a code with remarks by the collector. He gives the traditions which seem to him of juristic importance--about seventeen hundred in all--arranged according to subject, and follows up each section, when necessary, with remarks upon the usage of al-Madina, and upon his own view of the matter. When he cannot find either tradition or usage, he evidently feels himself of sufficient authority to follow his own opinion, and lay down on that basis a binding rule. This, however, as we have seen, is very different from allowing other people, outsiders to al-Madina, to do the same thing. The school founded by Malik ibn Anas on these principles is one of the surviving four. As that of Abu Hanifa spread eastward, so that of Malik spread westward, and for a time crushed out all others. The firm grip which it has especially gained in western North Africa may be due to the influence of the Idrisids whose founder had to flee from al-Madina when Malik was in the height of his reputation there, and also to hatred of the Abbasids who championed the school of Abu Hanifa.

But now we pass from simple development to development through conflict. Open conflict, so far as there had been any, had covered points of detail; for example, the kind of opinion professed by Abu Hanifa, on the one hand, and by Malik, on the other. One of the chiefest of the pupils of Abu Hanifa, the Muhammad ibn al-Hasan already mentioned, spent three years in study with Malik at al-Madina and found no difficulty in thus combining his schools. The conflict of the future was to be different and to touch the very basis of things. The muttering of the coming storm had been heard for long, but it was now to burst. Exact dates we cannot give, but the reaction must have been progressing in the latter part of the life of Malik ibn Anas.

The distinction drawn above between traditionists and lawyers will be remembered, and the promise of future collision which always has come between historical or empirical, and speculative or philosophical students of systems of jurisprudence. The one side points to the absurdities, crudities, and inadequacies of a system based upon tradition and developing by usage; the other says that we are not wise enough to rewrite the laws of our ancestors. These urge a necessity; those retort an inability. Add to this a belief on the part of the traditionists that they were defending a divine institution and the situation is complete as it now lay

[58]

902). Then there appeared among them Said, the son of Ahmad, the son of Abd Allah, the son of Maymun the oculist; but it was not under that name. He was now Ubayd Allah al-Mahdi himself, a descendant of Ali and of Muhammad ibn Isma'il, for whom his ancestors were supposed to have worked and builtup this conspiracy. In A.H. 296 (A.D. 909) he was saluted as Commander of the Faithful, with the title of al-Mahdi. So far the conspiracy had succeeded. This Fatimid dynasty, so they called themselves from Fatima, their alleged ancestress, the daughter of Muhammad, conquered Egypt and Syria half a century later and held them till A.H. 567 (A.D. 1171). When in A.H. 317 the Umayyads of Cordova also claimed the Khalifate and used the title, there were three Commanders of the Faithful at one time in the Muslim world. Yet it should be noticed that the constitutional position of these Umayyads was essentially different from that of the Fatimids. To the Fatimids, the Abbasids were usurpers. The Umayyads of Cordova, on the other hand, held, like the Zaydites and some jurisconsults of the highest rank, that, when Muslim countries were so far apart that the authority of the ruler of the one could not make itself felt in the other, it was lawful to have two Imams, each a true Successor of the Prophet. The good of the people of Muhammad demanded it. Still, the unity of the Khalifate is the more regular doctrine.

But only half of the work was done. Islam stood as firmly as ever and the conspiracy had only produced a schism in the faith and had not destroyed it. Ubayd Allah was in the awkward position, on the one hand, of ruling a people who were in great bulk fanatical Muslims and did not understand any jesting with their religion, and, on the other hand, of being head of a conspiracy to destroy that very religion. The Syrians and Arabs had apparently taken more degrees than the Egyptians and North Africans, and Ubayd Allah found himself between the devil and the deep sea. The Qarmatians in Arabia plundered the pilgrim caravans, stormed the holy city Mecca, and, most terrible of all, carried off the sacred black stone. When an enormous ransom was offered for the stone, they declined--they had orders not to send it back. Everyone understood that the orders were from Africa. So Ubayd Allah found it advisable to address them in a public letter, exhorting them to be better Muslims. The writing and reading of this letter must have been accompanied by mirth, at any rate no attention was paid to it by the Qarmatians. It was not till the time of the third Fatimid Khalifa that they were permitted to do business with that stone. Then they sent it back with the explanatory or apologetic remark that they had carried it off under orders and now sent it back under orders. Meanwhile the Fatimid dynasty was running its course in Egypt but without turning the people of Egypt from Islam. Yet it produced one strange personality and two sects, stranger even than the sect to which it itself owed its origin. The personality is that of al-Hakim Bi'amrillah, who still remains in Islam. The extreme right said that law should be based on Qur'an and tradition only; the extreme left, that it was better to leave untrustworthy and obscure traditions and work out a system of rules by logic and the necessities of the case. To and fro between these two extremes swayed the conflict to which we now come.

In that conflict three names stand out: ash-Shafi'i who died in 204, Ahmad ibn Hanbal who died in 241 and Da'ud az-Zahiri who died in 270. Strangely enough, the first of these, ash-Shafi'i, struck the mediating note and the other two diverged further and further from the via media thus shown toward a blank traditionism.

Ash-Shafi'i is without question one of the greatest figures in the history of law. Perhaps he had not the originality and keenness of Abu Hanifa; but he had a balance of mind and temper, a clear vision and full grasp of means and ends that enabled him to say what proved to be the last word in the matter. After him came attempts to tear down; but they failed. The fabric of the Muslim canon law stood firm. There is a tradition from the Prophet that he promised that with the end of every century would come a restorer of the faith of his people. At the end of the first century was the pious Khalifa, Umar ibn Abd al-Aziz, who by some accident strayed in among the Umayyads. At the end of the second came ash-Shafi'i. His work was to mediate and systematize and bore especially on the sources from which rules of law might be drawn. His position on the positive side may be stated as one of great reverence for tradition. "If you ever find a tradition from the Prophet saying one thing," he is reported to have said, "and a decision from me saying another thing, follow the tradition." An absolutely authentic--according to Muslim rules of evidence--and clear tradition from the Prophet he regarded as of equally divine authority with a passage in the Qur'an. Both were inspired utterances, if slightly different in form; the Qur'an was verbally inspired; such traditions were inspired as to their content. And if such a tradition contradicted a Qur'anic passage and came after it in time, then the written law of the Qur'an was abrogated by the oral law of the tradition. But this involved grave difficulties. The speculative jurists had defended their position from the beginning by pointing to the many contradictory traditions which were afloat, and asking how the house of tradition could stand when so divided against itself. A means of reconciling traditions had to be found, and to this ash-Shafi'i gave himself. We need not go over his methods here; they were the same that have always been used in such emergencies. The worship of the letter led to the straining of the letter, and to explaining away of the letter.

But there lay a rock in his course more dangerous than any mere contradiction in differing traditions. Usages had grown up and taken fast hold which were in the teeth of all traditions. These usages were in the individual life, in the constitution of the state, and in the rules and decisions of the law courts. The pious theologian and lawyer might rage against them as he chose; they were there, firmly rooted, immovable. They were not arbitrary changes, but had come about in the process of time through the revolutions of circumstances and varying conditions. Ash-Shafi'i showed his greatness by recognizing the inevitable and providing a remedy. This lay in an extension of the principle of agreement and the erection of it into 'a formal source. Whatever the community of Islam has agreed upon at any time, is of God. We have met this principle before, but never couched in so absolute and catholic a form. The agreement of the immediate Companions of Muhammad had weight with his first Successors. The agreement of these first Companions and of the first generation after them, had determining weight in the early church. The agreement of al-Madina had weight with Malik ibn Anas. The agreement of many divines and legists always had weight of a kind. Among lawyers, a principle, to the contrary of which the memory of man ran not, had been determining. But this was wider, and from this time on the unity of Islam was assured. The evident voice of the People of Muhammad was to be the voice of God. Yet this principle, if full of hope and value for the future, involved the canonists of the time in no small difficulties. Was it conceivable that the agreement could override the usage of the Prophet? Evidently not. There must, then, they argued, once have existed some tradition to the same effect as the agreement, although it had now been lost. Some such lost authority must be presupposed. This can remind us of nothing so much as of the theory of the inerrant but lost original of the Scriptures. And it had the fate of that theory. The weight of necessity forced aside any such trifling and the position was frankly admitted that the agreement of the community was a safer and more certain basis than traditions from the Prophet. Traditions were alleged to that effect. "My People will never agree in an error," declared Muhammad, or, at least, the later church made him so declare.

But ash-Shafi'i found that even the addition of agreement to Qur'an and Prophetic usage did not give him basis enough for his system. Opinion he utterly rejected; the preference of Abu Hanifa and the conception of the common welfare of Malik ibn Anas were alike to him. It is true also that both had beer practically saved under agreement. But he held fast by analogy, whether based on the Qur'an or on the usage of the Prophet. It was an essential instrument for his purpose. As was said, "The laws of the Qur'an and of the usage are limited; the possible cases are unlimited; that which is unlimited can never be contained in that which is limited." But in ash-Shafi'i's use of analogy there is a distinction to be observed. In seeking to establish a parallelism between a case that has arisen and a rule in the Qur'an or usage, which is similar in some points but not precisely parallel, are we to look to external points of resemblance, or may we go further and seek to determine the reason (illa) lying behind the rule and from that draw our analogy? The point seems simple enough and the early speculative jurists sought the reason. For that they were promptly attacked by the traditionists. Such a method was an attempt to look into the mysteries of God, they were told; man has no business to inquire after reasons, all he has to do is to obey. The point thus raised was fought over for centuries and schools are classified according to their attitude toward it. The position of ash-Shafi'i seems to have been that the reason for a command was to be considered in drawing an analogy, but that there must be some clear guide, in the text itself, pointing to the reason. He thus left himself free to consider the causes of the divine commands and yet produced the appearance of avoiding any irreverence or impiety in doing so.

Such then are the four sources or bases (asls) of jurisprudence as accepted and defined by ash-Shafi'i--Qur'an, prophetic usage, analogy, agreement. The last has come to bear more and more weight. Every Shafi'ite law book begins each section with words to this effect, "The basis of this rule, before the agreement (qabla-l-ijma), is" Qur'an or usage as the case may be. The agreement must put its stamp on every rule to make it valid. Further, all the now existing schools have practically accepted ash-Shafi'i's classification of the sources and many have contended that a lawyer, no matter what his school, who does not use all these four sources, cannot be permitted to act as a judge. Ash-Shafi'i has accomplished his own definition of a true jurist, "Not he is a jurist who gathers statements and prefers one of them, but he who establishes a new principle from which a hundred branches may spring."

But the extreme traditionists were little satisfied with this compromise. They objected to analogy and they objected to agreement; nothing but the pure law of God and the Prophet would satisfy them. And their numbers were undoubtedly large. The common people always heard traditions gladly, and it was easy to turn to ridicule the subtleties of the professional lawyers. How much simpler, it struck the average mind, it would be to follow some clear and unambiguous saying of the Prophet; then one could feel secure. This desire of the plain man to take traditions and interpret them strictly and liter-ally was met by the school of Da'ud az-Zahiri, David the literalist. He was born three or four years before the death of ash-Shafi'i, which occurred in 204. He was trained as a Shafi'ite and that, too, of the narrower, more traditional type; but it was not traditional enough for him. So he had to cut himself loose and form a school of his own. He rejected utterly analogy; he limited agreement, as a source, to the agreement of the immediate Companions of Muhammad, and in this he has been followed by the Wahhabites alone among moderns; he limited himself to Qur'an and prophetic usage.

In another point also, he diverged. Ash-Shafi'i had evidently exercised a very great personal influence upon his followers. All looked up to him and were prepared to swear to his words. So there grew up a tendency for a scholar to take a thing upon the word of his master. "Ash-Shafi'i taught so; I am a Shafi'ite and I hold so." This, too, Da'ud utterly rejected. The scholar must examine the proofs for himself and form his own opinion. But he had another peculiarity, and one which gained him the name of literalist. Everything, Qur'an and tradition, must be taken in the most exact sense, however absurd it might be. Of course, to have gone an inch beyond the very first meaning of the words would have been to stray in the direction of analogy. Yet, as fate would have it, to analogy, more or less, he had in the end to come. The inexorable law that the limited cannot bound the unlimited was proved again. "Analogy is like carrion," confessed a very much earlier traditionist, "when there is nothing else you eat it." Da'ud tried to make his meal more palatable by a change in name. He called it a proof (dalil) instead of a source (asl); but what difference of idea he involved in that it is hard to determine. This brought him to the doctrine of cause, already mentioned. Were we at liberty to seek the cause of a divine word or action and lead our "proof" from that? If the cause was directly stated, then Da'ud held that we must regard it as having been the cause in this case; but we were not at liberty, he added, to look for it, or on it, as cause in any other case.

It is evident that here we have to do with an impossible man and school, and so the Muslim world found. Most said roundly that it was illegal to permit a Zahirite to act as judge, on much the same grounds, that objection to circumstantial evidence will throw out a man now as juror. If they had been using modern language, they would have said that it was because he was a hopeless crank. Yet the Zahirite school lasted for centuries and drew long consequences, historical and theological, for which there is no space here. It never held rank as an acknowledged school of Muslim law.

We now come to the last of the four schools, and it, strange as its origin was, need not detain us long. The Zahirite reaction had failed through its very extremeness. It was left to a dead man and a devoted Shafi'ite to head the last attack upon the school of his master. Ahmad ibn Hanbal was a theologian of the first rank; he made no claim to be a constructive lawyer. His Musnad has already been dealt with. It is an immense collection of some thirty thousand traditions, but these are not even arranged for le gal purposes. He suffered terribly for the orthodox faith in the rationalist persecution under the Khalifa al-Ma'mun, and his sufferings gained him the position of a saint. But he never dreamed' of forming a school, least of all in opposition to his master, ash-Shafi'i. He died in 241, and after his death his disciples drew together and the fourth school was founded. It was simply reactionary and did not make progress in any way. It minimized agreement

[62]

and analogy and tended toward literal interpretation. As might be expected from its origin, its history has been one of violence, of persecution and counter-persecution, of insurrection and riot. Again and again the streets of Baghdad ran blood from its excesses. It has now the smallest following of the four surviving schools.

There is no need to pursue this history further. With ash-Shafi'i the great development of Muslim jurisprudence closes. Legislation, equity, legal fiction have done their parts; the hope for the future lay, and lies, in the principle of the agreement. The commonsense of the Muslim community, working through that expression of catholicity, has set aside in the past even the undoubted letter of the Qur'an, and in the future will still further break the grasp of that dead hand. It is the principle of unity in Islam. But there is a principle of variety as well. The four schools of law whose origin has been traced are all equally valid and their decisions equally sacred in Muslim eyes. The believer may belong to any one of these which he chooses; he must belong to one; and when he has chosen his school, he accepts it and its rules to the uttermost. Yet he does not cast out as heretics the followers of the other schools. In every chapter their codes differ more or less; but each school bears with the others; sometimes, it may be, with a superior tone, but still bears. This liberty of variety in unity is again undoubtedly due to the agreement. It has expressed itself, as it often does, in apocryphal traditions from the Prophet, the last rag of respect left to the traditionist school. Thus we are told that the Prophet said, "The disagreement of My People is a Mercy from God." This supplements and completes the other equally apocryphal but equally important tradition: "My People will never agree upon an error."

But there is a third principle at work which we cannot view with the same favor. As said above, every Muslim must attach himself to a legal school, and may choose any one of these four. But once he has chosen his school he is absolutely bound by the decisions and rules of that school. This is the principle against which the Zahirites protested, but their protest, the only bit of sense they ever showed, was in vain. The result of its working throughout centuries has been that now no one--except from a spirit of historical curiosity--ever dreams of going back from the text-books of the present day to the works of the older masters. Further, such an attempt to get behind the later commentaries would not be permitted. We have comment upon comment upon comment, abstract of this and expansion of that; but each hangs by his predecessor and dares not go another step backward. The great masters of the four schools settled the broad principles; they were authorities of the first degree (mujtahidun mutlaq), second to Muhammad in virtue of his inspiration only. Second,--one the masters who had authority within the separate schools (mujtahidun fi-l-madhahib) to determine the questions that arose there. Third, masters of still lesser rank for minor points (mujtahidun bilfatwa). And so the chain runs on. The possibility of a new legal school arising or of any considerable change among these existing schools is flatly denied. Every legist now has his place and degree of liberty fixed, and he must be content.

These three principles, then, of catholic unity and its ability to make and abrogate laws, of the liberty of diversity in that unity, and of blind subjection to the past within that diversity, these three principles must be our hope and fear for the Muslim peoples, What that future will be none can tell. The grasp of the dead hand of Islam is close, but its grip at many points has been forced to relax. Very early, as has already been pointed out, the canon law had to give way to the will of the sovereign, and ground once lost it has never regained. Now, in every Muslim country, except perhaps the Wahhabite state in central Arabia, there are two codes of law administered by two separate courts. The one judges by this canon law and has cognizance of what we may call private and family affairs, marriage, divorce, inheritance. Its judges, at whose head in Turkey stands the Shaykh al-Islam, a dignity first created by the Ottoman Sultan Muhammad II in 1453, after the capture of Constantinople, also give advice to those who consult them on such personal matters as details of the ritual law, the law of oaths and vows, etc. The other court knows no law except the custom of the country (urf, ada) and the will of the ruler, expressed often in what are called Qanuns, statutes. Thus, in Turkey at the present day, besides the codices of canon law, there is an accepted and authoritative corpus of such Qanuns. It is based on the Code Napoléon and administered by courts under the Minister of Justice. This is the nearest approach in Islam to the development by statute, which comes last in Sir Henry Maine's analysis of the growth of law. The court guided by these Qanuns decides all matters of public and criminal law, all affairs between man and man. Such is the legal situation throughout the whole Muslim world, from Sulu to the Atlantic and from Africa to China. The canon lawyers, on their side, have never admitted this to be anything but flat usurpation. There have not failed some even who branded as heretics and unbelievers those who took any part in such courts of the world and the devil. They look back to the good old days of the rightly guided Khalifas, when there was but one law in Islam, and forward to the days of the Mahdi when that law will be restored. There, between a dead past and a hopeless future, we may leave them. The real future is not theirs. Law is greater than lawyers, and it works in the end for justice and life.

Finally, it may be well to notice an important and necessary modification which holds as to the above statement that a Muslim may choose any one of the four schools and may then follow its rules. As might be expected, geographical influences weigh overwhelmingly in this choice. Certain countries are Hanifite or Shafi'ite; in each, adherents of the other sects are rare. This geographical position may be given roughly as follows: central Asia, northern India, and the Turks

[64]

everywhere are Hanifite. Lower Egypt, Syria, southern India and the Malay Archipelago are Shafi'ite. Upper Egypt and North Africa west of Egypt are Malikite. Practically, only the Wahhabites in central Arabia are Hanbalites. Further, the position holds in Islam that the country, as a whole, follows the legal creed of its ruler, just as it follows his religion. It is not only cuius regio eius religio, but cuius religio eius lex. Again and again, a revolution in the state has driven one legal school from power and installed another. Yet the situation occurs sometimes that a sovereign finds his people divided into two parties, each following a different rite, and he then recognizes both by appointing Qadis belonging to both, and enforcing the decisions of these Qadis. Thus, at Zanzibar, at present, there are eight Ibadite judges and two Shafi'ite, all appointed by the Sultan and backed by his authority. On the other hand, the Turkish government, ever since it felt itself strong enough, has thrown the full weight of its influence on the Hanifite side. In almost all countries under its rule it appoints Hanifite judges only; valid legal decisions can be pronounced only according to that rite. The private needs of non-Hanifites are met by the appointment of salaried Muftis- -givers of fatwàs, or legal opinions--of the other rites.

In the above sketch there have been of necessity two considerable omissions. The one is of Shi'ite and the other of Ibadite law. Neither seems of sufficient importance to call for separate treatment. The legal system of the Shi'ites is derived from that of the so-called Sunnites and differs in details only. We have seen already (p. 38) that the Shi'ites still have Mujtahids who are not bound to the words of a master, but can give decisions on their own responsibility. These seem to have in their hands the teaching power which strictly belongs only to the Hidden Imam. They thus represent the principle of authority which is the governing conception of the Shi'a. The Sunnites, on the other hand, have reached the point of recognizing that it is the People of Muhammad as a whole which rules through its agreement. In another point the Shi'ite conception of authority affects their legal system. They utterly reject the idea of co-ordinate schools of law; to the doctrine of the varying (ikhtilaf) as it is called, and the liberty of diversity which lies in it, they oppose the authority of the Imam. There can be only one truth and there can be no trifling with it even in details. Among the Shi'ites of the Zaydite sect this was affected also by their philosophical studies and a philosophical doctrine of the unity of truth; but to the Imamites it is an authoritative necessity and not one of thought. Thus on two important points the Shi'ites lack the possibility of freedom and development which is to be found with the Sunnites. Of the jurisprudence of the Ibadites we know comparatively little. A full examination of Ibadite fiqh would be of the highest interest, as the separation of its line of descent goes far back behind the formation of any of the orthodox systems and it must have been codified to a greater or less extent by Abd Allah ibn Ibad himself.

Its basis appears to be three-fold, Qur'an, prophetic usage, agreement--naturally that of the Ibadite community. There is no mention of analogy, and traditions seem to have been used sparingly and critically. Qur'an bore the principal emphasis. See above, (p. 26) for the Ibadite position on the form of the state and on the nature of its headship.

PART III

Theology

CHAPTER I

The three principles in the development; first religious questionings; Murji'ites, Kharijites, Qadarites; influence of Christianity; the Umayyads and Abbasids; the Mu'tazilites; the Qualities of God; the Vision of God; the creation of the Qur'an.

BEFORE entering upon a consideration of the development of the theology of Islam, it will be well to mark clearly the three principles which run continuously through that development, which conditioned it for evil and for good and which are still working in it. In dealing with jurisprudence and with the theory of the state, we have already seen abundantly how false is the current idea that Islam has ceased to grow and has no hope of future development. The organism of Islam, like every other organism, has periods of rest when it appears to have reached a cul de sac and to have outlived its life. But after these periods come others of renewed quickening and its vital energy pours itself forth again alter et idem. In the state, we saw how the old realms passed into decrepitude and decay, but new ones rose to take their places. The despotism by the grace of God of formal Islam was tempered by the sacred right of insurrection and revolution, and the People of Muhammad, in spite of kings and princes, asserted, from time to time, its unquenchable vitality.

In theology the spirit breathes through single chosen men more than through the masses; and, in consequence, our treatment of it will take biographical form wherever our knowledge renders that possible.

But whether we have men or naked movements, the begetters of which are names to us or less, three threads are woven distinctly through the web of Muslim religious thought. There is tradition (naql); there is reason (aql) and there is the unveiling of the mystic (kashf). They were in the tissue of Muhammad's brain and they have been in his church since he died. Now one would be most prominent, now another, according to the thinker of the time; but all were present to some degree. Tradition in its strictest form lives now only with the Wahhabites and the Brotherhood of as-Sanusi; reason has become a scholastic hand-maid of theology except among the modern Indian Mu'tazilites, whom orthodox Islam would no more accept as Muslims than a Trinitarian of the Westminster confession would give the name of Christian to a Unitarian of the left wing; the inner light of the mystic has assumed many forms, running from plainest pantheism to mere devout ecstasy.

But in the church of Muhammad they are all working still; and the catholicity of Islam, in spite of zealots, persecutions and counter-persecutions, has attained here, too, as in law, a liberty of variety in unity. Two of the principles we have met already in the students of hadith and of speculative law. The Hanbalites maintained in theology their devotion to tradition; they fought for centuries all independent thinking which sought to rise above what the fathers had told; they fought even scholastic theology of the strictest type and would be content with nothing but the rehearsal of the old dogmas in the old forms; they fought, too, the mystical life in all its phases. On the other hand, Abu Hanifa was tinged with rationalism and speculation in theology as in law, and his followers have walked in his path. Even the mystical light has been touched in our view of the theory of the state. It has flourished most among the Shi'ites, who are driven to seek and to find an inner meaning under the plain word of the Qur'an, and whose devotion to Ali and his house and to their divine mission has kept alive the thought of a continuous speaking of God to mankind and of an exalting of mankind into the presence of God. It is for the student, then, to watch and hold fast these three guiding threads.

The development of Muslim theology, like that of jurisprudence, could not begin till after the death of Muhammad. So long as he lived and received infallible revelations in solution of all questions of faith or usage that might come up, it is obvious that no system of theology could be formed or even thought of. Traditions, too, which have reached us, even show him setting his face against all discussions of dogma and repeating again and again, in answer to metaphysical and theological questions, the crude anthropomorphisms of the Qur'an. But these questions and answers are probably forgeries of the later traditional school, shadows of future warfare thrown back upon the screen of the patriarchal age. Again, in the first twenty or thirty years after Muhammad's death, the Muslims were too much occupied with the propagation of their faith to think what that faith exactly was. Thus, it seems that the questioning spirit in this direction was aroused comparatively late and remained for some time on what might be called a private basis. Individual men had their individual views, but sects did not quickly

[67]

arise, and when they did were vague and hard to define in their positions. It may be said, broadly, that everything which has reached us about the early Muslim heresies is uncertain, confused and unsatisfactory. Names, slates, influences and doctrines are all seen through a haze, and nothing more than an approximation to an outline can be attempted. Vague stories are handed down of the early questionings and disputings of certain ahl-al-ahwa, "people of wandering desires," a name singularly descriptive of the always flighty and sceptical Arabs; of how they compared Scripture with Scripture and got up theological debates, splitting points and defining issues, to great scandal and troubling of spirit among the simpler-minded pious. These were not yet heretics; they were the first investigators and systematizers.

Yet two sects loom up through the mist and their existence can be tolerably conditioned through the historical facts and philosophical necessities of the time. The one is that of the Murji'ites, and the other of the Qadarites. A Murji'ite is literally "one who defers or postpones," in this case postpones judgment until it is pronounced by God on the Day of Judgment. They arose as a sect during and out of the civil war between the Shi'ites, the Kharijites and the Umayyads. All these parties claimed to be Muslims, and most of them claimed that they were the only true Muslims and that the others were unbelievers. This was especially the attitude of the Shi'ites and Kharijites toward the Umayyads; to them, the Umayyads, as we have seen already, were godless heathen who professed Islam, but oppressed and slaughtered the true saints of God. The Murji'ites, on the other hand, worked out a view on which they could still support the Umayyads without homologating all their actions and condemning all their opponents. The Umayyads, they held, were de facto the rulers of the Muslim state; fealty had been sworn to them and they confessed the Unity of God and the apostleship of the Prophet. Thus, they were not polytheists, and there is no sin that can possibly be compared with the sin of polytheism (shirk). It was, therefore, the duty of all Muslims to acknowledge their sovereignty and to postpone until the secrets of the Last Day all judgment or condemnation of any sins they might have committed. Sins less than polytheism could justify no one in rising in revolt against them and in breaking the oath of fealty.

Such seems to have been the origin of the Murji'ites, and it was the origin also of the theory of the accomplished fact in the state, of which we have had to take account several times. Thus, between the fanatical venerators of the canon law, to whom all the Khalifas, after the first four, were an abomination, and the purely worldly lawyers of the court party, there came a group of pious theologians who taught that the good of the Muslim community required obedience to the ruler of the time, even though his personal unworthiness were plain. As a consequence, success can legitimate anything in the Muslim state.

[68]

But with the passing away of the situation which gave rise to Murji'ism, it itself changed from politics to theology. As a political party it had opposed the political puritanism of the Kharijites; it now came to oppose the uncompromising spirit in which these damned all who differed from them even in details and brandished the terrors of the wrath of God over their opponents. It is true that this came natural to Islam. The earlier Muslims seem in general to have been oppressed by a singularly gloomy fatalism. To use modern theological language, they labored under a terrible consciousness of sin. They viewed the world as an evil temptress, seducing men from heavenly things. Their lives were hedged about with sins, great and little, and each deserved the eternal wrath of God. The recollection of their latter end they kept ever before them and the terrors that it would bring, for they felt that no amount of faith in God and His Prophet could save them in the judgment to come. The roots of this run far back. Before the time of Muhammad and at his time there were among the Arab tribes, scattered here and there, many men who felt a profound dissatisfaction with heathenism, its doctrines and religious rites. The conception of God and the burden of life pressed heavily upon them. They saw men pass away and descend into the grave, and they asked whither they had gone and what had become of them. The thought of this fleeting, transitory life and of the ocean of darkness and mystery that lies around it, drove them away to seek truth in solitude and the deserts. They were called Hanifs--the word is of very doubtful derivation--and Muhammad himself, in the early part of his career, reckoned himself one of them. But we have evidence from heathen Arab poetry that these Hanifs were regarded as much the same as Christian monks, and that the term hanif was used as a synonym for rahib, monk.

And, in truth, the very soul of Islam sprang from these solitary hermits, scattered here and there throughout the desert, consecrating their lives to God, and fleeing from the wrath to come. Even in pre-Islamic Arabic poetry we feel how strong was the impression made on the Arab mind by the gaunt, weird men with their endless watchings and night prayers. Again and again there is allusion to the lamp of the hermit shining through the darkness, and we have pictures of the caravan or of the solitary traveller on the night journey cheered and guided by its glimmer. These Christian hermits and the long deserted ruins telling of old, forgotten tribes--judged and overthrown by God, as the Arabs held and hold--that lie throughout the Syrian waste and along the caravan routes were the two things that most stirred the imagination of Muhammad and went to form his faith. To Muhammad, and to the Semite always, the whole of life was but a long procession from the great deep to the great deep again. Where are the kings and rulers of the earth? Where are the peoples that were mighty in their day? The hand of God smote them and they are not. There is naught real in the world but God. From Him we

[69]

are, and unto Him we return. There is nothing for man but to fear and worship. The world is deceitful and makes sport of them that trust it.

Such is the oversong of all Muslim thought, the faith to which the Semite ever returns in the end. To this the later Murji'ites opposed a doctrine of Faith, which was Pauline in its sweep. Faith, they declared, saved, and Faith alone. If the sinner believed in God and His Prophet he would not remain in the fire. The Kharijites, on the other hand, held that the sinner who died unrepentant would remain therein eternally, even though he had confessed Islam with his lips. The unrepentant sinner, they considered, could not be a believer in the true sense. This is still the Ibadite position, and from it developed one of the most important controversies of Islam as to the precise nature of faith. Some extreme Murji'ites held that faith (iman) was a confession in the heart, private intercourse with God, as opposed to Islam, public confession with the lips. Thus, one could be a believer (mu'min), and outwardly confess Judaism or Christianity; to be a professed Muslim was not necessary. This is like the doctrine of the Imamites, called taqiya, that it is allowable in time of stress to dissemble one's religious views; and it is worth noticing that Jahm ibn Safwan (killed, 131?), one of these extreme Murji'ites, was a Persian proselyte in rebellion against the Arab rule, and of the loosest religious conduct. But these Antinomians were no more Muslims than the Anabaptists of Munster had a claim to be Christians. The other wing of the Murji'ites is represented by Abu Hanifa, who held that faith (iman) is acknowledgment with the tongue as well as the heart and that works are a necessary supplement. This is little different from the orthodox position which grew up, that persuasion, confession, and works made up faith. When Murji'ism dropped out of existence as a sect it left as its contribution to Islam a distinction between great and little sins (kabiras, saghiras), and the position that even great sins, if not involving polytheism (shirk), would not exclude the believer forever from the Garden.

The second sect, that of Qadarites, had its origin in a philosophical necessity of the human mind. A perception of the contradiction between man's consciousness of freedom and responsibility, on the one hand, and the absolute rule and predestination of God, on the other, is the usual beginning of the thinking life, both in individuals and in races. It was so in Islam. In theology as in law, Muhammad had been an opportunist pure and simple. On the one hand, his Allah is the absolute Semitic despot who guides aright and leads astray, who seals up the hearts of men and opens them again, who is mighty over all. On the other hand, men are exhorted to repentance, and punishment is threatened against them if they remain hardened in their unbelief. All these phases of a wandering and intensely subjective mind, which lived only in the perception of the moment, appear in the Qur'an. Muhammad was a poet rather than a theologian just as he was a prophet rather than a legislator. As soon, then, as the Muslims paused in

[70]

their career of conquest and began to think at all, they thought of this. Naturally, so long as they were fighting in the Path of God, it was the conception of God's absolute sovereignty which most appealed to them; by it their fates were fixed, and they charged without fear the ranks of the unbelievers. In these earliest times, the fatalistic passages bore most stress and the others were explained away. This helped, at least, to bring it about that the party which in time came to profess the freedom of man's will, began and ended as an heretical sect. But it only helped, and we must never loge sight of the fact that the eventual victory in Islam of the absolute doctrine of God's eternal decree was the victory of the more fundamental of Muhammad's conflicting conceptions. The other had been much more a campaigning expedient.

This sect of Qadarites, whose origin we have been conditioning, derived its name from their position that a man possessed qadar, or power, over his actions. One of the first of them was a certain Ma'bad al-Juhani, who paid for his heresy with his life in A.H. 80. Historians tell that he with Ata ibn Yassar, another of similar opinions, came one day to the celebrated ascetic, al-Hasan al-Basri (d. 110), and said, "O Abu Said, those kings shed the blood of the Muslims, and do grievous things and say that their works are by the decree of God." To this al-Hasan replied, "The enemies of God lie." The story is only important as showing how the times and their changes were widening men's thoughts. Very soon, now, we come from these drifting tendencies to a formal sect with a formal secession and a fixed name. The Murji'ites and the Qadarites melt from the scene, some of their tenets pass into orthodox Islam; some into the new sect.

The story of its founding again connects with the outstanding figure of al-Hasan al-Basri. He seems to have been the chief centre of the religious life and movements of his time; his pupils appear and his influence shows itself in all the later schools. Someone came to him as he sat among his pupils and asked what his view was between the conflicting Murji'ites and Wa'idites, the first holding that the committer of a great sin, if he had faith, was not an unbeliever, was to be accepted as a Muslim and his case left in the hands of God; the other laying more stress upon the threats (wa'id) in the Book of God and teaching that the committer of a great sin could not be a believer, that he had, ipso facto, abandoned the true faith, must go into the Fire and abide there. Before the master could reply, one of his pupils--some say Amr ibn Ubayd (d. circ. 141), others, Wasil ibn Ata (d. 131)--broke in with the assertion of an intermediate position. Such an one was neither a believer nor an unbeliever. Then he left the circle which sat round the master, went to another part of the mosque and began to develop his view to those who gathered round him. The name believer (mu'min), he taught, was a term of praise, and an evil-doer was not worthy of praise and could not have that name applied to him. But he was not an unbeliever, either, for he assented to the faith. If

[71]

he, then, died unrepentant, he must abide forever in the Fire--for there are only two divisions in the next world, heaven and hell--but his torments would be mitigated on account of his faith. The position to which orthodox Islam eventually came was that a believer could commit a great sin. If he did so, and died unrepentant, he went to hell; but after a time would be permitted to enter heaven. Thus, hell became for believers a sort of purgatory. On this secession, al-Hasan only said "I'tazala anna"--He has seceded from us. So the new party was called the Mu'tazila, the Secession. That, at least, is the story, which may be taken for what it is worth. The fixed facts are the rise at the beginning of the second century after the Hijra of a tolerably definite school of dissenters from the traditional ideas, and their application of reason to the dogmas of the Qur'an.

We have noted already the influence of Christianity on Muhammad through the hermits of the desert. From it sprang the asceticism of Islam and that asceticism grew and developed into quietism and thence into mysticism. The last step was still in the future, but already at this time there were wandering monks who imitated their Christian brethren in the wearing of a coarse woollen frock and were thence called Sufis, from suf, wool. It was not long before Sufi came to mean mystic, and the third of the three great threads was definitely woven into the fabric of Muslim thought. But that was not the limit of Christian influence. Those anchorites in their caves and huts had little training in the theology of the schools; the dogmas of their faith were of a practical simplicity. But in the development of the Murji'ites and Qadarites it is impossible to mistake the workings of the dialectic refinements of Greek theology as developed in the Byzantine and Syrian schools. It is worth notice, too, that, while the political heresies of the Shi'ites and Kharijites held sway mostly in Arabia, Mesopotamia, and Persia, these more religious heresies seem to have arisen in Syria first and especially at Damascus, the seat of the Umayyads.

The Umayyad dynasty, we should remember, was in many ways a return to pre-Muslim times and to an easy enjoyment of worldly things; it was a rejection of the yoke of Muhammad in all but form and name. The fear of the wrath of God had small part with the most of them; sometimes it appeared in the form of an insane rebellion and defiance. Further, as Muslim governments always have done, they sought aid in their task of governing from their non-Muslim subjects. So it came about that Sergius, the father of Johannes Damascenus, was treasurer under them and that after his death, this John of Damascus himself, the last great doctor of the Greek Church and the man under whose hands its theology assumed final form, became wazir and held that post until he withdrew from the world and turned to the contemplative life. In his writings and in those of his pupil, Theodorus Abucara (d. A.D. 826), there are polemic treatises on Islam, cast in the form of discussions between Christians and Muslims. These represent, there can be little

[72]

doubt, a characteristic of the time. The close agreement of Murji'ite and Qadarite ideas with those formulated and defended by John of Damascus and by the Greek Church generally can only be so explained. The Murji'ite rejection of eternal punishment and emphasis on the goodness of God and His love for His creatures, the Qadarite doctrine of free-will and responsibility, are to be explained in the same way as we have already explained the presence of sentences in the Muslim fiqh which seem to be taken bodily from the Roman codes. In this case, also, we are not to think of the Muslim divines as studying the writings of the Greek fathers, but as picking up ideas from them in practical intercourse and controversy. The very form of the tract of John of Damascus is significant, "When the Saracen says to you such and such, then you will reply. . . ." This, as a whole, is a subject which calls for investigation, but so far it is clear that the influence of Greek theology on Islam can hardly be overestimated. The one outstanding fact of the enormous emphasis laid by' both on the doctrine of the nature of God and His attributes is enough. It may even be conjectured that the harsher views developed by western Muslims, and especially by the theologians of Spain, were due, on the other hand, to Augustinian and Roman influence. It is, to say the least, a curious coincidence that Spanish Islam never took kindly to metaphysical or scholastic theology, in the exact sense, but gave almost all its energy to canon law.

But there were other influences to come. With the fall of the Umayyads and the rise of the Abbasids, the intellectual centre of the empire moved to the basin of the Euphrates and the Tigris. The story of the founding of Baghdad there, in 145, we have already heard. We have seen, too, that the victory of the Abbasids was, in a sense, a conquest of the Arabs by the Persians. Græcia capta and the rest came true here; the battles of al-Qadisiya and Nahawand were avenged; Persian ideas and Persian religion began slowly to work on the faith of Muhammad. At the court of the earliest Abbasids it was fashionable to affect a little free thought. People were becoming enlightened and played with philosophy and science. Greek philosophy, Zoroastrianism, Manichæism, the old heathenism of Harran, Judaism, Christianity--all were in the air and making themselves felt. So long as the adherents and teachers of these took them in a purely academic way, were good subjects and made no trouble, the earlier Abbasids encouraged their efforts, gathered in the scientific harvest, paid well for translations, instruments, and investigations, and generally posed as patrons of progress.

But a line had to be drawn somewhere and drawn tightly. The victory of the Abbasids had raised high hopes among the Persian nationalists. They had thought that they were rallying to the overthrow of the Arabs, and found, when all was done, that they had got only another Arab dynasty. So revolts had begun to break out afresh, and now, curiously enough, they were of a marked religious character. They were an expression of religious sects, Buddhistic, Zoroastrian, Manichean,

[73]

and parties with prophetic leaders of their own; all are swept together by Muslim writers as Zinadiqs, probably literally, "initiates," originally Manichæans, thereafter, practically non-Muslims concealing their unbelief. For when not in open revolt they must needs profess Islam. In 167, we find al-Mahdi, who was also, it is true, much more strict than his father, al-Mansur, appointing a grand inquisitor to deal with such heretics. Al-Mansur, however, had contented himself with crushing actual rebellion; and Christian, Jew, Zoroastrian, and heathen of Harran were tolerated so long as they brought to him the fruits of Greek science and philosophy.

That they did willingly, and so, through three intermediaries, science came to the Arabs. There was a heathen Syrian source with its centre at Harran, of which we know comparatively little. There was a Christian Syrian source working from the multitudinous monasteries scattered over the country. There was a Persian source by which natural science, and medicine especially, were passed on. Already in the fifth century A.D. an academy of medicine and philosophy had been founded at Gondeshapur in Khuzistan. One of the directors of this institution was summoned, in 148, to prescribe for al-Mansur, and from that time on it furnished court physicians to the Abbasids. On these three paths, then, Aristotle and Plato, Euclid and Ptolemy, Galen and Hippocrates reached the Muslim peoples.

The first hundred years of the Abbasid Khalifate was the golden age of Muslim science, the period of growth and development for the People of Muhammad fairly as a whole. Intellectual life did not cease with the close of that period, but the Khalifate ceased to aid in carrying the torch. Thereafter, learning was protected and fostered by individual rulers here and there, and individual investigators and scholars still went on their own quiet paths. But free intellectual life among the people was checked, and such learning as still generally flourished fell more and more between fixed bounds. Scholasticism, with its formal methods and systems, its subtle deductions and endless ramifications of proof and counter-proof, drew away attention from the facts of nature. The oriental brain studied itself and its own workings to the point of dizziness, and then turned and clung fast to the certainties of revelation. Under this spell heresy and orthodoxy proved alike sterile.

We return, now, to the beginnings of the Mu'tazilites. These served themselves heirs upon the Qadarites and denied that God predestined the actions of men. Death and life, sickness, health, and external vicissitudes came, they admitted, by God's qadar, but it was unthinkable that man should be punished for actions not in his control. The freedom of the will is an a priori certainty, and man possesses qadar over his own actions. This was the position of Wasil ibn Ata, of whom we have already heard. But to it he added a second doctrine, the origin of which is

[74]

obscure, although suggestive of discussions with Greek theologians. The Qur'an describes God as willing, knowing, decreeing, etc.--strictly as the Willing One, the Knowing One, the Decreeing One, etc.--and the orthodox hold that such expressions could only mean that God possesses as Qualities (sifat) Will, Knowledge, Power, Life, etc. To this Wasil raised objections. God was One, and such Qualities would be separate Beings. Thus, his party and the Mu'tazilites always called themselves the People of Unity and Justice (Ahl-at-tawhid wal'adl); the Unity being of the divine nature, the Justice consisting in that they opposed God's qadar over men and held that He must do for the creature that which was best for it. Orthodox Islam held and holds that there can be no necessity upon God, even to do justice; He is absolutely free, and what He does man must accept. It flatly opposes the position held by the Mu'tazilites in general, that good and evil can be perceived and distinguished by the intellect (aql). Good and evil have their nature by God's will, and man can learn to know them only by God's teachings and commands. Thus, except through revelation, there can be neither theology nor ethics.

The next great advance was made by Abu Hudhayl Muhammad al-Allaf (d. circa 226), a disciple of the second generation from Wasil. At his hands the doctrine of God's qualities assumed a more definite form. Wasil had reduced God to a vague unity, a kind of eternal oneness. Abu Hudhayl taught that the qualities were not in His essence, and thus separable from it, thinkable apart from it, but that they were His essence. Thus, God was omnipotent by His omnipotence, but it was His essence and not an His essence. He was omniscient by His omniscience and it was His essence. Further, he held that these qualities must be either negations or relations. Nothing positive can be asserted of them, for that would mean that there was in God the complexity of subject and predicate, being and quality; and God is absolute Unity. This view the Muslim theologians regard as a close approximation to the Christian Trinity; for them, the persons of the Trinity have always been personified qualities, and such seems really to have been the view of John of Damascus. Further, God's Will, according to Abu Hudhayl, as expressed in His Creative Word, did not necessarily exist in a subject (fi mahall, in subiecto). When God said, "Be!" creatively, there was no subject. Again, he endeavored-- and in this he was followed by most of the Mu'tazilites to cut down the number of God's attributes. His will, he said, was a form of His knowledge; He knew that there was good in an action, and that knowledge was His will.

His position on the qadar question was peculiar. With regard to this world, be was a Qadarite; but in the next world, both in heaven and in hell, he thought that all changes were by divine necessity. Otherwise, that is, if men were free, there would be obligation to observe a law (taklif); but there is no such obligation in the other world. Thus, whatever happened there happened by God's decree. Further, he taught that, eventually, nothing would happen there; that there would be no changes, but only an endless stillness in which those in heaven had all its joys and those in hell all its pains. This is a close approximation to the view of Jahm ibn Safwan, who held that after the judgment both heaven and hell would pass away and God remain alone as He was in the beginning. To these doctrines Abu Hudhayl seems to have been led by two considerations, both significant for the drift of the Mu'tazilites. First, there was about their reasonings a grimness of logic touched with utilitarianism. Thus, from their position that man could come by the light of his reason to the knowledge of God and of virtue, they drew the conclusion that it was man's duty so to attain, and that God would damn eternally every man who did not. Their utilitarianism, again, comes out strikingly in their view of heaven and hell. These, at present, were serving no useful purpose because they had no inhabitants; therefore, at present they did not exist. But this made difficulties for Abu Hudhayl. What has a beginning must have an end. So he explained the end as the ceasing of all changes. Second, he shows clear evidence of influence from Greek philosophy. The Qur'an teaches that the world has been created in time; Aristotle, that it is from eternity and to eternity. The creation, Abu Hudhayl applied to changes; before that, the world was, but in eternal rest. Hereafter, all changes will cease; rest will again enter and endure to all eternity. We shall see how largely this doctrine was advanced and developed by his successors.

But there were further complications in the doctrine of man's actions and into some of these we must enter, on account of their later importance. Not everything that comes from the action of a man is by his action. God has a creative part in it, apparently as regards the effects. Especially, knowledge in the mind of a pupil does not come from the teacher, but from God. The idea seems to be that they teacher may teach, but that the being taught in the pupil is a divine working. Similarly, he distinguished motions in the mind, which he held were not altogether due to the man, and external motions which were. There is given, too, to a man at the time of his performing an action an ability to perform the action, which is a special accident in him apart from any mere soundness of health or limb.

In these ways, Abu Hudhayl recognized God's working through man. Another of his positions had a similar basis and was a curious combination of historical criticism and mysticism, a combination which we shall find later in al-Ghazzali, a much greater man. The evidence of tradition for things dealing with the Unseen World (al-ghayb) he rejected. Twenty witnesses might hand on the tradition in question, but it was not to be received unless among them there was one, at least, of the People of Paradise. At all times, he taught, there were in the world these Friends of God (awliya Allah, sing. wali), who were protected against all greater sins and could not lie. It is the word of these that is the basis for belief, and the tradition is merely a statement of what they have said. This shows clearly how far the doctrine of the ecstatic life and of knowledge gained through direct intercourse between the believer and God had already advanced.

But Abu Hudhayl was only one in a group of daring and absolutely free-minded speculators. They were applying to the ideas of the Qur'an the keen solvent of Greek dialectic, and the results which they obtained were of the most fantastically original character. Thrown into the wide sea and utter freedom of Greek thought, their ideas had expanded to the bursting point and, more than even a German metaphysician, they had lost touch of the ground of ordinary life, with its reasonable probabilities, and were swinging loose on a wild hunt after ultimate truth, wielding as their weapons definitions and syllogisms. The lyric fervors of Muhammad in the Qur'an gave scope enough of strange ideas from which to start, or which had to be explained away. Their belief in the powers of the science of logic was unfailing, and, armed with Aristotle's "Analytics," they felt sure that certainty was within their reach. It was at the court and under the protection of al-Ma'mun that they especially flourished, and some account of the leading spirits among them will be necessary before we describe how they reached their utmost pride of power and how they fell.

An-Nazzam (d. 231) has the credit among later historians of having made use, to a high degree, of the doctrines of the Greek philosophers. He was one of the Satans of the Qadarites, say they; he read the books of the philosophers and mingled their teachings with the doctrines of the Mu'tazilites. He taught, in the most absolute way, that God could do nothing to a creature, either in this world or in the next, that was not for the creature's good and in accordance with strict justice. It was not only that God would not do it; He had not the power to do anything evil. Evidently the personality of God was fast vanishing behind an absolute law of right. To this, orthodox Islam opposed the doctrine that God could do anything; He could forgive whom He willed, and punish whom He willed. Further, he taught that God's willing a thing meant only that He did it in accordance with His knowledge; and when He willed the action of a creature that meant only that He commanded it. This is evidently to evade phrases in the Qur'an. Man, again, he taught, was spirit (ruh), and the body (badan) was only an instrument. But this spirit was a fine substance which flowed in the body like the essential oil in a rose, or butter in milk. In a universe determined by strict law, man alone was undetermined. He could throw a stone into the air, and by his action the stone went up; but when the force of his throw was exhausted it came again under law and fell. If he had only asked himself how it came to fall, strange things might have happened. But he, and all his fellows, were only playing with words like counters. Further, he taught that God had created all created things at once, but

[77]

that He kept them in concealment until it was time for them to enter on the stage of visible being and do their part. All things that ever will exist are thus existing now, but, in a sense, in retentis. This seems to be another attempt to solve the problem of creation in time, and it had important. consequences. Further, the Qur'an was no miracle (mu'jiz) to him. The only miraculous elements in it are the narratives about the Unseen World, and past things and things to come, and the fact that God deprived the Arabs of the power of writing anything like it. But for that, they could easily have surpassed it as literature. As a high Imamite he rejected utterly agreement and analogy. Only the divinely appointed Imam had the right to supplement the teaching of Muhammad. We pass over some of his metaphysical views, odd as they are. The Muslim writers on theological history have classified him rightly as more of a physicist than a metaphysician. He had a concrete mind and that fondness for playing with metaphysical paradoxes which often goes with it.

Another of the group was Bishr ibn al-Mu'tamir. His principal contribution was the doctrine of tawlid and tawallud, begetting and deriving. It is the transmission of a single action through a series of objects; the agent meant to affect the first object only; the effect on the others followed. Thus, he moves his hand, and the ring on his finger is moved. What relation of responsibility, then, does he bear to these derived effects? Generally, how are we to view a complex of causes acting together and across one another? The answer of later orthodox Islam is worth giving at this point. God creates in the man the will to move his hand; He creates the movement of the hand and also the movement of the ring. All is by God's direct creation at the time. Further, could God punish an infant or one who had no knowledge of the faith? Bishr's reply on the first point was simply a bit of logical jugglery to avoid saying frankly that there was anything that God could not do. His answer on the second was that God could have made a different and much better world than this, a world in which all men might have been saved. But He was not bound to make a better world--in this Bishr separates from the other Mu'tazilites--He was only bound to give man free-will and, then, either revelation to guide him to salvation or reason to show him natural law.

With Ma'mar ibn Abbad, the philosophies wax faster and more furious. He succeeded in reducing the conception of God to a bare, indefinable something. We could not say that God had knowledge. For it must be of something in Himself or outside of Himself. If the first, then there was a union of knower and known, and that is impossible; or a duality in the divine nature, and that was equally impossible. Here Ma'mar was evidently on the road to Hegel. If the second, then His knowledge depended on the existence of something other than Himself, and that did away with His absoluteness. Similarly, he dealt with God's Will. Nor could He be described as qadim, prior to all things, for that word, in

Arabic, suggested sequence and time. By all this, he evidently meant that our conceptions cannot be applied to God; that God is unthinkable by us. On creation, he developed the ideas of an-Nazzam. Substances (jisms) only were created by God, and by "substances" he seems to mean matter as a whole; all changes in them, or it, come either of necessity: its nature, as when fire burns, the sin warms; or of free-will, as always in the animal world. God has no part in these things. He has given the material and has nothing to do with the coming and going of separate bodies; such are simple changes, forms of existence, and proceed from the matter itself. Man is an incorporeal substance. The soul is the man and his body is but a cover. This true man can only know and will; the body perceives and does.

The last of this group whose views we need consider, is Thumama ibn Ashras. He was of very dubious morals; was imprisoned as a heretic by Harun ar-Rashid, but highly favored by al-Ma'mun, in whose Khalifate he died, A.H. 213. He held that actions produced through tawallud had no agent, either God or man. That knowledge of good and evil could be produced by tawallud through speculation, and is, therefore, an action without an agent, and required even before revelation. That Jews, Christians, Magians will be turned into dust in the next world and will not enter either Paradise or Hell; the same will be the fate of cattle and children. That any one of the unbelievers who does not know his Creator is excusable. That all knowledge is a priori. That the only action which men possess is will; everything besides that is a production without a producer. That the world is the act of God by His nature, i.e., it is an act which His nature compels Him to produce; is, therefore, from eternity and to eternity with Him. It may be doubted how far Thumama was a professional theologian and how far he was a free-thinking, easy-living man of letters.

In all this, the influence of Greek theology and of Aristotle can be clearly traced. With Aristotle had come to them the idea of the world as law, an eternal construction subsisting and developing on fixed principles. This conception of law shows itself in their thought frankly at strife with Muhammad's conception of God as will, as the sovereign over all. Hence, the crudities and devices by which they strove to make good their footing on strange ground and keep a right to the name of Muslim, while changing the essence of their faith. The anthropomorphic God of Muhammad, who has face and hands, is seen in Paradise by the believer and settles Himself firmly upon His throne, becomes a spirit, and a spirit, too; of the vaguest kind.

It remains now only to touch upon one or two points common to all the Mu'tazilites. First, the Beatific Vision of God in Paradise. It was a fixed agreement of the early Muslim Church, based on texts of the Qur'an and on

[79]

tradition, that some believers, at least, would see and gaze upon God in the other world; this was the highest delight held out to them. But the Mu'tazilites perceived that vision involved a directing of the eyes on the part of the seer and position on the part of the seen. God must, therefore, be in a place and thus limited. So they were compelled to reject the agreement and the traditions in question and to explain away the passages in the Qur'an. Similarly, in Qur'an vii. 52, we read that God settled Himself firmly upon His throne. This, with other anthropomorphisms of hands and feet and eyes, the Mu'tazilites had to explain away in a more or less cumbrous fashion.

With one other detail of this class we must deal at greater length. It was destined to be the vital point of the whole Mu'tazilite controversy and the test by which theologians were tried and had their places assigned. It had a weighty part also in bringing about the fall of the Mu'tazilites. There had grown up very early in the Muslim community an unbounded reverence and awe in the presence of the Qur'an. In it God speaks, addressing His servant, the Prophet; the words, with few exceptions, are direct words of God. It is, therefore, easily intelligible that it came to be called the word of God (kalam Allah). But Muslim piety went further and held that it was uncreated and had existed from all eternity with God. Whatever proofs of this doctrine may have been brought forward later from the Qur'an itself, we can have no difficulty in recognizing that it is plainly derived from the Christian Logos and that the Greek Church, perhaps through John of Damascus, has again played a formative part. So, in correspondence with the heavenly and uncreated Logos in the bosom of the Father, there stands this uncreated and eternal Word of God; to the earthly manifestation in Jesus corresponds the Qur'an, the Word of God which we read and recite. The one is not the same as the other, but the idea to be gained from the expressions of the one is equivalent to the idea which we would gain from the other, if the veil of the flesh were removed from us and the spiritual world revealed.

That this view grew up very early among the Muslims is evident from the fact that it is opposed by Jahm ibn Safwan, who was killed toward the end of the Umayyad period. It seems to have originated by a kind of transfusion of ideas from Christianity and not as a result of controversy or dialectic about the teachings of the Qur'an. We find the orthodox party vehemently opposing discussion on the subject, as indeed they did on all theological subjects. "Our fathers have told us; it is the faith received from the Companions;" was their argument from the earliest time we can trace. Malik ibn Anas used to cut off all discussions with "Bila kayfa" (Believe without asking how); and he held strongly that the Qur'an was uncreated. The same word kalam which we have found applied to the Word of God--both the eternal, uncreated Logos and its manifestation in the Qur'an--was used by them most confusingly for "disputation;" "he disputed" was takallam and "one who disputed" was mutakallim. All that was anathema to the pious, and it is amusing to see the origin of what became later the technical terms for scholastic theology and its students in their shuddering repulsion to all "talking about" the sacred mysteries.

This opposition appeared in two forms. First, they refused to go an inch beyond the statements in the Qur'an and tradition and to draw consequences, however near the surface these consequences might seem to lie. A story is told of al-Bukhari, (d. 257), late as he is, which shows how far this went and how long it lasted. An inquisition was got up against him out of envy by one of his fellow-teachers. The point of attack was the orthodoxy of his position on the lafz (utterance) of the Qur'an; was it created or uncreated? He said readily that the Qur'an was uncreated and was obstinately silent as to the utterance of it by men. At last, persistent questioning drove him to an outburst. "The Qur'an is the Word of God and is uncreated. The speech of man is created and inquisition (imtihan) is an innovation (bid'a)." But beyond that he would not go, even to draw the conclusion of the syllogism which he had indicated. Some, as we may gather from this story, had felt themselves driven to hold that not only the Qur'an in itself but also the utterance of it by the lips of men and the writing of it by men's hands--all between the boards, as they said--was uncreated. Others were coming to deny absolutely the existence of the eternal Logos and that this revealed Qur'an was uncreated in any sense. But others, as al-Bukhari, while holding tenaciously that the Qur'an was uncreated, refused to make any statement as to its utterance by men. There was nothing said about that in Qur'an or tradition.

The second form of opposition was to any upholding of their belief by arguments, except of the simplest and most apparent. That was an invasion by reason (aql) of the realm of traditional faith (naql). When the pious were eventually driven to dialectic weapons, their arguments show that these were snatched up to defend already occupied positions. They ring artificial and forced. Thus, in the Qur'an itself, the Qur'an is called "knowledge from God." It is, then, inseparable from God's quality of knowledge. But that is eternal and uncreated; therefore, so too, the Qur'an. Again, God created everything by the word, "Be." But this word cannot have been created, otherwise a created word would be a creator. Therefore, God's word is uncreated. Again, there stands in the Qur'an (vii, 52), "Are not the creation and the command His?" The command here is evidently different from the creation, i.e., not created. Further, God's command creates; therefore it cannot be created. But it is God's word in command. It will be noticed here how completely God's word is hypostatized. This appears still more strongly in the following argument. God said to Moses, (Qur. vii, 141), "I have chosen thee over mankind with my apostolate and my word." God, therefore, has a word. But, again (Qur. iv, 162), He addresses Moses with this word (kallama-llahu Musa taklima, evidently regarded as meaning that God's word addressed Moses) and said, "Lo, I am thy Lord." This argument is supposed to put the opponent in a dilemma. Either he rejects the fact of Moses being so addressed, which is rejecting what God has said, and is, therefore, unbelief; or he holds that the kalam which so addresses Moses is a created thing. Then, a created thing asserts that it is Moses' Lord. Therefore, God's kalam with which He addresses the prophets, or which addresses the prophets, is eternal, uncreated.

But if this doctrine grew up early in Islam, op-position to it was not slow in appearing, and that on different sides. Literary vanity, national pride, and philosophical scruples all made themselves felt. Even in Muhammad's lifetime, according to the legend of the poet Labid and the verses which he put up in challenge on the Ka'ba, the Qur'an had taken rank as inimitable poetry. At all points it was the Word of God and perfect in every detail. But, among the Arabs, a jealous and vain people, if there was one thing on which each was more jealous and vain than another, it was skill in working with words. The superiority of Muhammad as a Prophet of God they might endure, though often with a bad grace; but Muhammad as a rival and unapproachable literary artist they could not away with. So we find satire of the weaknesses of the Qur'an appearing here and there, and it came to be a sign of emancipation and freedom from prejudice to examine it in detail and balance it against other products of the Arab genius. The rival productions of Musaylima, the False Prophet, long enjoyed a semi-contraband existence, and Abu Ubayda (d. 208) found it necessary to write a treatise in defence of the metaphors of the Qur'an. Among the Persians this was still more the case. To them, Muhammad might be a prophet, but he was also an Arab; and while they accepted his mission, accepting his books in a literary way was too much for them. As a prophet, he was a man; as a literary artist, he was an Arab. So Jahm ibn Safwan may have felt; so, certainly, others felt later. The poet Bashshar ibn Burd (killed for satire, in 167), a companion of Wasil ibn Ata and a Persian of very dubious orthodoxy, used to amuse himself by comparing poems by himself and others with passages in the Qur'an, to the disadvantage of the latter. And Ibn al-Muqaffa (killed about 140), the translator of "Kalila and Dimna" and many other books into Arabic, and a Persian nationalist, is said to have planned an imitation of the Qur'an.

Added to all this came the influence of the Mu'tazilite theologians. They had a double ground for their opposition. The doctrine of an absolutely divine and perfect book limited them too much in their intellectual freedom. They were willing to respect and use the Qur'an, but not to accept its ipsissima verba. Regarded as the production of Muhammad under divine influence, it could have a human and a divine side, and things which needed to be dropped or changed in it could be ascribed to the human side. But that was not possible with a miraculous book come down from heaven. In a word, they were meeting the difficulty which has been met by Christianity in the latter half of the nineteenth century. The least they could do was to deny that the Qur'an was uncreated.

But they had a still more vital, if not more important, philosophical base of objection. We have seen already how they viewed the doctrine of God's qualities (sifat) and tried to limit them in every way. These qualities ran danger, they held, of being hypostatized into separate persons like those in the Christian Trinity, and we have just seen how near that danger really lay in the case of God's kalam. In orthodox Islam it has become a plain Logos.

The position in this of an-Nazzam has been given above. It is interesting as showing that the Qur'an, even then, was given as a probative miracle (mu'jiz) because it deprived all men of power (i'jaz) to imitate it. That is, its æsthetic perfection was raised to the miraculous degree and then regarded as a proof of its divine origin. But al-Muzdar, a pupil of Bishr ibn al Mu'tamir and an ascetic of high rank, called the Monk of the Mu'tazilites, went still further than an-Nazzam. He flatly damned as unbelievers all who held the eternity of the Qur'an; they had taken unto themselves two Gods. Further, he asserted that men were quite capable of producing a work even finer than the Qur'an in point of style. But the force of this opinion is somewhat diminished by the liberality with which he denounced his opponents in general as unbelievers. Stories are told of him very much like those in circulation with us about those who hold that few will be saved, and it is worth noticing that upon this point of salvability the Mu'tazilites were even narrower than the orthodox.

CHAPTER II

Al-Ma'mun and the triumph of the Mu'tazilites; the Mihna and Ahmad ibn Hanbal; al-Farabi; the Fatimids and the Ikhwan as-Safa; the early mystics, ascetic and pantheistic; al-Hallaj.

SUCH for long was the situation between the Mu'tazilites and their orthodox opponents. From time to time the Mu'tazilites received more or less protection and state favor; at other times, they had to seek safety in hiding. Popular favor they seem never to have enjoyed. As the Umayyads grew weak, they became more stiff in their orthodoxy; but with the Abbasids, and especially with al-Mansur, thought was again free. As has been shown above, encouragement of science and research was part of the plan of that great man, and he easily saw that the intellectual hope of the future was with these theological and philosophical questioners. So their work went slowly on, with a break under Harun ar-Rashid a magnificent but highly orthodox monarch, who understood no trifling with things of the faith. It is an interesting but useless question whether Islam could ever have been broadened and developed to the point of enduring in its midst free speculation and research. As the case stands in history, it has known periods of intellectual life, but only under the protection of isolated princes here and there. It has had Augustan ages; it has never had great popular yearnings after wider knowledge. Its intellectual leaders have lived and studied and lectured at courts; they have not gone down and taught the masses of the people. To that the democracy of Islam has never come. Hampered by scholastic snobbishness, it has never learned that the abiding victories of science are won in the village school.

But most unfortunately for the Mu'tazilites and for Islam, a Khalifa arose who had a relish for theological discussions and a high opinion of his own infallibility. This was al-Ma'mun. It did not matter that he ranged himself on the progressive side; his fatal error was that he invoked the authority of the state in matters of the intellectual and religious life. Thus, by enabling the conservative party to pose as martyrs, he brought the prejudices and passions of the populace still more against the new movement. He was that most dangerous of all beings, a doctrinaire despot. He had ideas and tried to make other people live up to them. Al-Mansur, though a bloody tyrant, had been a great statesman and had known how to bend people and things quietly to his will. He had sketched the firm outlines of a policy for the Abbasids, but had been cautious how he proclaimed his programme to the world. The world would come to him in time, and he could afford to wait and work in the dark. He knew, above all, that no people would submit to be school-mastered into the way in which they should go. Al-Ma'mun, for all his genius, was at heart a school-master. He was an enlightened patron of an enlightened Islam. Those who preferred to dwell in the darkness of the obscurant; he first scolded and then punished. Discussions in theology and comparative religion were his hobby. That some such interchange of letters between Muslims and Christians as that which crystallized in the Epistle of al-Kindi took place at his court seems certain. Bishr al-Marisi, who had lived in hiding in ar-Rashid's time on account of his heretical views, disputed, in 209, before al-Ma'mun on the nature of the Qur'an. He founded at Baghdad an academy with library, laboratories, and observatory. All the weight of his influence was thrown on the side of the Mu'tazilites. It appeared as though he were determined to pull his people up by force from their superstition and ignorance.

At last, he took the final and fatal step. In 202 a decree appeared proclaiming the doctrine of the creation of the Qur'an as the only truth, and as binding upon all Muslims. At the same time, as an evident sop to the Persian nationalists and the Alids, Ali was proclaimed the best of creatures after Muhammad. The Alids, it should be remembered, had close points of contact with the Mu'tazilites. Such a theological decree as this was a new thing in Islam; never before had the individual consciousness been threatened by a word from the throne. The Mu'tazilites through it practically became a state church under erastian control. But the system of Islam never granted to the Imam, or leader of the Muslim people, any position but that of a protector and representative. Its theology could only be formed, as we have seen in the case of its law, by the agreement of the whole community. The question then naturally was what effect such a new thing as this decree could have except to exasperate the orthodox and the masses. Practically, there was no other effect. Things went on as before. All that it meant was that one very prominent Muslim had stated his opinion and thrown in his lot with heretics.

For six years this continued, and then a method was devised of bringing the will of the Khalifa home upon the people. In 217 a distinguished Mu'tazilite, Ahmad ibn Abi Duwad, was appointed chief qadi, and in 218 the decree was renewed. But this time it was accompanied by what we would call a test-act, and an inquisition (mihna) was instituted. The letter of directions for the conduct of this matter, written by al-Ma'mun to his lieutenant at Baghdad, is decisive as to the character of the man and the nature of the movement. It is full of railings against the common people who know not the law and are accursed. They are too stupid to understand philosophy or argument. It is the duty of the Khalifa to guide them and especially to show them the distinction between God and His book. He who holds otherwise than the Khalifa is either too blind or too lying and deceitful to be trusted in any other thing. Therefore, the qadis must be tested as to their views. If they hold that the Qur'an is uncreated, they have abandoned tawhid, the doctrine of God's Unity, and can no longer hold office in a Muslim land. Also, the qadis must apply the same test to all the witnesses in cases before them. If these do not hold that the Qur'an is created, they cannot be legal witnesses. Other letters followed; the Mihna was extended through the Abbasid empire and applied to other doctrines, e.g., that of free-will and of the vision of God. The Khalifa also commanded that the death penalty for unbelief (kufr) should be inflicted on those who refused to take the test. They were to be regarded as idolaters and polytheists. The death of al-Ma'mun in the same year relieved the pressure. It is true that the Mihna was continued by his successor, al-Mu'tasim, and by his successor, al-Wathiq, but without energy; it was more a handy political weapon than anything else. In 234, the second year of al-Mutawakhil, it was abolished and the Qur'an decreed untreated. At the same time the Alids and all Persian nationalism came under a ban. Practically, the status quo ante was restored and Mu'tazilism was again left a struggling heresy. The Arab party and the pure faith of Muhammad had re-asserted themselves.

In this long conflict, the most prominent figure was certainly that of Ahmad ibn Hanbal. He was the trust and strength of the orthodox; that he stood fast through imprisonment and scourging defeated the plans of the Mu'tazilites. In dealing with the development of law, we have seen what his legal position was. The same held in theology. Scholastic theology (kalam) was his abomination. Those who disputed over doctrines he cast out. That their dogmatic position was the same as his made no difference. For him, theological truth could not be reached by reasoning (aql); tradition (naql) from the fathers (as-salaf) was the only ground on which the dubious words of the Qur'an could be explained. So, in his long examinations before the officials of al-Ma'mun and al-Mu'tasim, he contented himself with repeating either the words of the Qur'an which for him were proofs or such traditions as he accepted. Any approach to drawing a consequence he utterly rejected. When they argued before him, he kept silence.

What, then, we may ask, was the net result of this incident? for it was nothing more. The Mu'tazilites dropped back into their former position, but under changed conditions. The sympathy of the populace was further from them than ever. Ahmad ibn Hanbal, saint and ascetic, was the idol of the masses; and he, in their eyes, had maintained single-handed the honor of the Word of God. For his persecutors there was nothing but hatred. And after he had passed away, the conflict was taken up with still fiercer bitterness by the school of law founded by his pupils. They continued to maintain his principles of Qur'an and tradition long after the Mu'tazilites themselves had practically vanished from the scene, and all that was left for them to contend against was the modified system of scholastic theology which is now the orthodox theology of Islam. With these reactionary Hanbalites we shall have to deal later.

The Mu'tazilites, on their side, having seen the shipwreck of their hopes and the growing storm of popular disfavor, seem to have turned again to their scholastic studies. They became more and more theologians affecting a narrower circle, and less and less educators of the world at large. Their system became more metaphysical and their conclusions more unintelligible to the plain man. The fate which has fallen on all continued efforts of the Muslim mind was coming upon them. Beggarly speculations and barren hypotheses, combats of words over names, sapped them of life and reality. What the ill-fated friendship of al-Ma'mun had begun was carried on and out by the closed circle of Muslim thought. They separated into schools, one at al-Basra and another at Baghdad. At Baghdad the point especially developed was the old question, What is a thing (shay)? They defined a thing, practically, as a concept that could be known and of which something could be said. Existence (wujud) did not matter. It was only a quality which could be there or not. With it, the thing was an entity (mawjud); without it, a non-entity (ma'dum), but still a thing with all equipment of substance (jawhar) and accident (arad), genus and species. The bearing of this was especially upon the doctrine of creation. Practically, by God's adding a single quality, things

[86]

entered the sphere of existence and were for us. Here, then, is evidently an approach to a doctrine of pre-existent matter. At al-Basra the relation of God to His qualities was especially discussed, and there it came to be pretty nearly a family dispute between al-Jubba'i (d. 303) and his son Abu Hashim. Orthodox Islam held that God has qualities, existent, eternal, added to His essence; thus, He knows, for example, by such a quality of knowledge. The students of Greek philosophy and the Shi'ites denied this and said that God knew by His essence. We have seen already Mu'tazilite views as to this point. Abu Hudhayl held that these qualities were God's essence and not in it. Thus, He knew by a quality of knowledge, but that quality was His essence. Al-Jubba'i contented himself with safe-guarding this statement. God knew in accordance with His essence, but it was neither a quality nor a state (hal) which required that He should be a knower. The orthodox had said the first; his son, Abu Hashim, said the second. He held that we know an essence and know it under different conditions. The conditions varied but the essence remained. These conditions are not thinkable by themselves, for we know them only in connection with the essence. These are states; they are different from the essence, but do not exist apart from it. Al-Jubba'i opposed to this a doctrine that these states were really subjective in the mind of the perceiver, either generalizations or relationships existing mentally but not externally. This controversy spun itself out at great length through centuries. It eventually resolved itself into the fundamental metaphysical inquiry, What is a thing? A powerful school came to a conclusion that would have delighted the soul of Mr. Herbert Spencer. Things are four, they said, entities, non-entities, states and relationships. As we have seen above, al-Jubba'i denied the reality of both states and relationships. Orthodox Islam has been of a divided opinion.

But all this time, other movements had been in progress, some of which were to be of larger future importance than this fossilizing intellectualism. In 255 al-Jahiz died. Though commonly reckoned a Mu'tazilite he was really a man of letters, free in life and thought. He was a maker of books, learned in the writings of the philosophers and rather inclined to the doctrines of the Tabi'iyun, deistic naturalists. His confession of faith was of the utmost simplicity. He taught that whoever held that God had neither body nor form, could not be seen with the eyes, was just and willed no evil deeds, such was a Muslim in truth. And, further, if anyone was not capable of philosophical reflection, but held that Allah was his Lord and that Muhammad was the Apostle of Allah, he was blameless and nothing more should be required of him. Here we have evidently in part a reaction from the subtilties of controversy, and in part an attempt to broaden theology enough to give even the unsettled a chance to remain in the Muslim Church. Something of the same kind we shall find, later, in the case of Ibn Rushd. Finally, we have probably to see in his remark that the Qur'an was a body, turned at one time into a man and at another into a beast, a satirical comment on the great controversy of his time.

Al-Jahiz may be for us a link with the philosophers proper, the students of the wisdom of the Greeks. He represents the standpoint of the educated man of the time, and was no specialist in anything but a general scepticism. In the first generation of the philosophers of Islam, in the narrower sense, stands conspicuously al-Kindi, commonly called the Philosopher of the Arabs. The name belongs to him of right, for he is almost the only example of a student of Aristotle, sprung from the blood of the desert. But he was hardly a philosopher in any independent sense. His rôle was translating, and during the reigns of al-Ma'mun and al-Mu'tasim a multitude of translations and original works de omni scibili came from his hands; the names of 265 of these have come down to us. In the orthodox reaction under al-Mutawakhil he fared ill; his library was confiscated but afterward restored. He died about 260, and with him dies the brief, golden century of eager acquisition, and the scholastic period enters in philosophy as in theology.

That the glory was departing from Baghdad and the Khalifate is shown by the second important name in philosophy. It is that of al-Farabi, who was born at Farab in Turkestan, lived and worked in the brilliant circle which gathered round Sayf ad-Dawla, the Hamdanid, at his court at Aleppo. In music, in science, in philology, and in philosophy, he was alike master. Aristotle was his passion, and his Arabic contemporaries and successors united in calling him the second teacher, on account of his success in un-knotting the tangles of the Greek system. It was in truth a tangled system which came to him, and a tangled system which he left. The Muslim philosophers began, in their innocence, with the following positions: The Qur'an is truth and philosophy is truth; but truth can only be one; therefore, the Qur'an and philosophy must agree. Philosophy they accepted in whole-hearted faith, as it came to them from the Greeks through Egypt and Syria. They took it, not as a mass of more or less contradictory speculation, but as a form of truth. They, in fact, never lost a certain theological attitude. Under such conditions, then, Plato came to them; but it was mostly Plato as interpreted by Porphyrius, that is, as neo-Platonism. Aristotle, too, came to them in the guise of the later Peripatetic schools. But in Aristotle, especially, there entered a perfect knot of entanglement and confusion. During the reign of al-Mu'tasim, a Christian of Emessa in the Lebanon--the history in details is obscure--translated parts of the "Enneads" of Plotinus into Arabic and entitled his work "The Theology of Aristotle." A more unlucky bit of literary mischief and one more far-reaching in its consequences has never been. The Muslims took it all as solemnly as they took the text of the Qur'an. These two great masters, Plato and Aristotle, they said, had expounded the truth, which is one. Therefore, there must be some way of bringing them into agreement. So generations of toilers labored valiantly with the welter of translations and pseudographs to get out of them and into them the one truth. The more pious added the third element of the Qur'an, and it must remain a marvel and a magnificent testimonial to their skill and patience that they got even so far as they did and that the whole movement did not end in simple lunacy. That al-Farabi should have been so incisive a writer, so wide a thinker and student; that Ibn Sina should have been so keen and clear a scientist and logician; that Ibn Rushd should have known--really known--and commented his Aristotle as he did, shows that the human brain, after all, is a sane brain and has the power of unconsciously rejecting and throwing out nonsense and falsehood.

But it is not wonderful that, dealing with such materials and contradictions, they developed a tendency to mysticism. There were many things which they felt compelled to hold which could only be defended and rationalized in that cloudy air and slanting light. Especially, no one but a mystic could bring together the emanations of Plotinus, the ideas of Plato, the spheres of Aristotle and the seven-storied heaven of Muhammad. With this matter of mysticism we shall have to deal immediately. Of al-Farabi it is enough to say that he was one of the most patient of the laborers at that impossible problem. It seems never to have occurred to him, or to any of the others, that the first and great imperative was to verify his references and sources. The oriental, like the mediæval scholastic, tests minutely the form of his syllogism, but takes little thought whether his premises state facts or not. With a scrupulous scepticism in deduction, he combines a childlike acceptance on tradition or on the narrowest of inductions.

But there are other and more ominous signs in al-Farabi of the scholastic decline. There appears first in him that tendency toward the writing of encyclopædic compends, which always means superficiality and the commonplace. Al-Farabi himself could not be accused of either, but that he thus claimed all knowledge for his portion showed the risk of the premature circle and the small gain. Another is mysticism. He is a neo-Platonist, more exactly a Plotinian; although he himself would not have recognized this title. He held, as we have seen, that he was simply retelling the doctrines of Plato and Aristotle. But he was also a devout Muslim. He seems to have taken in earnest all the bizarre details of Muslim cosmography and eschatology; the Pen, the Tablet, the Throne, the Angels in all their ranks and functions mingle picturesquely with the system of Plotinus, his ἕν, his ψυχή, his νοῦς, his receptive and active intellects. But to make tenable this position he had to take the great leap of the mystic. Unto us these things are impossible; with God, i.e., on another plane of existence, they are the simplest realities. If the veil were taken from our eyes we would see them. This has always been the refuge of the devout Muslim who has tampered with science. We shall look for it more in detail when we come to al-Ghazzali, who has put it into classical form.

Again, he was, in modern terms, a monarchist and a clericalist. His conception of the model state is a strange compound of the republic of Plato and Shi'ite dreams of an infallible Imam. Its roots lie, of course, in the theocratic idea of the Muslim state; but his city, which is to take in all mankind, a Holy Roman Empire and a Holy Catholic Church at once, a community of saints ruled by sages, shows a later influence than that of the mother city of Islam, al-Madina, under Abu Bakr and Umar. The influence is that of the Fatimids with their capital, al-Mahdiya, near Tunis. The Hamdanids were Shi'ites and Sayf ad-Dawla, under whom al-Farabi enjoyed peace and protection, was a vassal of the Fatimid Khalifas.

This brings us again to the great mystery of Muslim history. What was the truth of the Fatimid movement? Was the family of the Prophet the fosterer of science from the earliest times? What degree of contact had they with the Mu'tazilites? With the founders of grammar, of alchemy, of law? That they were themselves the actual beginners of everything--and everything has been claimed for them--we may put down to legend. But one thing does stand fast. Just as al-Ma'mun combined the establishment of a great university at Baghdad with a favoring of the Alids, so the Fatimids in Cairo erected a great hall of science and threw all their influence and authority into the spreading and extending of knowledge. This institution seems to have been a combination of free public library and university, and was probably the gateway connecting between the inner circle of initiated Fatimid leaders and the outside, uninitiated world. We have already seen how unhappy were the external effects of the Shi'ite, and especially of the Fatimid, propaganda on the Muslim world. But from time to time we become aware of a deep undercurrent of scientific and philosophical labor and investigation accompanying that propaganda, and striving after knowledge and truth. It belongs to the life below the surface, which we can know only through its occasional outbursts. Some of these are given above; others will follow. The whole matter is obscure to the last degree, and dogmatic statements and explanations are not in place. It may be that it was only a natural drawing together on the part of all the different forces and movements that were under a ban and had to live in secrecy and stillness. It may be that the students of the new sciences passed over, simply through their studies and political despair--as has often happened in our day--into different degrees of nihilism, or, at the other extreme, into a passionate searching for, and dependence on, some absolute guide, an infallible Imam. It may be that we have read wrongly the whole history of the Fatimid movement; that it was in reality a deeply laid and slowly ripened plan to bring the rule of the world into the control of a band of philosophers, whose task it was to be to rule the human race and gradually to educate it into self-rule; that they saw--these unknown devotees of science and truth--no other way of breaking down the barriers of Islam and setting free the spirits of men. A wild hypothesis! But in face of the real mystery no hypothesis can seem wild.

Closely allied with both al-Farabi and the Fatimids is the association known as the Sincere Brethren (Ikhwan as-safa). It existed at al-Basra in the middle of the fourth century of the Hijra during the breathing space which the free intellectual life enjoyed after the capture of Baghdad by the Buwayhids in 334. It will be remembered how that Persian dynasty was Shi'ite by creed and how it, for the time, completely clipped the claws of the orthodox and Sunnite Abbasid Khalifas. The only thing, thereafter, which heretics and philosophers had to fear was the enmity of the populace, but that seems to have been great enough. The Hanbalite mob of Baghdad had grown to be a thing of terror. It was, then, an educational campaign on which this new philosophy had to enter. Their programme was by means of clubs, propagating themselves and spreading over the country from al-Basra and Baghdad, to reach all educated people and introduce among them gradually a complete change in their religious and scientific ideas. Their teaching was the same combination of neo-Platonic speculation and mysticism with Aristotelian natural science, wrapped in Mu'tazilite theology, that we have already known. Only there was added to it a Pythagorean reverence for numbers, and everything, besides, was treated in an eminently superficial and popularized manner. Our knowledge of the Fraternity and its objects is based on its publication, "The Epistles of the Sincere Brethren" (Rasa'il ikhwan as-safa) and upon scanty historical notices. The Epistles are fifty or fifty-one in number and cover the field of human knowledge as then conceived. They form, in fact, an Arabic Encyclopédie. The founders of the Fraternity, and authors, presumably, of the Epistles, were at most ten. We have no certain knowledge that the Fraternity ever took even its first step and spread to Baghdad. Beyond that almost certainly the development did not pass. The division of members into four--learners, teachers, guides, and drawers near to God in supernatural vision--and the plan of regular meetings of each circle for study and mutual edification remained in its paper form. The society was half a secret one and lacked, apparently, vitality and energy. There was among its founders no man of weight and character. So it passed away and has left only these Epistles which have come down to us in numerous MSS., showing how eagerly they have been read and copied and how much influence they at least must have exercised. That influence must have been very mixed. It was, it is true, for intellectual life, yet it carried with it in a still higher degree the defects we have already noticed in al-Farabi. To them must be added the most simple skimming of all real philosophical problems and a treatment of nature and natural science which had lost all connection with facts.

It has been suggested, and the suggestion seems luminous and fertile, that this Fraternity was simply a part of the great Fatimid propaganda which, as we know, honey-combed the ground everywhere under the Sunnite Abbasids. Descriptions which have reached us of the methods followed by the leaders of the Fraternity agree exactly with those of the missionaries of the Isma'ilians. They raised difficulties and suggested serious questionings; hinted at possible answers but did not give them; referred to a source where all questions would be answered. Again, their catch-words and fixed phrases are the same as those afterward used by the Assassins, and we have traces of these Epistles forming a part of the sacred library of the Assassins. It is to be remembered that the Assassins were not simply robber bands who struck terror by their methods. Both the western and the eastern branches were devoted to science, and it may be that in their mountain fortresses there was the most absolute devotion to true learning that then existed. When the Mongols captured Alamut, they found it rich in MSS. and in instruments and apparatus of every kind. It is then possible that the elevated eclecticism of the Ikhwan as-safa was the real doctrine of the Fatimids, the Assassins, the Qarmatians and the Druses; certainly, wherever we can test them there is the most singular agreement. It is a mechanical and æsthetic pantheism, a glorification of Pythagoreanism, with its music and numbers; idealistic to the last degree; a worship and pursuit of a conception of a harmony and beauty in all the universe, to find which is to find and know the Creator Himself. It is thus far removed from materialism and atheism, but could easily be misrepresented as both. This, it is true, is a very different explanation from the one given in our first Part; it can only be put alongside of that and left there. The one expresses the practical effect of the Isma'ilians in Islam; the other what may have been their ideal. However we judge them, we must always remember that somewhere in their teaching, at its best, there was a strange attraction for thinking and troubled men. Nasir ibn Khusraw, a Persian Faust, found peace at Cairo between 437 and 444 in recognizing the divine Imamship of al-Mustansir, and after a life of persecution died in that faith as a hermit in the mountains of Badakhshan in 481. The great Spanish poet, Ibn Rani, who died in 362, similarly accepted al-Mu'izz as his spiritual chief and guide.

Another eclectic sect, but on a very different principle, was that of the Karramites, founded by Abu Abd Allah ibn Karram, who died in 256. Its teachings had the honor to be accepted and protected by no less a man than the celebrated Mahmud of Ghazna (388-421), Mahmud the Idol-breaker, the first invader of India and the patron of al-Beruni, Firdawsi, Ibn Sina and many another. But that, to which we will return, belongs to a later date and, probably, to a modified form of Ibn Karram's teaching. For himself, he was an ascetic of Sijistan and, according to the story, a man of no education. He lost himself in theological subtleties which he seems to have failed to understand. However, out of them all he put together a book which he called "The Punishment of the Grave," which spread widely in

Khurasan. It was, in part, a frank recoil to the crassest anthropomorphism. Thus, for him, God actually sat upon the throne, was in a place, had direction and so could move from one point to another. He had a body with flesh, blood, and limbs; He could be embraced by those who were purified to the requisite point. It was a literal acceptance of the material expressions of the Qur'an along with a consideration of how they could be so, and an explanation by comparison with men--all opposed to the principle bila kayfa. So, apparently, we must understand the curious fact that he was also a Murji'ite and held faith to be only acknowledgment with the tongue. All men, except professed apostates, are believers, he said, because of that primal covenant, taken by God with the seed of Adam, when He asked, "Am I not your Lord?" (Alastu bi-rabbikum) and they, brought forth from Adam's loins for the purpose, made answer, "Yea, verily, in this covenant we remain until we formally cast it off." This, of course, involved taking God's qualities in the most literal sense. So, if we are to see in the Mu'tazilites scholastic commentators trying to reduce Muhammad, the poet, to logic and sense, we must see in Ibn Karram one of those wooden-minded literalists, for whom a metaphor is a ridiculous lie if it cannot be taken in its external meaning. He was part of the great stream of conservative reaction, in which we find also such a man as Ahmad ibn Hanbal. But the saving salt of Ahmad's sense and reverence kept him by the safe proviso "without considering how and without comparison." All Ahmad's later followers were not so wise. In his doctrine of the state Ibn Karram inclined to the Kharijites.

Before we return to al-Jubba'i and the fate of the Mu'tazilites, it remains to trace more precisely the thread of mysticism, that kashf, revelation, which we have already mentioned several times. Its fundamental fact is that it had two sides, an ascetic and a speculative, different in degree, in spirit and in result, and yet so closely entangled that the same mystic has been assigned, in good and in bad faith, as an adherent of both.

It is to the form of mysticism which sprang from asceticism that we must first turn. Attention has been given above to the wandering monks and hermits, the sa'ihs (wanderers) and rahibs who caught Muhammad's attention and respect. We have seen, too, how Muslim imitators began in their turn to wander through the land, clad in the coarse woollen robes which gave them the name of Sufis, and living upon the alms of the pious. How early these appeared in any number and as a fixed profession is uncertain, but we find stories in circulation of meetings between such mendicant friars and al-Hasan al-Basri himself. Women, too, were among them, and it is possible that to their influence a development of devotional love-poetry was due. At least, many verses of this kind are ascribed to a certain Rabi'a, an ascetic and ecstatic devotee of the most extreme other-worldliness, who died in 135. Many other women had part in the contemplative life. Among

[93]

them may be mentioned, to show its grasp and spread, A'isha, daughter of Ja'far as-Sadiq, who died in 145; Fatima of Naysabur, who died in 223, and the Lady Nafisa, a contemporary and rival in learning with ash-Shafi'i and the marvel of her time in piety and the ascetic life. Her grave is one of the most venerated spots in Cairo, and at it wonders are still worked and prayer is always answered. She was a descendant of al-Hasan, the martyred ex-Khalifa, and an example of how the fated family of the Prophet was an early school for women saints. Even in the Heathenism we have traces of female penitents and hermits, and the tragedy of Ali and his sons and descendants gave scope for the self-sacrifice, loving service and religious enthusiasm with which women are dowered.

All these stood and stand in Islam on exactly the same footing as men. The distinction in Roman Christendom that a woman cannot be a priest there falls away, for in Islam is neither priest nor layman. They lived either as solitaries or in conventual life exactly as did the men. They were called by the same terms in feminine form; they were Sufiyas beside the Sufis; Zahidas (ascetics) beside the Zahids; Waliyas (friends of God) beside the Walis; Abidas (devotees) beside the Abids. They worked wonders (karamat, closely akin to the χαρίσματα of 1 Cor. xii, 9) by the divine grace, and still, as we have seen, at their own graves such are granted through them to the faithful, and their intercession (shafa'a) is invoked. Their religious exercises were the same; they held dhikrs and women darwishes yet dance to singing and music in order to bring on fits of ecstasy. To state the case generally, whatever is said hereafter of mysticism and its workings among men must be taken as applying to women also.

To return: one of the earliest male devotees of whom we have distinct note is Ibrahim ibn Adham. He was a wanderer of royal blood, drifted from Balkh in Afghanistan to al-Basra and to Mecca. He died in 161. Contempt for the learning of lawyers and for external forms appears in him; obedience to God, contemplation of death, death to the world formed his teaching. Another, Da'ud ibn Nusayr, who died in 165, was wont to say, "Flee men as thou fleest a lion. Fast from the world and let the breaking of thy fast be when thou diest." Another, al-Fudayl ibn Iyad of Khurasan, who died in 187, was a robber converted by a heavenly voice; he cast aside the world, and his utterances show that he lapsed into the passivity of quietism.

Reference has already been made in the chapter on jurisprudence to the development of asceticism which came with the accession of the Abbasids. The disappointed hopes of the old believers found an outlet in the contemplative life. They withdrew from the world and would have nothing to do with its rulers; their wealth and everything connected with them they regarded as unclean. Ahmad ibn Hanbal in his later life had to use all his obstinacy and ingenuity to keep free of the court and its contamination. Another was this al-Fudayl. Stories-- chronologically impossible--are told how he rebuked Harun al-Rashid for his luxury and tyranny and denounced to his face his manner of life. With such an attitude to those round him he could have had little joy in his devotion. So it was said, "When al-Fudayl died, sadness was removed from the world."

But soon the recoil came. Under the spur of such exercises and thoughts, the ecstatic oriental temperament began to revel in expressions borrowed from human love and earthly wine. Such we find by Ma'ruf of al-Karkh, a district of Baghdad, who died in 200, and whose tomb, saved by popular reverence, is one of the few ancient sites in modern Baghdad; and by his greater disciple, Sari as-Saqati, who died in 257. To this last is ascribed, but dubiously, the first use of the word tawhid to signify the union of the soul with God. The figure that the heart is a mirror to image back God and that it is darkened by the things of the body appears in Abu Sulayman of Damascus, who died in 215. A more celebrated ascetic, who died in 227, Bishr al-Hafi (bare-foot), speaks of God directly as the Beloved (habib). Al-Harith al-Muhasibi was a contemporary of Ahmad ibn Hanbal and died in 243. The only thing in him to which Ahmad could take exception was that he made use of kalam in refuting the Mu'tazilites; even this suspicion against him he is said to have abandoned. Sari and Bishr, too, were close friends of Ahmad's. Dhu-n-Nun, the Egyptian Sufi, who died in 245, is in more dubious repute. He is said to have been the first to formulate the doctrine of ecstatic states (hals, maqamas); but if he went no further than this, his orthodoxy, in the broad sense, should be above suspicion. Islam has now come to accept these as right and fitting. Perhaps the greatest name in early Sufiism is that of al-Junayd (d. 297); on it no shadow of heresy has ever fallen. He was a master in theology and law, reverenced as one of the greatest of the early doctors. Questions of tawhid he is said to have discussed before his pupils with shut doors. But this was probably tawhid in the theological and not in the mystical sense--against the Mu'tazilites and not on the union of the soul with God. Yet he, too, knew the ecstatic life and fell fainting at verses which struck into his soul. Ash-Shibli (d. 334) was one of his disciples, but seems to have given himself more completely to the ascetic and contemplative life. In verses by him we find the vocabulary of the amorous intercourse with God fully developed. The last of this group to be mentioned here shall be Abu Talib al-Makki, who died in 386. It is his distinction to have furnished a text-book of Sufiism that is in use to this day. He wrote and spoke openly on tawhid, now in the Sufi sense, and got into trouble as a heretic, but his memory has been restored to orthodoxy by the general agreement of Islam. When, in 488, al-Ghazzali set himself to seek light in Sufiism, among the treatises he studied were the books of four of those mentioned above, Abu Talib, al-Muhasibi, al-Junayd, and ash-Shibli.

In the case of these and all the others already spoken of there was nothing but a very simple and natural development such as could easily be paralleled in Europe. The earliest Muslims were burdened, as we have seen, with the fear of the terrors of an avenging God. The world was evil and fleeting; the only abiding good was in the other world; so their religion became an ascetic other-worldliness. They fled into the wilderness from the wrath to come. Wandering, either solitary or in companies, was the special sign of the true Sufi. The young men gave themselves over to the guidance of the older men; little circles of disciples gathered round a venerated Shaykh; fraternities began to form. So we find it in the case of al-Junayd, so in that of Sari as-Saqati. Next would come a monastery, rather a rest-house; for only in the winter and for rest did they remain fixed in a place for any time. Of such a monastery there is a trace at Damascus in 150 and in Khurasan about 200. Then, just as in Europe, begging friars organized themselves. In faith they were rather conservative than anything else; touched with a religious passivism which easily developed into quietism. Their ecstasies went little beyond those, for instance, of Thomas à Kempis, though struck with a warmer oriental fervor.

The points on which the doctors of Islam took exception to these earlier Sufis are strikingly different from what we would expect. They concern the practical life far more than theological speculation. As was natural in the case of professional devotees, a constantly prayerful attitude began to assume importance beside and in contrast to the formal use of the five daily prayers, the salawat. This development was in all probability aided by the existence in Syria of he Christian sect of the Euchites, who exalted the duty of prayer above all other religious obligations. These, also, abandoned property and obligations and wandered as poor brethren over the country. They were a branch of Hesychasts, the quietistic Greek monks who eventually led to the controversy concerning the uncreated light manifested at the transfiguration on Mount Tabor and added a doctrine to the Eastern Church. Considering these points, it can hardly be doubted that there was some historical connection and relation here, not only with earlier but also with later Sufiism. There is a striking resemblance between the Sufis seeking by patient introspection to see the actual light of God's presence in their hearts, and the Greek monks in Athos, sitting solitarily in their cells and seeking the divine light of Mount Tabor in contemplation of their navels.

But our immediate point is the matter of constant, free prayer. In the Qur'an (xxxiii, 41) the believers are exhorted to "remember (dhikr) God often;" this command the Sufis obeyed with a correlative depreciation of the five canonical prayers. Their meetings for the purpose, much like our own prayer-meetings, still more like the "class-meetings" of the early Methodists, as opposed to stated public worship, were called dhikrs. These services were fiercely attacked by the orthodox theologians, but survived and are the darwish functions which tourists still go to see at Constantinople and Cairo. But the more private and personal dhikrs of individual Sufis, each in his house repeating his Qur'anic litanies through the night, until to the passer-by it sounded like the humming of bees or the unceasing drip of roof-gutters, these seem, in the course of the third century, to have fallen before ridicule and accusations of heresy.

Another point against the earlier Sufis was their abuse of the principle of tawakkul, dependence upon God. They gave up their trades and professions; they even gave up the asking for alms. Their ideal was to be absolutely at God's disposal, utterly cast upon His direct sustenance (rizq). No anxiety for their daily bread was permitted to them; they must go through the world separated from it and its needs and looking up to God. Only one who can do this is properly an acknowledger of God's unity, a true Muwahhid. To such, God would assuredly open the door of help; they were at His gate; and the biographies of the saints are full of tales how His help used to come.

To this it may be imagined that the more sober, even among Sufis, made vehement objection. It fell under two heads. One was that of leash, the gaining of daily bread by labor. The examples of the husbandman who casts his seed into the ground and then depends upon God, of the merchant who travels with his wares in similar trust, were held up against the wandering but useless monk. As always, traditions were forged on both sides. Said a man--apparently in a spirit of prophecy--one day to the Prophet, "Shall I let my camel run free and trust in God?" Replied the Prophet, or someone for him with a good imitation of his humorous common-sense, "Tie up your camel and trust in God." The other head was the use of remedies in sickness. The whole controversy parallels strikingly the "mental science" and "Christian science" of the present day. Medicine, it was held, destroyed tawakkul. In the fourth century in Persia this insanity ran high and many books were written for it and against it. The author of one on the first side was consulted in an obstinate case of headache. "Put my book under your pillow," he said, "and trust in God." On both these points the usage of the Prophet and the Companions was in the teeth of the Sufi position. They had notoriously earned their living, honestly or dishonestly, and had possessed all the credulity of semi-civilization toward the most barbaric and multifarious remedies. So the agreement of Islam eventually righted itself, though the question in its intricacies and subtilties remained for centuries a thing of delight for theologians. In the end only the wildest fanatics held by absolute tawakkul.

But all this time the second form of Sufiism had been slowly forcing its way. It was essentially speculative and theological rather than ascetic and devotional. When it gained the upper hand, zahid (ascetic) was no longer a convertible term with Sufi. We pass over the boundary between Thomas à Kempis and St. Francis to Eckhart and Suso. The roots of this movement cannot be hard to find in the light of what has preceded. They lie partly in the neo-Platonism which is the foundation of the philosophy of Islam. Probably it did not come to the Sufis along the same channels by which it reached al-Farabi. It was rather through the Christian mystics and, perhaps, especially through the Pseudo-Dionysius the Areopagite, and his asserted teacher, Stephen bar Sudaili with his Syriac "Book of Hierotheos." We need not here consider whether the Monophysite heresy is to be reckoned in as one of the results of the dying neo-Platonism. It is true that outlying forms of it meant the frank deifying of a man and thus raised the possibility of the equal deifying of any other man and of all men. But there is no certainty that these views had an influence in Islam. It is enough that from A.D. 533 we find the Pseudo-Dionysius quoted and his influence strong with the ultra Monophysites, and still more, thereafter, with the whole mystical movement in Christendom. According to it, all is akin in mature to the Absolute, and all this life below is only a reflection of the glories of the upper sphere, where God is. Through the sacraments and a hierarchy of angels man is led back toward Him. Only in ecstasy can man come to a knowledge of Him. The Trinity, sin and the atonement fade out of view. The incarnation is but an example of how the divine and the human can join. All is an emanation or an emission of grace from God; and the yearnings of man are back to his source. The revolving spheres, the groaning and travailing nature are striving to return to their origin. When this conception had seized the Oriental Church, when it had passed into Islam and dominated its emotional and religious life; when through the translation of the Pseudo-Dionysius by Scotus Erigena in 850, it had begun the long contest of idealism in Europe, the dead school of Plotinus had won the field, and its influence ruled from the Oxus to the Atlantic.

But the roots of Sufiism struck also in another direction. We have already seen an early tendency to regard Ali and, later, members of his house as incarnations of divinity. In the East, where God comes near to man, the conception of God in man is not difficult. The Semitic prophet through whom God speaks easily slips over into a divine being in whom God exists and may be worshipped. But if with one, why not with another? May it not be possible by purifying exercises to reach this unity? If one is a Son of God, may not all become that if they but take the means? The half-understood pantheism which always lurks behind oriental fervors claims its due. From his wild whirling dance, the darwish, stung to cataleptic ecstasy by the throbbing of the drums and the lilting chant, sinks back into the unconsciousness of the divine oneness. He has passed temporarily from this scene of multiplicity into the sea of God's unity and, at death, if he but persevere, he will reach that haven where he fain would be and will abide there forever. Here, we have not to do with calm philosophers rearing their systems in labored speculations, but with men, often untaught, seeking the salvation of their souls earnestly and with tears.

One of the earliest of the pantheistic school was Abu Yazid al-Bistami (d. 261). He was of Persian parentage, and his father had been a follower of Zarathustra. As an ascetic he was of the highest repute; he was also an author of eminence on Sufiism (al-Ghazzali used his books) and he joined to his devout learning and self-mortification clear miraculous gifts. But equally clear was his pantheistic drift and his name has come down linked to the saying, "Beneath my cloak there is naught else than God." It is worth noticing that certain other of his sayings show that, even in his time, there were Sufi saints who boasted that they had reached such perfection and such miraculous powers that the ordinary moral and ceremonial law no longer applied to them. The antinomianism which haunted the later Sufiism and darwishdom had already appeared.

But the greatest name of all among these early pantheists was that of al-Hallaj (the cotton carder), a pupil of al-Junayd, who was put to death with great cruelty in 309. It is almost impossible to reach any certain conclusion as to his real views and aims. In spite of what seem to be utterances of the crassest pantheism, such as, "I am the Truth," there have not been wanting many in later Islam who have reverenced his memory as that of a saint and martyr. To Sufis and darwishes of his time and to this day he has been and is a patron saint. In his life and death he represents for them the spirit of revolt against dogmatic scholasticism and formalism. Further, even such a great doctor of the Muslim Church as al-Ghazzali defended him and, though lamenting some incautious phrases, upheld his orthodoxy. At his trial itself before the theologians of Baghdad, one of them refused to sign the fatwa declaring him an unbeliever; he was not clear, he said, as to the case. And it is true that such records as we have of the time suggest that his condemnation was forced by the government as a matter of state policy. He was a Persian of Magian origin, and evidently an advanced mystic of the speculative type. He carried the theory to its legitimate conclusion, and proclaimed the result publicly. He dabbled in scholastic theology; had evident Mu'tazilite leanings; wrote on alchemy and things esoteric. But with this mystical enthusiasm there seem to have united in him other and more dangerous traits. The stories which have reached us show him of a character fond of excitement and change, surrounding himself with devoted adherents and striving by miracle-working of a commonplace kind to add to his following. His popularity among the people of Baghdad and their reverence for him rose to a perilous degree. He may have had plans of his own as a Persian nationalist; he may have had part in one of the Shi'ite conspiracies; he may have been nothing but a rather weak-headed devotee, carried off his feet by a sudden tide of public excitement, the greatest trial and

[99]

danger that a saint has to meet. But the times were not such then in Baghdad that the government could take any risks. Al-Muqtadir was Khalifa and in his weak hands the Khalifate was slipping to ruin. The Fatimids were supreme in North Africa; the Qarmatians held Syria and Arabia, and were threatening Baghdad itself. In eight years they were to take Mecca. Persia was seething with false prophets and nationalists of every shade. Thirteen years later Ibn ash-Shalmaghani was put to death in Baghdad on similar grounds; in his case, Shi'ite conspiracy against the state was still more clearly involved. We can only conclude in the words of Ibn Khallikan (d. 681), "The history of al-Hallaj is long to relate; his fate is well known; and God knoweth all secret things." With him we must leave, for the present, consideration of the Sufi development and return to the Mu'tazilites and to the people tiring of their dry subtilties.

CHAPTER III

The rise of orthodox kalam; al-Ash'ari; decline of the Mu'tazilites; passing of heresy into unbelief; development of scholastic theology by Ash'arites; rise of Zahirite kalam; Ibn Hazm; persecution of Ash'arites; final assimilation of kalam.

As we have already seen, the traditionalist party at first refused to enter upon any discussion of sacred things. Malik ibn Anas used to say, "God's istiwa (settling Himself firmly upon His throne) is known; how it is done is unknown; it must be believed; questions about it are an innovation (bid'a)." But such a position could not be held for any length of time. The world cannot be cut in two and half assigned to faith and half to reason. So, as time went on, there arose on the orthodox side men who, little by little, were prepared to give a reason for the faith that was in them. They thus came to use kalam in order to meet the kalam of the Mu'tazilites; they became mutakallims, and the scholastic theology of Islam was founded. It is the history of this transfer of method which we have now to consider.

Its beginnings are wrapped in a natural obscurity. It was at first a gradual, unconscious drift, and people did not recognize its existence. Afterward, when they looked back upon it, the tendency of the human mind to ascribe broad movements to single men asserted itself and the whole was put under the name of al-Ash'ari. It is true that with him, in a sense, the change suddenly leaped to self-consciousness, but it had already been long in progress. As we have seen, al-Junayd discussed the unity of God, but it was behind closed doors. Ash-Shafi'i held that there should be a certain number of men trained thus to defend and purify the faith, but that it would be a great evil if their arguments should become known to the mass of the people. Al-Muhasibi, a contemporary of Ahmad ibn Hanbal, was suspected, and rightly, of defending his faith with argument, and

[100]

thereby incurred Ahmad's displeasure. Another contemporary of Ahmad's, al-Karabisi (d. 345), incurred the same displeasure, and the list might easily be extended. But the most significant fact of all is that the movement came to the surface and showed itself openly at the same time in the most widely separated lands of Islam. In Mesopotamia there was al-Ash'ari, who died after 320; in Egypt there was at-Tahawi, who died in 331; in Samarqand there was al-Mataridi, who died in 333. Of these at-Tahawi is now little more than a name; al-Mataridi's star has paled before that of al-Ash'ari; al-Ash'ari has come in popular view to be the solitary hero before whom the Mu'tazilite system went down. It will perhaps be sufficient if we take his life and experiences as our guide in this period of change; the others must have followed very much in the same path.

He was born at al-Basra in 260, the year in which al-Kindi died and Muhammad al-Muntazar vanished from the sight of men. He came into a world full of intellectual ferment; Alids of different camps were active in their claim to be possessors of an infallible Imam; Zaydites and Qarmatians were in revolt; the decree of 234 that the Qur'an was uncreated had had little effect, so far, in silencing the Mu'tazilites; in 261 the Sufi pantheist, Abu Yazid, died. Al-Ash'ari himself was of the best blood of the desert and of a highly orthodox family which had borne a distinguished part in Muslim history. Through some accident he came in early youth into the care of al-Jubba'i, the Mu'tazilite, who, according to one story, had married al-Ash'ari's mother; was brought up by him and remained a stanch Mu'tazilite, writing and speaking on that side, till he was forty years old.

Then a strange thing happened. One day he mounted the pulpit of the mosque in al-Basra and cried aloud, "He who knows me, knows me; and he who knows me not, let him know that I am so and so, the son of so and so. I have maintained the creation of the Qur'an and that God will not be seen in the world to come with the eyes, and that the creatures create their actions. Lo, I repent that I have, been a Mu'tazilite and turn to opposition to them." It was a voice full of omen. It told that the intellectual supremacy of the Mu'tazilites had publicly passed and that, hereafter, they would be met with their own weapons. What led to this change of mind is strictly unknown; only legends have reached us. One, full of psychological truth, runs that one Ramadan, the fasting month, when he was worn with prayer and hunger, the Prophet appeared to him three times in his sleep, and commanded him to turn from his vain kalam and seek certainty in the traditions and the Qur'an. If he would but give himself to that study, God would make clear the difficulties and enable him to solve all the puzzles. He did so, and his mind seemed to be opened; the old contradictions and absurdities had fled, and he cursed the Mu'tazilites and all their works.

It can easily be seen that in some such way as this the blood of the race may have led him back to the God of his fathers, the God of the desert, whose word must be accepted as its own proof. The gossips of the time told strange tales of rich relatives and family pressure; we can leave these aside. When he had changed he was terribly in earnest. He met his old teacher, al-Jubba'i, in public discussions again and again till the old man withdrew. One of these discussions legend has handed down in varying forms. None of them may be exactly true, but they are significant of the change of attitude. He came to al-Jubba'i and said, "Suppose the case of three brothers; one being God-fearing, another godless and a third dies as a child. What of them in the world to come?

Al-Jubba'i replied, "The first will be rewarded in Paradise; the second punished in Hell, and the third will be neither rewarded nor punished." Al-Ash'ari continued, "But if the third said, 'Lord, Thou mightest have granted me life, and then I would have been pious and entered Paradise like my brother,' what then? "Al-Jubba'i replied, "God would say, 'I knew that if thou wert granted life thou wouldst be godless and unbelieving and enter Hell.'" Then al-Ash'ari drew his noose, "But what if the second said, 'Lord, why didst Thou not. make me die as a child? Then had I escaped Hell.'" Al-Jubba'i was silenced, and Al-Ash'ari went away in triumph. Three years after his pupil had left him the old man died. The tellers of this story regard it as disproving the Mu'tazilite doctrine of "the best"--al-aslah--namely, that God is constrained to do that which may be best and happiest for His creatures. Orthodox Islam, as we have seen, holds that God is under no such constraint, and is free to do good or evil as He chooses.

But the story has also another and somewhat broader significance. It is a protest against the religious rationalism of the Mu'tazilites, which held that the mysteries of the universe could be expressed and met in terms of human thought. In this way it represents the essence of al-Ash'ari's position, a recoil from the impossible task of raising a system of purely rationalistic theology to reliance upon the Word of God, and the tradition (hadith) and usage (sunna) of the Prophet and the pattern of the early church (salaf).

The stories told above represent the change as sudden. According to the evidence of his books that was not so. In his return there were two stages. In the first of these he upheld the seven rational Qualities (sifat aqliya) of God, Life, Knowledge, Power, Will, Hearing, Seeing, Speech: but explained away the Qur'anic anthropomorphisms of God's face, hands, feet, etc. In the second stage, which fell, apparently, after he had moved to Baghdad and come under the strong Hanbalite influences there, he explained away nothing, but contented himself with the position that the anthropomorphisms were to be taken, bila kayfa wala tashbih, without asking how and without drawing any comparison. The first phrase is directed against the Mu'tazilites, who inquired persistently into the nature and possibility of such things in God; the second, against the anthropomorphists (mushabbihs, comparers; mujassims, corporealizers), mostly ultra Hanbalites and Karramites, who said that these things in God were like the corresponding things in men. At all stages, however, he was prepared to defend his conclusions and assail those of his adversaries by dint of argument.

The details of his system will be best understood by reading his creed and the creed of al-Fudali, which is essentially Ash'arite. Both are in the Appendix of Translated Creeds. Here, it is necessary to draw attention to two, only, of the obscurer points. On the vexed question, "What is a thing?" he anticipated Kant. The early theologians, orthodox and theoretical, and those later ones also who did not follow him, regarded, as we have seen, existence (wujud) as only one of the qualities belonging to an existing thing (mawjud). It was there all the time, but it lacked the quality of "existence"; then that quality was added to its other qualities and it became existent. But al-Ash'ari and his followers held that existence was the "self" (ayn) of the entity and not a quality or state, however personal or necessary. See, on the whole, Appendix of Creeds.

On the other vexed question of free-will, or, rather, as the Muslims chose to express it, on the ability of men to produce actions, he took up a mediating position. The old orthodox position was absolutely fatalistic; the Mu'tazilites, following their principle of Justice, gave to man an initiative power. Al-Ash'ari struck a middle path. Man cannot create anything; God is the only creator. Nor does man's power produce any effect on his actions at all. God creates in His creature power (qudra) and choice (ikhtiyar). Then He creates in him his action corresponding to the power and choice thus created. So the action of the creature is created by God as to initiative and as to production; but it is acquired by the creature. By acquisition (kasb) is meant that it corresponds to the creature's power and choice, previously created in him, without his having had the slightest effect on the action. He was only the locus or subject of the action. In this way al-Ash'ari is supposed to have accounted for free-will and entailed responsibility upon men. It may be doubted whether the second point occupied him much. It was open to his God to do good or evil as He chose; the Justice of the Mu'tazilites was left behind. He may have intended only to explain the consciousness of freedom, as some have done more recently. The closeness with which al-Ash'ari in this comes to the pre-established harmony of Leibnitz and to the Kantian conception of existence shows how high a rank he must take as an original thinker. His abandoning of the Mu'tazilites was due to no mere wave of sentiment but to a perception that their speculations were on too narrow a basis and of a too barren scholastic type. He died after 320 with a curse on them and their methods as his last words.

A few words only need be given to al-Mataridi. The creed of an-Nasafi in the Appendix of Creeds, pp. 308-315 belongs to his school. He and at-Tahawi were followers of the broad-minded Abu Hanifa, who was more than suspected of Mu'tazilite and Murji'ite leanings. Muslim theologians usually reckon, up some thirteen points of difference between al-Mataridi and al-Ash'ari and admit that seven of these are not much more than combats of words. Those which occur in an-Nasafi's creed are marked with a star.

We are now in a position to finish shortly with the Mu'tazilites. Their work, as a constructive force, is done. From this time on there is kalam among the orthodox, and the term mutakallim denotes nothing but a scholastic theologian, whether of one wing or another. And so, like any other organ which has done its part and for the existence of which there is no longer any object, they gradually and quietly dropped into the background. They had still, sometimes, to suffer persecution, and for hundreds of years there were men who continued to call themselves Mu'tazilites; but their heresies came to be heresies of the schools and not burning questions in the eyes of the masses. We need now draw attention to only a few incidents and figures in this dying movement. The Muslim historians lay much stress on the orthodox zeal of the Khalifa al-Qadir, who reigned 381-422, and narrate how he persecuted the Mu'tazilites, Shi'ites and other heretics and compelled them, under oath, to conform.

But there are several difficulties in the way of this persecution, which make it probable that it was more nominal than otherwise. Al-Qadir was bitterly orthodox; he had written a treatise on theology and compelled his unhappy courtiers to listen to a public reading of it every week. But he enjoyed, outside of his palace, next to no power. He was in the control of the Shi'ite Buwayhids, who, as we have seen, ruled Baghdad and the Khalifate from 320 to 447. These dubious persecutions are said to have fallen in 408 and 420. Again, a Muslim pilgrim from Spain visited Baghdad about 390 and has left us a record of the state of religious things there. He found in session what may perhaps best be described as a Parliament of Religions. It seems to have been a free debate between Muslims of all sects, orthodox and heretical, Parsees and atheists, Jews and Christians--unbelievers of every kind. Each party had a spokesman, and at the beginning of the proceedings the rule was rehearsed that no one might appeal to the sacred books of his creed but might only adduce arguments founded upon reason. The pious Spanish Muslim went to two meetings but did not peril his soul by any further visits. In his narrative we recognize the horror with which the orthodox of Spain viewed such proceedings--Spain, Muslim and Christian, has always favored the straitest sect; but when such a thing was permitted in Baghdad, religious liberty there at least must have been tolerably broad. Possibly it was sittings of the Ikhwan as-safa upon which this scandalized Spaniard stumbled. He himself speaks of them as meetings of mutakallims.

But if the mixture of Sunnite and Shi'ite authority in Baghdad gave all the miscellaneous heretics a chance for life, it was different in the growing dominions of Mahmud of Ghazna. That iconoclastic monarch had embraced the anthropomorphic faith of the Karramites, the most literal-minded of all the Muslim sects. In consequence, all forms of Mu'tazilism and all kinds of mutakallims were an abomination to him, and it was a very real persecution which they met at his hands. That al-Qadir, his spiritual suzerain, urged him on is very probable; it is also possible that respect for the growing power of Mahmud may have protected al-Qadir to some extent from the Buwayhids. In 420 Mahmud took from them Ispahan and held there a grand inquisition on Shi'ites and heretics of all kinds.

To proceed with the Mu'tazilites; when we come to al-Ghazzali and his times we shall find that they have ceased to be a crying danger to the faith. Though their views might, that doctor held, be erroneous in some respects, they were not to be considered as damnable. Again, in 538, there died az-Zamakhshari, the great grammarian, who is often called the last of the Mu'tazilites. He was not that by any means, but his heresies were either mild or were regarded mildly. A single point will show this, His commentary on the Qur'an, the Kashshaf, was revised and expurgated in the orthodox interest by al-Baydawi (d. 688) and in that form is now the most popular and respected of all expositions. The Kashshaf itself, in its original, unmodified form, has been printed several times at Cairo. Again, Ibn Rushd, the Aristotelian, who died in 595, when he is combating the arguments of the mutakallims, makes little difference between the Mu'tazilites and the others. They are only, to him, another variety of scholastic theologian, with a rather better idea, perhaps, of logic and argument. He considered, as we shall find later, all the mutakallims as sadly to seek in such matters. Since then, and into quite modern times, there have been sporadic cases of theologians called Mu'tazilites by themselves or others. Practically, they have been scholastics of eccentric views. Finally, the use of this name for themselves by the present-day broad school Muslims of India is absolutely unhistorical and highly misleading.

We turn now to suggest, rather than to trace, some of the non-theological consequences of the preceding theology.

Increasingly, from this time on, it is not heresy which has to be met so much as simple unbelief, more or less frank. It is evident that the heretics of the earlier period are now dividing in two directions, one part inclining toward milder forms of heresy and the other toward doubt in the largest sense, passing over to

Aristotelian + neo-Platonic philosophy, and thence dividing into materialists, deists, and theists. Thus we have seen earlier the workings of al-Farabi and of the Ikhwan as-safa. The teachings of the latter pass on to the Isma'ilians who developed them in the mountain fortresses, the centres of their power, scattered from Persia to Syria. These were otherwise called Assassins; otherwise Batinites in the narrower sense--in the broader that term meant only those who found under the letter of the Qur'an a hidden, esoteric meaning; otherwise Ta'limites or claimers of a ta'lim, a secret teaching by a divinely instructed Imam, and with them we shall have much to do later. It is sufficient here to notice how the peaceful and rather watery philosophy of the "Sincere Brethren" was transmuted through ambition and fanaticism into belligerent politics at the hands and daggers of these fierce sectaries. Into this period, too, fall some well-known names of dubious and more than dubious orthodoxy. Al-Beruni (d. 440) even at the court of Mahmud of Ghazna managed to keep his footing and his head. Yet it may be doubted how far he was a Karramite or even a Muslim. He was certainly the first scientific student of India and Indica and of chronology and calendars, a man whose attainments and results show that our so-called modern methods are as old as genius. On religion, he maintained a prudent silence, but earned the favor of Mahmud by an unsparing exposure of the weakness in the Fatimid genealogy. In this sketch he has a place as a man of science who went his own way without treading on the religious toes of other people.

His contemporary Ibn Sina (d. 428), for us Avicenna, was of a different nature, and his lines were cast in different places. He was a wanderer through the courts of northern Persia. The orthodox and stringent Mahmud he carefully avoided; the Buwayhids and those of their ilk took such heresies as his more easily. Endowed with a gigantic memory and an insatiable intellectual appetite, he was the encyclopædist of his age, and his scientific work, and especially that in medicine, went further than anything else to put the Muslim East and mediæval Europe in the strait waistcoat from which the first has not yet emerged and the second only shook itself free in the seventeenth century. He was a student of Aristotle and a mystic, as all Muslim students of Aristotle have been. How far his mysticism enabled him to square the Qur'an with his philosophy is not clear; such men seldom said exactly what they meant and all that they thought. He was also a diligent student and reader of the Qur'an and faithful in his public religious duties. Yet the Muslim world asserts that he left behind him a testamentary tractate (wasiya) defending dissimulation as to the religion of the country in which we might be; that it was not wrong for the philosopher to go through religious rites which for him had no meaning. He, too, is significant for his time, and, if our interest were philosophy, would call for lengthened treatment. As it is, he marks

[106]

for us the accomplished separation between students of theology and students of philosophy.

An equally well known and by us much better loved name is that of Umar al-Khayyam, who died later, about 515, but who may fitly be grouped with Ibn Sina. He, too, was a bon vivant, but of a deeper, more melancholy strain. His wine meant more than friendly cups; it was a way of escape from the world and its burden. His science, too, went deeper. He was not a gatherer and arranger of the wisdom of the past; his reformed calendar is more perfect than that which we even now use. His faith is a riddle to us, as it was to his comrades. But it was because he had no certain truth to proclaim that Umar did not speak out clearly. His last words were almost those of Rabelais, "I go to meet the great Perhaps." Anecdotage connects his name with that of al-Ghazzali. Neither had escaped the pall of universal scepticism which must have descended upon their time. But al-Ghazzali, by God's grace, as he himself reverently says, was enabled to escape. Umar died under it.

A very different man was Abu-l-Ala al-Ma'arri, the blind poet and singer of intellectual freedom. In Arabic literature there is no other voice like his, clear and confident. He was a man of letters; no philosopher nor theologian nor scientist, though at one time he seems to have come in contact with a circle like that of Ikhwan as-safa, perhaps the same; and his spirit was like that of one of the heroic poets of the old desert life, whose hand was taught to keep his head, whose tongue spared nothing from heaven to earth, and who lived his own life out in his own way, undaunted. In his darkness he nourished great thoughts and flung out a sæva indignatio on hypocrisy and subservience which reminds of Lessing. But Abu-l-Ala was a great poet, and his scorn of priests and courtiers and their lies, his pity for suffering humanity and his confidence in the light of reason are thrown into scraps of burning, echoing verse without their like in Arabic. He died at the town of his birth, Ma'arrat an-Nu'man, in northern Syria, in 449. The problem is how he was suffered to live out his long life of eighty-six years.

We can now return to the development of scholastic theology in the orthodox church at the hands of the followers of al-Ash'ari. They had to fight their way against many and most differing opponents. At the one extreme were the dwindling Mu'tazilites, passing slowly into comparatively innocuous heretics, and the growing party of unbelievers, philosophical and otherwise, open and secret. At the other extreme was the mob of Hanbalites, belonging to the only legal school which laid theological burdens on its adherents. The theologians, in this case, certainly varied as to the weight of their own anathemas against all kalam, but were at one in that they carried the bulk of the multitude with them and could enforce their conclusions with the cudgels of rioters. In the midst were the rival orthodox (pace the Hanbalites) developers of kalam, among whom the Mataridites probably held the most important place. Thus, the Ash'arite school was the nursling as well as the child of controversy.

It was, then, fitting that the name joined, at least in tradition, with the final form of that system, should be that of a controversialist. But this man, Abu Bakr al-Baqilani the Qadi, was more than a mere controversialist. It is his glory to have contributed most important elements to and put into fixed form what is, perhaps, the most fantastic and daring metaphysical scheme, and almost certainly the most thorough theological scheme, ever thought out. On the one hand, the Lucretian atoms raining down through the empty void, the self-developing monads of Leibnitz, pre-established harmony and all, the Kantian "things in themselves" are lame and impotent in their consistency beside the parallel Ash'arite doctrines; and, on the other, not even the rigors of Calvin, as developed in the Dutch confessions, can compete with the unflinching exactitude of the Muslim conclusions.

First, as to ontology. The object of the Ash'arites was that of Kant, to fix the relation of knowledge to the thing in itself. Thus, al-Baqilani defined knowledge (ilm) as cognition (ma'rifa) of a thing as it is in itself. But in reaching that "thing in itself" they were much more thorough than Kant. Only two of the Aristotelian categories survived their attack, substance and quality. The others, quantity, place, time and the rest, were only relationships (i'tibars) existing subjectively in the mind of the knower, and not things. But a relationship, they argued, if real, must exist in something, and a quality cannot exist in another quality, only in a substance. Yet it could not exist in either of the two things which it brought together; for example, in the cause or the effect. It must be in a third thing. But to bring this third thing and the first two together, other relationships would be needed and other things for these relationships to exist in. Thus we would be led back in an infinite sequence, and they had taken over from Aristotle the position that such an infinite series backward (tasalsal) is inadmissible. Relationships, then, had no real existence but were mere phantoms, subjective nonentities. Further, the Aristotelian view of matter was now impossible for them. All the categories had gone except substance and quality; and among them, passion. Matter, then, could not have the possibility of suffering the impress of form. A possibility is neither an entity nor a non-entity, but a subjectivity purely. But with the suffering matter, the active form and all causes must also go. They, too, are mere subjectivities. Again, qualities, for these thinkers, became mere accidents. The fleeting character of appearances drove them to the conclusion that there was no such thing as a quality planted in the nature of a thing; that the idea "nature" did not exist. Then this drove them further. Substances exist only with qualities, i.e., accidents. These qualities may be positive or they may be negative; the ascription to things of negative qualities is one of their most fruitful conceptions. When, then, the qualities fall out of existence, the substances themselves must also cease to exist. Substance as well as quality is fleeting, has only a moment's duration.

But when they rejected the Aristotelian view of matter as the possibility of receiving form, their path of necessity led them straight to the atomists. So atomists they became, and, as always, after their own fashion. Their atoms are not of space only, but also of time. The basis of all the manifestation, mental and physical, of the world in place and time, is a multitude of monads. Each has certain qualities but has extension neither in space nor time. They have simply position, not bulk, and do not touch one another. Between them is absolute void. Similarly as to time. The time-atoms, if the expression may be permitted, are equally unextended and have also absolute void--of time--between them. Just as space is only in a series of atoms, so time is only in a succession of untouching moments and leaps across the void from one to the other with the jerk of the hand of a clock. Time, in this view, is in grains and can exist only in connection with change. The monads differ from those of Leibnitz in having no nature in themselves, no possibility of development along certain lines. The Muslim monads are, and again are not, all change and action in the world are produced by their entering into existence and dropping out again, not by any change in themselves.

But this most simple view of the world left its holders in precisely the same difficulty, only in a far higher degree, as that of Leibnitz. He was compelled to fall back on a pre-established harmony to bring his monads into orderly relations with one another; the Muslim theologians, on their side, fell back upon God and found in His will the ground of all things.

We here pass from their ontology to their theology, and as they were thorough-going metaphysicians, so now they are thorough-going theologians. Being was all in the one case; now it is God that is all. In truth, their philosophy is in its essence a scepticism which destroys the possibility of a philosophy in order to drive men back to God and His revelations and compel them to see in Him the one grand fact of the universe. So, when a darwish shouts in his ecstasy, "Huwa-l-haqq," he does not mean, "He is the Truth," in our Western sense of Verity, or our New Testament sense of "The Way, the Truth, and the Life," but simply, "He is the Fact"--the one Reality.

To return: from their ontology they derived an argument for the necessity of a God. That their monads came so and not otherwise must have a cause; without it there could be no harmony or connection between them. And this cause must be one with no cause behind it; otherwise we would have the endless chain. This cause, then, they found in the absolutely free will of God, working without any matter beside it and unaffected by any laws or necessities. It creates and annihilates the atoms and their qualities and, by that means, brings to pass all the motion and change of the world. These, in our sense, do not exist. When a thing seems to us to be moved, that really means that God has annihilated--or permitted to drop out of existence, by not continuing to uphold, as another view held--the atoms making up that thing in its original position, and has created them again and again along the line over which it moves. Similarly of what we regard as cause and effect. A man writes with a pen and a piece of paper. God creates in his mind the will to write; at the same moment he gives him the power to write and brings about the apparent motion of the hand, of the pen and the appearance on the paper. No one of these is the cause of the other. God has brought about by creation and annihilation of atoms the requisite combination to produce these appearances. Thus we see that free-will for the Muslim scholastics is simply the presence, in the mind of the man, of this choice created there by God. This may not seem to us to be very real, but it has, certainly, as much reality as anything else in their world. Further, it will be observed how completely this annihilates the machinery of the universe. There is no such thing as law, and the world is sustained by a constant, ever-repeated miracle. Miracles and what we regard as the ordinary operations of nature are on the same level. The world and the things in it could have been quite different. The only limitation upon God is that He cannot produce a contradiction. A thing cannot be and not be at the same time. There is no such thing as a secondary cause; when there is the appearance of such, it is only illusional. God is producing it as well as the ultimate appearance of effect. There is no nature belonging to things. Fire does not burn and a knife does not cut. God creates in a substance a being burned when the fire touches it and a being cut when the knife approaches it.

In this scheme there are certainly grave difficulties, philosophical and ethical. It establishes a relationship between God and the atoms; but we have already seen that relationships are subjective illusions. That, however, was in the case of the things of the world, perceived by the senses--contingent being, as they would put it. It does not hold of necessary being. God possesses a quality called Difference from originated things (al-mukhalafa lil-hawadith). He is not a natural cause, but a free cause; and the existence of a free cause they were compelled by their principles to admit. The ethical difficulty is perhaps greater. If there is no order of nature and no certainty, or nexus, as to causes and effects; if there is no regular development in the life, mental, moral, and physical of a man--only a series of isolated moments; how can there be any responsibility, any moral claim or duty? This difficulty seems to have been recognized more clearly than the philosophical

[110]

one. It was met formally by the assertion of a certain order and regularity in the will of God. He sees to it that a man's life is a unity, and, for details, that the will to eat and the action always coincide. But such an answer must have been felt to be inadequate and to involve grave moral dangers for the common mind. Therefore, as we have seen, the study of kalam was hedged about with difficulties and restrictions. Theologians recognized its trap-falls and doubts, even for themselves, and lamented that they were compelled by their profession to study it. The public discussion of its questions was regarded as a breach of professional etiquette. Theologians and philosophers alike strove to keep these deeper mysteries hidden from the multitude. The gap between the highly educated and the great mass--that fundamental error and greatest danger in Muslim society-- comes here again to view. Further, even among theologians, there was some difference in degree of insight, and books and phrases could be read by different men in very different ways. To one, they would suggest ordinary, Qur'anic doctrines; another would see under and behind them a trail of metaphysical consequences bristling with blasphemous possibilities. Thus, Muslim science has been always of the school; it has never learned the vitalizing and disinfecting value of the fresh air of the market-place. This applies to philosophers even more than to theologians. The crowning accusation which Ibn Rushd, the great Aristotelian commentator, brought against al-Ghazzali was that he discussed such subtilties in popular books.

This, then, was the system which seems to have reached tolerably complete form at the hands of al-Baqilani, who died in 403. But with the completion of the system there went by no means its universal or even wide-spread acceptance in the Muslim world. That of al-Mataridi held its own for long, and, even yet, the Mataridite creed of an-Nasafi is used largely in the Turkish schools. In the fifth century it was considered remarkable that Abu Dharr (d. 434), a theologian of Herat, should be an Ash'arite rather than, apparently, a Mataridite. It was not till al-Ghazzali (d. 505) that the Ash'arite system came to the orthodox hegemony in the East, and it was only as the result of the work of Ibn Tumart, the Mahdi of the Muwahhids (d. 524), that it conquered the West. For long its path was darkened by suspicion and persecution. This came almost entirely from the Hanbalites. The Mu'tazilites had no force behind them, and while the views of deists and materialists were steadily making way in secret, their public efforts appeared only in very occasional disputes between theologians and philosophers. As we have seen, Muslim philosophy has always practised an economy of teaching.

The Hanbalite crisis seems to have come to a head toward the close of the reign of Tughril Beg, the first Great Saljuq. In 429, as we have seen, the Saljuqs had taken Merv and Samarqand, and in 447 Tughril Beg had entered Baghdad and freed the Khalifa from the Shi'ite domination of the Buwayhids who had so long enforced toleration. It was natural that he, a theologically unschooled Turk, should be captured by the simplicity and concreteness of the Hanbalite doctrines.

Added to this political factor there was a theological movement at work which was deeply hostile to the Ash'arites as they had developed. An important point in the method of al-Ash'ari himself, and, after him, of his followers, was to put forth a creed, expressed in the old-fashioned terms and containing the old-fashioned doctrines as nearly as was at all possible, and to accompany it with a spiritualizing interpretation which was, naturally, accessible to the professional student only. Accordingly what had at first seemed a weapon against the Mu'tazilites came to be viewed with more and more suspicion by the holders to the old, unquestioning orthodoxy. The duty also of religious investigation and speculation (nazr) came to have more and more stress laid upon it. The bila kayfa dropped into the background. A Muslim must have a reason for the faith that was in him, they said; otherwise, he was no true Muslim, was in fact an unbeliever. Of course, they limited carefully the extent to which he should go. For the ordinary man a series of very simple proofs would be prepared; the student, on the other hand, when carefully led, could work his way through the system sketched above. All this, naturally, was anathema to the party of tradition.

It is significant that at this time the Zahirite school of law (fiqh) developed into a school of kalam and applied its literal principles unflinchingly to its new victim. The leader in this was Ibn Hazm, a theologian of Spain. He died in 456, after a stormy life filled with controversy. The remorseless sting of his vituperative style coupled him, in popular proverb, with al-Hajjaj, the blood-thirsty lieutenant of the Umayyads in al-Iraq. "The sword of al-Hajjaj and the tongue of Ibn Hazm," they said. But for all his violence of language and real weight of character and brain, he made little way for his views in his lifetime. It was almost one hundred years after his death before they came into any prominence. The theologians and lawyers around him in the West were devoted to the study of fiqh in the narrowest and most technical sense. They labored over the systems and treatises of their predecessors and neglected the great original sources of the Qur'an and the traditions. The immediate study of tradition (hadith) had died out. Ibn Hazm, on the other hand, went straight back to hadith. Taqlid he absolutely rejected, each man must draw from the sacred texts his own views. So the whole system of the canon lawyers came down with a crash and they, naturally, did not like it. Analogy (qiyas), their principal instrument, he swept away. It had no place either in law or theology. Even on the principle of agreement (ijma) he threw a shadow of doubt.

But it was in theology rather than in law that Ibn Hazm's originality lay. Strictly, his Zahirite principles when applied there should have led him to anthropomorphism (tajsim). The literal meaning of the Qur'an, as we have seen, assigns to God hands and feet, sitting on and descending from His throne. But to Ibn Hazm, anthropomorphism was an abomination only less than the speculative arguments with which the Ash'arites tried to avoid it. His own method was purely grammatical and lexicographical. He hunted in his dictionary until he found some other meaning for "hand" or "foot," or whatever the stumbling-block might be.

But the most original point in his system is his doctrine of the names of God, and his basing of that doctrine upon God's qualities. The Ash'arites, he contended with justice, had been guilty of a grave inconsistency in saying that God was different in nature, qualities, and actions from all created things, and yet that the human qualities could be predicated of God, and that men could reason about God's nature. He accepted the doctrine of God's difference (mukhalafa) on highly logical, but, for us, rather startling grounds. The Qur'an applies to Him the words, "The Most Merciful of those that show mercy," but God, evidently, is not merciful. He tortures children with all manner of painful diseases, with hunger and terror. Mercy, in our human sense, which is high praise applied to a man, cannot be predicated of God. What then does the Qur'an mean by those words? Simply that they--arhamu-rrahimin--are one of God's names, applied to Him by Himself and that we have no right to take them as descriptive of a quality, mercy, and to use them to throw light on God's nature. They form one of the Ninety-nine Most Beautiful Names (al-asma al-husna) of which the Prophet has spoken in a tradition. Similarly, we may call God the Living One (al hayy), because He has given us that as one of His names, not because of any reasoning on our part. Do we not say that His life is different from that of all other living beings? These names then, are limited to ninety-nine and no more should be formed, however full of praise such might be for God, or however directly based on His actions. He has called Himself al-Wahib, the Giver, and so we may use that term of Him. But He has not called Himself al-Wahhab the Bountiful Giver, so we may not use that term of Him, though it is one of praise. Of course, you may describe His action and say that He is the guider of His saints. But you must not make from that a name, and call Him simply the Guider. Further, if we regard these names as expressing qualities in God, we involve multiplicity in God's nature; there is the quality and the thing qualified. Here we are back at the old Mu'tazilite difficulty and it is intelligible that Ibn Hazm dealt more gently with the Mu'tazilites than with the Ash'arites. The one party were Muslims and sinned in ignorance-- invincible ignorance, a Roman Catholic would call it; the others were unbelievers. They had turned wilfully from the way. The Mu'tazilites had tried to limit the qualities as much as possible. At the best they had said that they were God's essence and not in His essence. Al-Ash'ari and his school had fairly revelled in qualities and had mapped out the nature of God with the detail--and daring--of a phrenological chart.

Naturally, Ibn Hazm made his ethical basis the will of God only. God has willed that this should be a sin and that a good deed. Lying, he concedes, is always saying what does not agree with the truth. But, still, God may pronounce that one lie is a sin, and one not. Muslim ethics, it is true, have never branded lying as sinful in itself.

For the Shi'ites and their doctrine of an infallible Imam, Ibn Hazm cannot find strong enough expressions of contempt.

In Ibn Hazm's time, and he praises God for it, there were but few Ash'arites in the West. Theology generally did not find many students. So things went on till long after his death. To this fiery controversialist the worst blow of all would have been if he could have known that the men who were at last to bring his system, in part and for a time, into public acceptance and repute, were also to complete the conquest of Islam for the Ash'arite school. That was still far in the future, and we must return to the persecution,

The accounts of the persecution which set in are singularly conflicting. Some assign it to Hanbalite influence; others tell of a Mu'tazilite wazir of Tughril Beg. That the traditionalist party was the main force in it seems certain. In all probability, however, all the other anti-Ash'arite sects, from the Mu'tazilites on, took their own parts. The Ash'arite party represented a via media and would be set upon with zest by all the extremes. They were solemnly cursed from the pulpits and, what added peculiar insult to it, the Rafidites, an extreme Kharijite sect, were joined in the same anathema. Al-Juwayni, the greatest theologian of the time, fled to the Hijaz and gained the title of Imam of the two Harams (Imam al-Haramayn), by living for four years between Mecca and al-Madina. Al-Qushayri, the author of a celebrated treatise on Sufiism, was thrown into prison. The Ash'arite doctors generally were scattered to the winds. Only with the death of Tughril Beg in 455 did the cloud pass. His successor, Alp-Arslan, and especially the great wazir, Nizam al-Mulk, favored the Ash'arites. In 459 the latter founded the Nizamite Academy at Baghdad to be a defence of Ash'arite doctrines. This may fairly be regarded as the turning-point of the whole controversy. The Hanbalite mob of Baghdad still continued to make itself felt, but its excesses were promptly suppressed. In 510 ash-Shahrastani was well received there by the people, and in 516 the Khalifa himself attended Ash'arite lectures.

It is needless to spend more time over the other theologians who were links in the chain between al-Ash'ari and the Imam al-Haramayn. Their views wavered, this

[114]

way and that, only the rationalizing tendency became stronger and stronger. There was danger that the orthodox system would fossilize and lose touch with life as that of the Mu'tazilites had done. It is true that Sufiism still held its ground. All theologians practically were touched by it in its simpler form; and the cause of the higher Sufiism of ecstasy, wonders by saints (karamat) and communion of the individual soul with God had been eloquently and effectively urged by al-Qushayri (d. 465) in his Risala. But in spite of the labors of so many men of high ability, the religious outlook was growing ever darker. Keen observers recognized that some change was bound to come. That it might be an inflowing of new life by a new al-Ash'ari was their prayer. It is more than dubious whether even the keenest mind of the time could have recognized what form the new life must take. They had not the perspective and could only feel a vague need. But from what has gone before it will be plain that Islam had again to assimilate to itself something from without or perish. Such had been its manner of progress up till now. New opinions had arisen; had become heresies; conflict had followed; part of the new thought had been absorbed into the orthodox church; part had been rejected; through it all the life of the church had gone on in fuller and richer measure, being always, in spite of everything, the main stream; the heresy itself had slowly dwindled out of sight. So it had been with Murji'ism; so with Mu'tazilism. With the orthodox, tradition (naql) still stood fast, but reason (aql) had taken a place beside it. Kalam, in spite of Hanbalite clamors, had become fairly a part of their system. What was to be the new element, and who was to be its champion?

CHAPTER IV

Al-Ghazzali, his life, times, and work; Sufiism formally accepted into Islam.

WITH the time came the man. He was al-Ghazzali, the greatest, certainly the most sympathetic figure in the history of Islam, and the only teacher of the after generations ever put by a Muslim on a level with the four great Imams. The equal of Augustine in philosophical and theological importance, by his side the Aristotelian philosophers of Islam, Ibn Rushd and all the rest, seem beggarly compilers and scholiasts. Only al-Farabi, and that in virtue of his mysticism, approaches him. In his own person he took up the life of his time on all its sides and with it all its problems. He lived through them all and drew his theology from ms experience. Systems and classifications, words and arguments about words, he swept away; the facts of life as he had known them in his own soul he grasped. When his work was done the revelation of the mystic (kashf) was not only a full part but the basal part in the structure of Muslim theology. That basis, in spite, or rather on account of the work of the mutakallims had previously been lacking. Such a scepticism as their atomic system had practically amounted to, could disprove much but could prove little. If all the categories but substance and quality are mere subjectivities, existing in the mind only, what can we know of things? An ultra-rational basis had to be found and it was found in the ecstasy of the Sufis. But al-Ghazzali brought another element into fuller and more effective working. With him passes away the old-fashioned kalam, a thing of shreds and patches, scraps of metaphysics and logic snatched up for a moment of need, without grasp of the full sweep of philosophy, and incapable, in the long run, of meeting it. Even its atomic system is a philosophy of amateurs, with all their fantastic one-sidedness, their vigor and rigor. But al-Ghazzali was no amateur. His knowledge and grasp of the problems and objects of philosophy were truer and more vital than in any other Muslim up to his time--perhaps after it, too. Islam has not fully understood him any more than Christendom fully understood Augustine, but until long after him the horizon of Muslims was wider and their air clearer for his work. Then came a new scholasticism, reigning to this day.

So much by way of preface. We must now give some account of the life and experiences, the ideas and sensations, of this great leader and reformer. For his life and his work were one. Everything that he thought and wrote came with the weight and reality of personal experience. He recognized this connection himself, and has left us a book--the Munqidh min ad-dalal, "Rescuer from Error"--almost unique in Islam, which, in the form of an apology for the faith, is really an Apologia pro vita sua. This book is our main source for what follows.

Al-Ghazzali was born at Tus in 450. He lost his father when young and was educated and brought up by a trusted Sufi friend. He early turned to the study of theology and canon law, but, as he himself confesses, it was only because they promised wealth and reputation. Very early he broke away from taqlid, simple acceptance of religious truth on authority, and he began to investigate theological differences before he was twenty. His studies were of the broadest, embracing canon law, theology, dialectic, science, philosophy, logic and the doctrines and practices of the Sufis. It was a Sufi atmosphere in which he moved, but their religious fervors do not seem to have laid hold of him. Pride in his own intellectual powers, ambition and contempt for others of less ability mastered him. The latter part of his life as a student was spent at Naysabur as pupil and assistant of the Imam al-Haramayn. Through the Imam he stood in the apostolic succession of Ash'arite teachers, being the fourth from al-Ash'ari himself. There he remained till the death of the Imam in 478, when he went out to seek his fortune and found it with the great wazir, Nizam al-Mulk. By him al-Ghazzali was appointed, in 484, to teach in the Nizamite Academy at Baghdad. There he had the greatest success as a teacher and consulting lawyer, and his worldly hopes seemed safe. But suddenly he was struck down by mysterious disease. His speech became hampered; his appetite and digestion failed. His physicians gave him up; his malady, they said, was mental and could only be mentally treated. His only hope lay in peace of mind. Then he suddenly quitted Baghdad, in 488, ostensibly on pilgrimage to Mecca. This flight, for it was so in effect, of al-Ghazzali was unintelligible to the theologians of the time; since that time it has marked the greatest epoch in the church of Islam after the return of al-Ash'ari.

That it should be unintelligible was natural. No cause could be seen on the surface, except some possible political complications; the cause in reality lay in al-Ghazzali's mind and conscience. He was wandering in the labyrinth of his time. From his youth he had been a sceptical, ambitious student, playing with religious influences yet unaffected by them. But the hollowness of his life was ever present with him and pressing upon him. Like some with us, he sought to be converted and could not bring it to pass. His religious beliefs gradually gave way and fell from him, piece by piece.

At last, the strain became too great and at the court of Nizam al-Mulk he touched for two months the depths of absolute scepticism. He doubted the evidence of the senses; he could see plainly that they often deceived. No eye could perceive the movement of a shadow, but still the shadow moved; a gold piece would cover any star, but a star was a world larger than the earth. He doubted even the primary ideas of the mind. Is ten more than three? Can a thing be and not be? Perhaps; he could not tell. His senses deceived him, why not his mind? May there not be something behind the mind and transcending it, which would show the falsity of its convictions even as the mind showed the falsity of the information given by the senses? May not the dreams of the Sufis be true, and their revelations in ecstasy the only real guides? When we awake in death, may it not be into a true but different existence? All this--perhaps. And so he wandered for two months. He saw clearly that no reasoning could help him here; he had no ideas on which he could depend, from which he could begin. But the mercy of God is great; He sends His light to whom He wills, a light that flows in, and is given by no reasoning. By it al-Ghazzali was saved; he regained the power to think, and the task which he now set before him was to use this power to guide himself to truth.

When he looked around, he saw that those who gave themselves to the search for truth might be divided into four groups. There were the scholastic theologians, who were much like the theologians of all times and faiths. Second, there were the Ta'limites, who held that to reach truth one must have an infallible living teacher, and that there was such a teacher. Third, there were the followers of philosophy, basing on logical and rational proofs. Fourth, there were the Sufis, who held that they, the chosen of God, could reach knowledge of Him directly in ecstasy. With all these he had, of course, been acquainted to a greater or less degree; but now he settled down to examine them one by one, and find which would lead him to a certainty to which he could hold, whatever might come. He felt that he could not

[117]

go back to the unconscious faith of his childhood; that nothing could restore. All his mental being must be made over before he could find rest. He began with scholastic theology, but found no help there. Grant the theologians their premises and they could argue; deny them and there was no common ground on which to meet. Their science had been founded by al-Ash'ari to meet the Mu'tazilites; it had done that victoriously, but could do no more. They could hold the faith against heretics, expose their inconsistencies; against the sceptic they availed nothing. It is true that they had attempted to go further back and meet the students of philosophy on their own ground; to deal with substances and attributes and first principles generally; but their efforts had been fruitless. They lacked the necessary knowledge of the subject, had no scientific basis, and were constrained eventually to fall back on authority. After study of them and their methods it became clear to al-Ghazzali that the remedy for his ailment was not in scholastic theology.

Then he turned to philosophy. He had seen already that the weakness of the theologians lay in their not having made a sufficient study of primary ideas and the laws of thought. Three years he gave up to this. He was at Baghdad at the time, teaching law and writing legal treatises, and probably the three years extended from the beginning of 484 to the beginning of 487. Two years he gave, without a teacher, to the study of the writings of the different schools. of philosophy, and almost another to meditating and working over his results. He felt that he was the first Muslim doctor to do this with the requisite thoroughness. And it is noteworthy that at this stage he seems to have again felt himself to be a Muslim, and in an enemy's country when he was studying philosophy. He speaks of the necessity of understanding what is to be refuted; but this may be only a confusion between his attitude when writing after 500, and his attitude when investigating and seeking truth, fifteen years earlier. He divides the followers of philosophy in his time into three: Materialists, Deists (Tabi'is, i.e. Naturalists), and Theists. The materialists reject a creator; the world exists from all eternity; the animal comes from the egg and the egg from the animal. The wonder of creation compels the deists to admit a creator, but the creature is a machine, has a certain poise (i'tidal) in itself which keeps it running; its thought is a part of its nature and ends with death. They thus reject a future life, though admitting God and His attributes.

He deals at much greater length with the teachings of those whom he calls theists, but through all his statements of their views his tone is not that of a seeker but that of a partisan; he turns his own experiences into a warning to others, and makes of their record a little guide to apologetics. Aristotle he regards as the final master of the Greek school; his doctrines are best represented for Arabic readers in the books of Ibn Sina and al-Farabi; the works of their predecessors on this subject are a mass of confusion. Part of these doctrines must be stamped as unbelief, part

[118]

as heresy, and part as theologically indifferent. He then divides the philosophical sciences into six, mathematics, logic, physics, metaphysics, political economy, ethics; and discusses these in detail, showing what must be rejected, what is indifferent, what dangers arise from each to him who studies or to him who rejects without study.

Throughout, he is very cautious to mark nothing as unbelief that is not really so; to admit always those truths of mathematics, logic, and physics that cannot intellectually be rejected; and only to warn against an attitude of intellectualism and a belief that mathematicians, with their success in their own department, are to be followed in other departments, or that all subjects are susceptible of the exactness and certainty of a syllogism in logic. The damnable errors of the theists are almost entirely in their metaphysical views. Three of their propositions mark them as unbelievers. First, they reject the resurrection of the body and physical punishment hereafter; the punishments of the next world will be spiritual only. That there will be spiritual punishments, al-Ghazzali admits, but there will be physical as well. Second, they hold that God knows universals only, not particulars. Third, they hold that the world exists from all eternity and to all eternity. When they reject the attributes of God and hold that He knows by His essence and not by something added to His essence, they are only heretics and not unbelievers. In physics he accepts the constitution of the world as developed and explained by them; only all is to be regarded as entirely submitted to God, incapable of self-movement, a tool of which the Creator makes use. Finally, he considers that their system of ethics is derived from the Sufis. At all times there have been such saints, retired from the world--God has never left himself without a witness; and from their ecstasies and revelations our knowledge of the human heart, for good and for evil, is derived.

Thus in philosophy he found little light. It did not correspond entirely to his needs, for reason cannot answer all questions nor unveil all the enigmas of life. He would probably have admitted that he had learned much in his philosophical studies--so at least we may gather from his tone; he never speaks disrespectfully of philosophy and science in their sphere; his continual exhortation is that he who would understand them and refute them must first study them; that to do otherwise, to abuse what we do not know, brings only contempt on ourselves and on the cause which we champion. But with his temperament he could not found his religion on intellect. As a lawyer he could split hairs and define issues; but once the religious instinct was aroused, nothing could satisfy him but what he eventually found. And so, two possibilities and two only were before him, though one was hardly a real possibility, if we consider his training and mental powers. He might fall back on authority. It could not be the authority of his childish faith, "Our fathers have told us," he himself confesses, could never again have weight with him. But it might be some claimer of authority in a new form, some infallible teacher with a doctrine which he could accept for the authority behind it. As the Church of Rome from time to time gathers into its fold men of keen intellect who seek rest in submission, and the world marvels, so it might have been with him. Or again, he might turn directly to God and to personal intercourse with Him; he might seek to know Him and to be taught of Him without any intermediary, in a word to enter on the path of the mystic.

He came next to examine the doctrine of the Ta'limites. They, a somewhat outlying wing of the Fatimid propaganda, had come at this time into alarming prominence. In 483 Hasan ibn as-Sabbah had seized Alamut and entered on open rebellion. The sect of the Assassins was applying its principles. But the poison of their teaching was also spreading among the people. The principle of authority in religion, that only by an infallible teacher could truth be reached and that such an infallible teacher existed if he could only be found, was in the air. For himself, al-Ghazzali found the Ta'limites and their teaching eminently unsatisfactory: They had a lesson which they went over parrot-fashion, but beyond it they were in dense ignorance. The trained theologian and scholar had no patience with their slackness and shallowness of thought. He labored long, as ash-Shahrastani later confesses that he, too, did, to penetrate their mystery and learn something from them; but beyond the accustomed formulæ there was nothing to be found. He even admitted their contention of the necessity of a living, infallible teacher, to see what would follow--but nothing followed. "You admit the necessity of an Imam," they would say. "It is your business now to seek him; we have nothing to do with it." But though neither al-Ghazzali nor ash-Shahrastani, who died 43 (lunar) years after him, could be satisfied with the Ta'limites, many others were. The conflict was hot, and al-Ghazzali himself wrote several books against them.

The other possibility, the path of the mystic, now lay straight before him. In the Munqidh he tells us how, when he had made an end of the Ta'limites, he began to study the books of the Sufis, without any suggestion that he had had a previous acquaintance with them and their practices. But probably this means nothing more than it does when he speaks in a similar way of studying the scholastic theologians; namely, that he now took up the study in earnest and with a new and definite purpose. He therefore read carefully the works of al-Harith al-Muhasibi, the fragments of al-Junayd, ash-Shibli, and Abu Yazid al-Bistami. He had also the benefit of oral teaching; but it became plain to him that only through ecstasy and the complete transformation of the moral being could he really understand Sufiism. He saw that it consisted in feelings more than in knowledge, that he must be initiated as a Sufi himself; live their life and practise their exercises, to attain his goal.

[120]

On the way upon which he had gone up to this time, he had gained three fixed points of faith. He now believed firmly in God, in prophecy, and in the fast judgment. He had also gained the belief that only by detaching himself from this world, its life, enjoyments, honors, and turning to God could he be saved in the world to come. He looked on his present life, his writing and his teaching, and saw of how little value it was in the face of the great fact of heaven and hell. All he did now was for the sake of vainglory and had in it no consecration to the service of God. He felt on the edge of an abyss. The world held him back; his fears urged him away. He was in the throes of a conversion wrought by terror; his religion, now and always, in common with ail Islam, was other-worldly. So he remained in conflict with himself for six months from the middle of 488. Finally, his health broke down under the strain. In his feebleness and overthrow he took refuge with God, as a man at the end of his resources. God heard him and enabled him to make the needed sacrifices. He abandoned all and wandered forth from Baghdad as a Sufi. He had put his brilliant present and brilliant future absolutely behind him; had given up everything for the peace of his soul. This date, the end of 488, was the great era in his life; but it marked an era, too, in the history of Islam. Since al-Ash'ari went back to the faith of his fathers in 300, and cursed the Mu'tazilites and all their works, there had been no such epoch as this flight of al-Ghazzali. It meant that the reign of mere scholasticism was over; that another element was to work openly in the future Church of Islam, the element of the mystical life in God, of the attainment of truth by the soul in direct vision.

He went to Syria and gave himself up for two years to the religious exercises of the Sufis. Then he went on pilgrimage, first to Jerusalem; then to the tomb of Abraham at Hebron; finally to Mecca and al-Madina. With this religious duty his life of strict retirement ended. It is evident that he now felt that he was again within the fold of Islam. In spite of his former resolution to retire from the world, he was drawn back. The prayers of his children and his own aspirations broke in upon him, and though he resolved again and again to return to the contemplative life, and did often actually do so, yet events, family affairs, and the anxieties of life, kept continually disturbing him.

This went on, he tells us, for almost ten years, and in that time there were revealed to him things that could not be reckoned and the discussion of which could not be exhausted. He learned that the Sufis were on the true and only path to the knowledge of God; that neither intelligence nor wisdom nor science could change or improve their doctrine or their ethics. The light in which they walk is essentially the same as the light of prophecy; Muhammad was a Sufi when on his way to be a prophet. There is none other light to light any man in this world. A complete purifying of the heart from all but God is their Path; a seeking to plunge the heart completely in the thought of God, is its beginning, and its end is complete passing away in God. This last is only its end in relation to what can be entered upon and grasped by a voluntary effort; in truth, it is only the first step in the Path, the vestibule to the contemplative life. Revelations (mukashafas, unveilings) came to the disciples from the very beginning; while awake they see angels and souls of prophets, hear their voices and gain from them guidance. Then their State (hal, a Sufi technicality for a state of ecstasy) passes from the beholding of forms to stages where language fails and any attempt to express what is experienced must involve some error. They reach a nearness to God which some have fancied to be a hulul, fusion of being, others an ittihad, identification, and others a wusul, union; but these are all erroneous ways of indicating the thing. Al-Ghazzali notes one of his books in which he has explained wherein the error lies. But the thing itself is the true basis of all faith and the beginning of prophecy; the karamat of the saints lead to the miracles of the prophets. By this mea is the possibility and the existence of prophecy can be proved, and then the life itself of Muhammad proves that he was a prophet. Al-Ghazzali goes on to deal with the nature of prophecy, and how the life of Muhammad shows the truth of his mission; but enough has been given to indicate his attitude and the stage at which he had himself arrived.

During this ten years he had returned to his native country and to his children, but had not undertaken public duty as a teacher. Now that was forced upon him. The century was drawing to a close. Everywhere there was evident a slackening of religious fervor and faith. A mere external compliance with the rules of Islam was observed, men even openly defended such a course. He adduces as an example of this the Wasiya of Ibn Sina. The students of philosophy went their way, and their conduct shook the minds of the people; false Sufis abounded, who taught antinomianism; the lives of many theologians excited scandal; the Ta'limites were still spreading. A religious leader to turn the current was absolutely needed, and his friends looked to al-Ghazzali to take up that duty; some distinguished saints had dreams of his success; God had promised a reformer every hundred years and the time was up. Finally, the Sultan laid a command upon him to go and teach in the academy at Naysabur, and he was forced to consent. His departure for Naysabur fell at the end of 499, exactly eleven years after his flight from Baghdad. But he did not teach there long. Before the end of his life we find him back at Tus, his native place, living in retirement among his disciples, in a Madrasa or academy for students and a Khanqah or monastery for Sufis.

There he settled down to study and contemplation. We have already seen what theological position he had reached. Philosophy had been tried and found wanting. In a book of his called Tahafut, or "Destruction," he had smitten the philosophers hip and thigh; he had turned, as in earlier times al-Ash'ari, their own weapons against them, and had shown that with their premises and methods no certainty could be reached. In that book he goes to the extreme of intellectual scepticism, and, seven hundred years before Hume, he cuts the bond of causality with the edge of his dialectic and proclaims that we can know nothing of cause or effect, but simply that one thing follows another. He combats their proof of the eternity of the world, and exposes their assertion that God is its creator. He demonstrates that they cannot prove the existence of the creator or that that Creator is one; that they cannot prove that He is incorporeal, or that the world has any creator or cause at all; that they cannot prove the nature of God or that the human soul is a spiritual essence. When he has finished there is no intellectual basis left for life; he stands beside the Greek sceptics and beside Hume. We are thrown back on revelation, that given immediately by God to the individual soul or that given through prophets. All our real knowledge is derived from these sources. So it was natural that in the latter part of his life he should turn to the traditions of the Prophet. The science of tradition must certainly have formed part of his early studies, as of those of all Muslim theologians, but he had not specialized in it; his bent had lain in quite other directions. His master, the Imam al-Haramayn, had been no student of tradition; among his many works is not one dealing with that subject. Now he saw that the truth and the knowledge of the truth lay there, and he gave himself, with all the energy of his nature, to the new pursuit.

The end of his wanderings came at Tus, in 505. There he died while seeking truth in the traditions of Muhammad, as al-Ash'ari, his predecessor, had done. The stamp of his personality is ineffaceably impressed on Islam. The people of his time reverenced him as a saint and wonder-worker. He himself never claimed to work karamat and always spoke modestly of the light which he had reached in ecstasy. After his death legends early began to gather round him, and the current biographies of him are untrustworthy to a degree. It says much for the solidity of his work that he did not pass into a misty figure of popular superstition. But that work remained and remains among his disciples and in his books. We must now attempt to estimate its bearing and scope.

For him, as for the mutakallims in general, the fundamental thing in the world and the starting-point of all speculation is will. The philosophers in their intellectualism might picture God as thought--thought thinking itself and evolving all things thereby. Their source was Plotinus; that of the Muslims was the terrific "Be!" of creation. But how can we know this will of God if we are simply part of what it has produced? In answering this, al-Ghazzali and his followers have diverged from the rest of Islam, but not into heresy. Their view is admitted to be a possible interpretation of Qur'anic passages, if not that commonly held. The soul of man, al-Ghazzali taught, is essentially different from the rest of the created things. We read in the Qur'an (xv, 29; xxxviii, 72) that God breathed into man of

[123]

His spirit (ruh). This is compared with the rays of the sun reaching a thing on the earth and warming it. In virtue of this, the soul of man is different from everything else in the world. It is a spiritual substance (jawhar ruhani), has no corporeality, and is not subject to dimension, position or locality. It is not in the body or outside of the body; to apply such categories to it is as absurd as to speak of the knowledge or ignorance of a stone. Though created, it is not shaped; it belongs to the spiritual world and not to this world of sensible things. It contains some spark of the divine and it is restless till it rests again in that primal fire; but, again, it is recorded in tradition that the Prophet said, "God Most High created Adam in His own form (sura)." Al-Ghazzali takes that to mean that there is a likeness between the spirit of man and God in essence, quality, and actions. Further, the spirit of man rules the body as God rules the world. Man's body is a microcosm beside the macrocosm of this world, and they correspond, part by part. Is, then, God simply the anima mundi? No, because He is the creator of all by His will, the sustainer and destroyer by His will. Al-Ghazzali comes to this by a study of himself. His primary conception is, volo ergo sum. It is not thought which impresses him, but volition. From thought he can develop nothing; from will can come the whole round universe. But if God, the Creator, is a Willer, so, too, is the soul of man. They are kin, and, therefore, man can know and recognize God. "He who knows his own soul, knows his Lord," said another tradition.

This view of the nature of the soul is essential to the Sufi position and is probably borrowed from it. But there are in it two possibilities of heresy, if the view be pushed any further. It tends (1) to destroy the important Muslim dogma of God's Difference (mukhalafa) from all created things, and (2) to maintain that the souls of men are partakers of the divine nature and will return to it at death. Al-Ghazzali labored to safeguard both dangers, but they were there and showed themselves in time. Just as the Aristotelian + neo-Platonic philosophers reached the position that the universe with all its spheres was God, so, later, Sufis came to the other pantheistic position that God was the world. Before the atomic scholastics the same danger also lay. It is part of the irony of the history of Muslim theology that the very emphasis on the transcendental unity should lead thus to pantheism. Al-Ghazzali's endeavor was to strike the via media. The Hegelian Trinity might have appealed to him.

To return, his views on science, as we have already seen, were the same as those of the contemporary students of natural philosophy. Their teachings he accepted, and, so far, he can be compared to a theologian of the present day, who accepts evolution and explains it to suit himself. His world was framed on what is commonly called the Ptolemaic system. He was no fiat-earth man like the present Ulama of Islam; God had "spread out the earth like a carpet," but that did not hinder him from regarding it as a globe. Around it revolve the spheres of the seven planets and that of the fixed stars; Alphonso the Wise had not yet added the crystalline sphere and the primum mobile. All that astronomers and mathematicians teach us of the laws under which these bodies move is to be accepted. Their theory of eclipses and of other phenomena of the heavens is true, whatever the ignorant and superstitious may clamor. Yet it is to be remembered that the most important facts and laws have been divinely revealed. As the weightiest truths of medicine are to be traced back to the teaching of the prophets, so there are conjunctions in the heavens which occur only once in a thousand years and which man can yet calculate because God has taught him their laws. And all this structure of the heavens and the earth is the direct work of God, produced out of nothing by His will, guided by His will, ever dependent for existence on His will, and one day to pass away at His command. So al-Ghazzali joins science and revelation. Behind the order of nature lies the personal, omnipotent God who says; "Be!" and it is. The things of existence do not proceed from Him by any emanation or evolution, but are produced directly by Him.

Further, there is another side of al-Ghazzali's attitude toward the physical universe that deserves attention, but which is very difficult to grasp or express. Perhaps it may be stated thus: Existence has three modes; there is existence in the alam al-mulk, in the alam al-jabarut, and in the alam al-malakut. The first is this world of ours which is apparent to the senses; it exists by the power (qudra) of God, one part proceeding from another in constant change. The alam al-malakut exists by God's eternal decree, without development, remaining in one state without addition or diminution. The alam al-jabarut comes between these two; it seems externally to belong to the first, but in respect of the power of God which is from all eternity (al-qudra al-azaliya) it is included in the second. The soul (nafs) belongs to the alam al-malakut, is taken from it and returns to it. In sleep and in ecstasy, even in this world, it can come into contact with the world from which it is derived. This is what happens in dreams--"sleep is the brother of death," says al-Ghazzali; and thus, too, the saints and the prophets attain divine knowledge. Some angels belong to the world of malakut; some to that of jabarut, apparently those who have shown themselves here as messengers of God. The things in the heavens, the preserved tablet, the pen, the balance, etc., belong to the world of malakut. On the one hand, these are not sensible, corporeal things, and, on the other, these terms for them are not metaphors. Thus al-Ghazzali avoids the difficulty of Muslim eschatology with its bizarre concreteness. He rejects the right to allegorize--these things are real, actual; but he relegates them to this world of malakut. Again, the Qur'an, Islam, and Friday (the day of public worship) are personalities in the world of malakut and jabarut. So, too, the world of mulk must appear as a personality at the bar of these other worlds at the last day. It will come as an ugly old woman, but Friday as a beautiful young bride. This personal Qur'an belongs to the world of jabarut, but Islam to that of malakut.

But just as those three worlds are not thought of as separate in time, so they are not separate in space. They are not like the seven heavens and seven earths of Muslim literalists, which stand, story-fashion, one above the other. Rather they are, as expressed above, modes of existence, and might be compared to the speculations on another life in space of n dimensions, framed, from a very different starting-point and on a basis of pure physics, by Balfour Stewart and Tait in their "Unseen Universe." On another side they stand in close kinship to the Platonic world of ideas, whether through neo-Platonism or more immediately. Sufism at its best, and when stripped of the trap-pings of Muslim tradition and Qur'anic exegesis, has no reason to shrink from the investigation either of the physicist or of the metaphysician. And so it is not strange to find that all Muslim thinkers have been tinged with mysticism to a greater or less degree, though they may not all have embraced formal Sufiism and accepted its vocabulary and system. This is true of al-Farabi, who was avowedly a Sufi; true also of Ibn Sina, who, though nominally an Aristotelian, was essentially a neo-Platonist, and admitted the possibility of intercourse with superior beings and with the Active Intellect, of miracles and revelations; true even of Ibn Rushd, who does not venture to deny the immediate knowledge of the Sufi saints, but only argues that experience of it is not sufficiently general to be made a basis for theological science.

In ethics, as we have already seen, the position of al-Ghazzali is a simple one. All our laws and theories upon the subject, the analysis of the qualities of the mind, good and bad, the tracing of hidden defects to their causes--all these things we owe to the saints of God to whom God Himself has revealed them. Of these there have been many at all times and in all countries, and without them and their labors and the light which God has vouchsafed to them, we could never know ourselves. Here, as everywhere, comes out al-Ghazzali's fundamental position that the ultimate source of all knowledge is revelation from God. It may be major revelation, through accredited prophets who come forward as teachers, divinely sent and supported by miracles and by the evident truth of their message appealing to the human heart, or it may be minor revelation--subsidiary and explanatory--through the vast body of saints of different grades, to whom God has granted immediate knowledge of Himself. Where the saints leave off, the prophets begin; and, apart from such teaching, man, even in physical science, would be groping in the dark.

This position becomes still more prominent in his philosophical system. His agnostic attitude toward the results of pure thought has been already sketched. It

[126]

is essentially the same as that taken up by Mansell in his Bampton lectures on "The Limits of Religious Thought." Mansell, a pupil and continuator of Hamilton, developed and emphasized Hamilton's doctrine of the relativity of knowledge, and applied it to theology, maintaining that we cannot know or think of the absolute and infinite, but only of the relative and finite. Hence, he went on to argue, we can have no positive knowledge of the attributes of God. This, though disguised by the methods and language of scholastic philosophy, is al-Ghazzali's attitude in the Tahafut. Mansell's opponents said that the was like a man sitting on the branch of a tree and sawing off his seat. Al-Ghazzali, for the support of his seat, went back to revelation, either major, in the books sent down to the prophets, or minor, in the personal revelations of God's saints. Further, it was not only in the Muslim schools that this attitude toward philosophy prevailed. Yehuda Halevi (d. A.D. 1145; al-Ghazzali, d. 1111) also maintains in his Kusari the insufficiency of philosophy in the highest questions of life, and bases religious truth on the incontrovertible historical facts of revelation. And Maimonides (d. A.D. 1204) in his Moreh Nebuchim takes essentially the same position.

Of his views on dogmatic theology little need be said. Among modern theologians he stands nearest to Ritschl. Like Ritschl, he rejects metaphysics and opposes the influence of any philosophical system on his theology. The basis must be religious phenomena, simply accepted and correlated. Like Ritschl, too, he was emphatically ethical in his attitude; he lays stress on the value for us of a doctrine or a piece of knowledge. Our source of religious knowledge is revelation, and beyond a certain point we must not inquire as to the how and why of that knowledge. To do so would be to enter metaphysics and the danger-zone where we lose touch with vital realities and begin to use mere words. On one point he goes beyond Ritschl, and, on another, Ritschl goes beyond him. In his devotion to the facts of the religious consciousness Ritschl did not go so far as to become a mystic, indeed rejected mysticism with a conscious indignation; al-Ghazzali did become a mystic. But, on the other hand, Ritschl refused absolutely to enter upon the nature of God or upon the divine attributes--all that was mere metaphysics and heathenism; al-Ghazzali did not so far emancipate himself, and his only advance was to keep the doctrine on a strictly Qur'anic basis. So it stands written; not, so man is compelled by the nature of things to think.

His work and influence in Islam may be summed up briefly as follows: First, he led men back from scholastic labors upon theological dogmas to living contact with, study and exegesis of, the Word and the traditions. What happened in Europe when the yoke of mediæval scholasticism was broken, what is happening with us now, happened in Islam under his leadership. He could be a scholastic with scholastics, but to state and develop theological doctrine on a Scriptural basis was emphatically his method. We should now call him a Biblical theologian.

[127]

Second, in his teaching and moral exhortations he reintroduced the element of fear. In the Munqidh and elsewhere he lays stress on the need of such a striking of terror into the minds of the people. His was no time, he held, for smooth, hopeful preaching; no time for optimism either as to this world or the next. The horrors of hell must be kept before men; he had felt them himself. We have seen how other-worldly was his own attitude, and how the fear of the Fire had been the supreme motive in his conversion; and so he treated others.

Third, it was by his influence that Sufiism attained a firm and assured position in the Church of Islam.

Fourth, he brought philosophy and philosophical theology within the range of the ordinary mind. Before his time they had been surrounded, more or less, with mystery. The language used was strange; its vocabulary and terms of art had to be specially learned. No mere reader of the Arabic of the street or the mosque or the school could understand at once a philosophical tractate. Greek ideas and expressions, passing through a Syriac version into Arabic, had strained to the uttermost the resources of even that most flexible tongue. A long training had been thought necessary before the elaborate and formal method of argumentation could be followed. All this al-Ghazzali changed, or at least tried to change. His Tahafut is not addressed to scholars only; he seeks with it a wider circle of readers, and contends that the views, the arguments, and the fallacies of the philosophers should be perfectly intelligible to the general public.

Of these four phases of al-Ghazzali's work, the first and the third are undoubtedly the most important. He made his mark by leading Islam back to its fundamental and historical facts, and by giving a place in its system to the emotional religious life. But it will have been noticed that in none of the four phases was he a pioneer. He was not a scholar who struck out a new path, but a man of intense personality who entered on a path already blazed and made it the common highway. We have here his character. Other men may have been keener logicians, more learned theologians, more gifted saints; but he, through his personal experiences, had attained so overpowering a sense of the divine realities that the force of his character--once combative and restless, now narrowed and intense--swept all before it, and the Church of Islam entered on a new era of its existence.

So much space it has been necessary to give to this great man. Islam has never outgrown him, has never fully understood him. In the renaissance of Islam which is now rising to view his time will come and the new life will proceed from a renewed study of his works.

From this time on, the Ash'arites may be fairly regarded as the dominant school so far as the East is concerned. Saladin (d. 589) did much to aid in the establishment of this hegemony. He was a devout Muslim with the taste of an amateur for theological literature. Anecdotes tell how he had a special little catechism composed, and used himself to instruct his children in it. He founded theological academies in Egypt at Alexandria and Cairo, the first there except the Fatimid Hall of Science. One of the few blots on his name is the execution of the pantheistic Sufi, Shihab ad-Din as-Suhrawardi, at Aleppo in 587. Meanwhile, in the farther East, Fakhr ad-Din ar-Razi (d. 606) was writing his great commentary on the Qur'an, the Mafatih al-Ghayb, "The Keys of the Unseen," and carrying on the work of al-Ghazzali. The title of his commentary itself shows the dash of mysticism in his teaching, and he was in correspondence with Ibn Arabi, the arch-Sufi of the time. He studied philosophy, too, commented on works of Ibn Sina, and fought the philosophers on their own ground as al-Ghazzali had done. Kalam and philosophy are now, in the eyes of the theologians, a true philosophy and a false. Philosophy has taken the place of Mu'tazilism and the other heresies. The enemies of the faith are outside its pale, and the scholasticizing of philosophy goes on steadily. According to some, a new stage was marked by al-Baydawi (d. 685), who confused inextricably philosophy and kalam, but the newness can have been comparative only. A century later al-Iji (d. 756) writes a book, al-Mawagif, on kalam, half of which is

given to metaphysics and the other half to dogmatics. At-Taftazani is another name worthy of mention. He died in 791, after a laborious life as a controversialist and commentator. When we reach Ibn Khaldun (d. 808), the first philosophical historian and the greatest until the nineteenth century of our era, we find that kalam has fallen again from its high estate. It has become a scholastic discipline, useful only to repel the attacks of heretics and unbelievers; and of heretics, says Ibn Khaldun, there are now none left. Reason, he goes on, cannot grasp the nature of God; cannot weigh His unity nor measure His qualities. God is unknowable and we must accept what we are told about Him by His prophets. Such was the result of the destruction of philosophy in Islam.

CHAPTER V

Islam in the West; Ibn Tumart and the Muwahhids; philosophy in the West under Muwahhid protection; Ibn Bajja; Ibn Tufayl; Ibn Rushd; Ibn Arabi; Ibn Sa'bin.

WE have now anticipated one of the strangest and most characteristic figures and movements in the history of Islam. The preceding account, except as relates to Ibn Khaldun, has told of the triumphs of the Ash'arites in the East only. In the West the movement was slower, and to it we must now turn. The Maghrib--the

Occident, as the Arabs called all North Africa beyond Egypt--had been slow from the first to take on the Muslim impress. The invading army had fought its way painfully through, but the Berber tribes remained only half subdued and one-tenth Islamized. Egypt was conquered in A.H. 20, and Samarqand had been reached in 56; but it was not till 74 that the Muslims were at Carthage. And even then and for long after there arose insurrection after insurrection, and the national spirit of the Berbers remained unbroken. Broadly, but correctly, Islam in North Africa for more than three centuries was a failure. The tribal constitutions of the Berbers were unaffected by the conception of the Khalifate and their primitive religious aspirations by the Faith of Muhammad. Not till the possibility came to them to construct Muslim states out of their own tribes did their opposition begin to weaken. And then it was rather political Islam that had weakened. When the Fatimids conquered Egypt in 356 and moved the seat of their empire from al-Mahdiya to the newly founded Cairo, Islam assumed a new meaning for North Africa. The Fatimid empire there quickly melted away, and in its place arose several independent states, Berber in blood though claiming Arab descent and bearing Arab names. Islam no longer meant foreign oppression, and it began at last to make its way. Again, in the preceding period of insurrection the Berber leaders had frequently appeared in the guise and with the claim of prophets, men miraculously gifted and with a message from God. These wild tribesmen, with all their fanaticism for their own tribal liberties, have always been peculiarly accessible to the genius which claims its mission from heaven. So they had taken up the Fatimid cause and worshipped Ubayd Allah the Mahdi. And so they continued thereafter, and still continue to be swayed by saints, darwishes, and prophets of all degrees of insanity and cunning. The latest case in point is that of the Shaykh as-Sanusi, with whom we have already dealt. As time went on, there came a change in these prophet-led risings and saint-founded states. They gradually slipped over from being frankly anti-Muhammadan, if also close imitations of Muhammad's life and methods, to being equally frankly Muslim. The theology of Islam easily afforded them the necessary point of connection. All that the prophet of the day need do was to claim the position of the Mahdi, that Guided One, who according to the traditions of Muhammad was to come before the last day, when the earth shall be filled with violence, and to fill it again with righteousness. It was easy for each new Mahdi to select from the vast and contradictory mass of traditions in Muslim eschatology those which best fitted his person and his time. To the story and the doctrine of one of these we now come.

At the beginning of the sixth century a certain Berber student of theology, Ibn Tumart by name, travelled in the East in search of knowledge. An early and persistent western tradition asserts that he was a favorite pupil of al-Ghazzali's, and was marked out by him as showing the signs of a future founder of empire.

This may be taken for what it is worth. What is certain is that Ibn Tumart went back to the Maghrib and there brought about the triumph of a doctrine which was derived, if modified, from that of the Ash'arites. Previously all kalam had been under a cloud in the West. Theological studies had been closely limited to fiqh, or canon law, and that of the narrowed school of Malik ibn Anas. Even the Qur'an and the collections of traditions had come to be neglected in favor of systematized law-books. The revolt of Ibn Hazm against this had apparently accomplished little. It had been too one-sided and negative, and had lacked the weight of personality behind it. Ibn Hazm had assailed the views of others with a wealth of vituperative language. But he had been a controversialist only. There is a story, tolerably well authenticated, that the books of al-Ghazzali were solemnly condemned by the Qadis of Cordova, and burnt in public. Yet, against that is to be set that all the Spanish theologians did not approve of this violence.

Ibn Tumart started in life as a reformer of the corruptions of his day, and seems to have slipped from that into the belief that he had been appointed by God as the great reformer for all time. As happens with reformers, from exhortation it came to force; from preaching at the abuses of the government to rebellion against the government. That government, the Murabit, went down before Ibn Tumart and his successors, and the pontifical rule of the Muwahhids, the asserters of God's tawhid or unity, rose in its place. The doctrine which he preached bears evident marks of the influence of al-Ghazzali and of Ibn Hazm. Tawhid, for him, meant a complete spiritualizing of the conception of God. Opposed to tawhid, he set tajsim, the assigning to God of a jism or body having bulk. Thus, when the theologians of the West took the anthropomorphic passages of the Qur'an literally, he applied to them the method of ta'wil, or interpretation, which he had learned in the East, and explained away these stumbling-blocks. Ibn Hazm, it will be remembered, resorted to grammatical and lexicographical devices to attain the same end, and had regarded ta'wil with abhorrence. To Ibn Tumart, then, this tajsim was flat unbelief and, as Mahdi, it was his duty to oppose it by force of arms, to lead a jihad against its maintainers. Further, with Ibn Hazm, he agreed in rejecting taqlid. There was only one truth, and it was man's duty to find it for himself by going to the original sources.

This is the genuine Zahirite doctrine which utterly rejects all comity with the four other legal rites; but Ibn Tumart, as Mahdi, added another element. It is based on a very simple Imamite philosophy of history. There has always been an Imam in the world, a divinely appointed leader, guarded by isma, protection against error. The first four Khalifas were of such divine appointment; thereafter came usurpers and oppressors. Theirs was the reign of wickedness and lies in the earth. Now he, the Mahdi, was come of the blood of the Prophet and bearing plainly all the necessary, accrediting signs to overcome these tyrants and anti-Christs. He thus

[131]

was an Imamite, but stood quite apart from the welter of conflicting Shi'ite sects the Seveners, Twelvers, Zaydites and the rest--as far as do the present Sharifs of Morocco with their Alid-Sunnite position. The Mahdi, it is to be remembered, is awaited by Sunnites as by Shi'ites, and is guarded against error as much as an Imam, since he partakes of the general isma which in divine things belongs to prophets. Such a leader, then, could claim from the people absolute obedience and credence. His word must be for them the source of truth. There was, therefore, no longer any need of analogy (qiyas) as a source, and we accordingly find that Ibn Tumart rejected it in all but legal matters and there surrounded it with restrictions. Analogical argument in things theological was forbidden.

But where he absolutely parted company from the Ash'arites was with regard to the qualities of God. In that, too, he followed the view of Ibn Hazm sketched above. We must take the Qur'anic expressions as names and not as indicating attributes to us. It is true that his creed shows signs of a philosophical width lacking in Ibn Hazm. Like the Mu'tazilites, e.g. Abu Hudhayl, he defines largely by negations. God is not this; is not affected by that. It is even phrased so as to be capable of a pantheistic explanation, and we find that Ibn Rushd wrote a commentary on it. But it may be doubted whether Ibn Tumart was himself a pantheist. All phases of Islam, as we have seen, ran toward that; and here there is only a little indiscretion in the wording. But it may easily have been that he had besides, like the Fatimids, a secret teaching or exposition of those simpler declarations which were intended for the mass of the people. Among his successors distinct traces of such a thing appear; both Aristotelian philosophers and advanced Sufis are connected with the Muwahhid movement. That, however, belongs to the sequel.

The success of Ibn Tumart, if halting at first, was eventually complete. As a simple lawyer who felt called upon to protest--as, indeed, are all good Muslims in virtue of a tradition from Muhammad--against the abuses of the time, he accomplished comparatively little. As Mahdi, he and his supporter and successor, Abd al-Mu'min, swept the country. For his movement was not merely Imamite and Muslim, but an expression as well of Berber nationalism. Here was a man, sprung from their midst, of their own stock and tongue, who, as Prophet of God, called them to arms. They obeyed his call, worshipped him and fought for him. He translated the Qur'an for them into Berber; the call to prayers was given in Berber; functionaries of the church had to know Berber; his own theological writings circulated in Berber as well as in Arabic. As Persia took Islam and moulded it to suit herself, so now did the Berber tribes. And a strange jumble they made of it. With them, the Zahirite system of canon law, rejected by all other Muslim peoples, enjoyed its one brief period of power and glory. Shi'ite legends and superstitions mingled with philosophical free thought. The book of mystery,

[132]

al-Jafr, written by Ali, and containing the history of the world to the end of time, was said to have passed from the custody of al-Ghazzali at his death to the hands of the Mahdi and was by him committed to his successors. If only in view of the syncretism practised by both, it was fitting that al-Ghazzali and Ibn Tumart should be brought closely together. Yet it is hard to explain the persistence with which the great Ash'arite is made the teacher and guide of the semi-Zahirite. There must have been something, now obscure to us, in their respective systems which suggested to contemporaries such intimate connection.

The rule of the Muwahhids lasted until 667, nearly one hundred years, and involved in its circle of influence many weighty personalities. With some of these we will now deal shortly.

It has been told above how narrow in general were the intellectual interests of the West. Canon law, poetry, history, geography were eagerly pursued, but little of original value was produced. Originality and the breaking of ground in new fields were under a ban. Subtilty of thought and luxury of life took their place. Above all, and naturally, this applied to philosophy. And so it comes that the first philosophic name in the Muslim West is that of Abu Bakr ibn Bajja, for mediæval Europe Avenpace, who died comparatively young in 533. For him, as for all, and still more in the West than in the East, the problem of the philosopher was how to gain and maintain a tenable position in a world composed mostly of the philosophically ignorant and the religiously fanatical. This problem had two sides, internal and external. The inner and the nobler one was how such a mind could in its loneliness rise to its highest level and purify itself to the point of knowing things as they really are and so reach that eternal life in which the individual spirit loses itself in the Active Intellect (νοῦς ποιητικός, al-aql al-fa''al) which is above all and behind all. The other, and baser, was how to so present his views and adapt his life that the life and the views might be possible in a Muslim community.

Ibn Bajja was a close disciple of al-Farabi, who is to be regarded as the spiritual father of the later Arabic philosophy; Ibn Sina practically falls out. In logic, physics, and metaphysics he followed al-Farabi closely. But we can see how the times have moved and the philosophies with them. The essential differences have appeared and Ibn Bajja can no longer, with a good conscience, appear as a pious Muslim. The Sufi strain also is much weaker. The greatest joy and the closest truth are to be found in thought, and not in the sensuous ecstasies of the mystic. The intellect is the highest element in man's being, but is only immortal as it joins itself to the one Active Intellect, which is all that is left of God. Here we have the beginning of the doctrine which, later, under the name of Averroism and pampsychism ran like wild fire through the schools of Europe. Further, only by

[133]

the constant exercise of its own functions can the intellect of man be thus raised. He must live rationally at all points; be able to give a reason for every action. This may compel him to live in solitude; the world is so irrational and will not suffer reason. Or some of the disciples of reason may draw together and form a community where they may live the calm life of nature and of the pursuit of knowledge and self-development. So they will be at one with nature and the eternal, and far removed from the frenzied life of the multitude with its lower aims and conceptions. It is easy to see how the iron of a fight against overwhelming odds had entered this soul. Only the friendship of some of the Murabit princes saved him; but he died in the end, says a story, by poison.

With the next names we find ourselves at a Muwahhid court, and there the atmosphere has changed. It is evident that, whatever might be the temper of the people, the chiefs of the Muwahhids viewed philosophy with no disfavor. Their problem, as in the case of the Fatimids, seems rather to have been how much the people might be taught with safety. Their solution of the problem--here we proceed on conjecture, but the basis is tolerably sound--was that the bulk of the people should be taught nothing but the literal sense of the Qur'an, metaphors, anthropomorphisms and all; that the educated lay public, which had already some inkling of the facts, should be assured that there was really no difference between philosophy and theology that they were two phases of one truth; and that the philosophers should have a free hand to go on their own way, always provided that their speculations did not spread beyond their own circle and agitate the minds of the commonalty. It was a beautiful scheme, but like all systems of obscurantism it did not work. On the one hand, the people refused to be blindfolded, and, on the other, philosophy died out of inanition.

In accordance with this, we find the Muwahhid chiefs installing the Zahirite fiqh as the official system and sternly stopping all speculative discussing either of canon law or of theology. "The Word so stands written; take it or the sword," is the significant utterance which has come to us from Abu Ya'qub (reg. 558-580), son of Abd al-Mu'min. The same continued under his son Abu Yusuf al-Mansur (reg. 580-595), who added a not very carefully concealed contempt for the Mahdiship of Ibn Tumart. All such things were ridiculous in his philosophic eyes.

Under these men and in adjustment with their system lived and worked Ibn Tufayl and Ibn Rushd, the last of the great Aristotelians. Ibn Tufayl was wazir and physician to Abu Ya'qub and died a year after him, in 531. His was a calm, contemplative life, secluded in princely libraries. But his objects were the same as those of Ibn Bajja. He has evidently no hope that the great body of the people can ever be brought to the truth. A religion, sensuous and sensual alike, is needed to restrain the wild beast in man, and the masses should be left to the guidance of that religion. For a philosopher to seek to teach them better is to expose himself to peril and them to the loss of that little which they have. But in his methods, on the other hand, Ibn Tufayl is essentially at one with al-Ghazzali. He is a mystic who seeks in Sufi exercises, in the constant purifying of mind and body and in the unwearying search for the one unity in the individual multiplicity around him, to find a way to lose his self in that eternal and one spirit which for him is the divine. So at last he comes to ecstasy and reaches those things which eye hath not seen nor ear heard. The only difference between him and al-Ghazzali is that al-Ghazzali was a theologian and saw in his ecstasy Allah upon His throne and around Him the things of the heavens, as set forth in the Qur'an, while Ibn Tufayl was a philosopher, of nee-Platonic+ Aristotelian stamp, and saw in his ecstasy the Active Intellect and Its chain of causes reaching down to man and back to Itself.

The book by which his name has lived, and which has had strange haps, is the romance of Hayy ibn Yaqzan, "The Living One, Son of the Waking One." In it he conceives two islands, the one inhabited and the other not. On the inhabited island we have conventional people living conventional lives, and restrained by a conventional religion of rewards and punishments. Two men there, Salaman and Asal, have raised themselves to a higher level of self-rule.Salaman adapts himself externally to the popular religion and rules the people; Asal, seeking to perfect himself still further in solitude, goes to the other island. But there he finds a man, Hayy ibn Yaqzan, who has lived alone from infancy and has gradually, by the innate and uncorrupted powers of the mind, developed himself to the highest philosophic level and reached the Vision of the Divine. He has passed through all the stages of knowledge until the universe lies clear before him, and now he finds that his philosophy thus reached, without prophet or revelation, and the purified religion of Asal are one and the same. The story told by Asal of the people of the other island sitting in darkness stirs his soul and he goes forth to them as a missionary. But he soon learns that the method of Muhammad was the true one for the great masses, and that only by sensuous allegory and concrete things could they be reached and held. He retires to his island again to live the solitary life.

The bearing of this on the system of the Muwahhids cannot be mistaken. If it is a criticism of the finality of historical revelation, it is also a defence of the attitude of the Muwahhids toward both people and philosophers. By the favor of Abu Ya'qub, Ibn Tufayl had practically been able to live on an island and develop himself by study. So, too, Abu Ya'qub might stand for the enlightened but practical Salaman. Yet the meaning evidently is that between them they failed and must fail. There could only be a solitary philosopher here and there, and happy for him if he found a princely patron. The people which knew not the truth were accursed. Perhaps, rather, they were children and had to be humored and guided as such in an endless childhood.

[135]

It is evident that such a solitary possessor of truth had two courses open to him. He could either busy himself in his studies and exercises, as had done Ibn Bajja and Ibn Tufayl, or he could boldly enter public life and trust to his dialectic ingenuity and resource--perhaps, also, to his plasticity of conscience--to carry him past all whispers of heresy and unbelief. The latter course was chosen by Ibn Rusted. He was born at Cordova, in 520, of a family of jurists and there studied law. From his legal studies only a book on the law of inheritance has reached us, and it, though frequently commented on, has never been printed. In 548 he was presented to Abu Ya'qub by Ibn Tufayl and encouraged by him in the study of philosophy. In it his greatest work was done. In spite of the shreds and patches of neo-Platonism which clung to him, he was the greatest mediaeval commentator on Aristotle. It is only part of the eternal puzzle of the Muslim mind that the utility of Greek for a student of Aristotle seems never to have struck him. Thereafter he acted as judge in different places in Spain and was court physician for a short time in 578 to Abu Ya'qub. In 575 he had written his tractates, to which we shall come immediately, mediating between philosophy and theology. Toward the end of his life he was condemned by Abu Yusuf al-Mansur for heresy and banished from Cordova. This was in all likelihood a truckling on the part of al-Mansur to the religious prejudices of the people of Spain, who were probably of stiffer orthodoxy than the Berbers. He was in Spain, at Cordova, at the time, and was engaged in carrying on a religious war with the Christians. On his return to Morocco the decree of exile was recalled and Ibn Rushd restored to favor. We find him again at the court in Morocco, and he died there in 595.

This is not the place to enter upon Ibn Rushd's philosophical system. He was a thorough-going Aristotelian, as he knew Aristotle. That was probably much better than any of his predecessors; but even he had not got clear from the fatal influence of Plotinus. Above all, he is essentially a theologian just as much as they. In Aristotle there had been given what was to all intents a philosophical revelation. Only in the knowledge and acceptance of it could truth and life be found. And some must reach it; one at least there must always be. If a thing is not seen by someone it has existed in vain; which is impossible. If someone at least does not know the truth, it also has existed in vain, which is still more impossible. That is Ibn Rushd's way of saying that the esse is the percipi and that there must be a perceiver. And he has unlimited faith in his means of reaching that Truth-- only by such capitalization can we express his theologic attitude. The logic of Aristotle is infallible and can break through to the supreme good itself. Ecstasy and contemplation play no part with him; there he separates from Ibn Tufayl. Such intercourse with the Active Intellect may exist; but it is too rare to be taken into account. Obviously, Ibn Rushd himself, who to himself was the percipient of truth for his age, had never reached that perception. Solitary meditation he cannot away with; for him the market-place and contact with men; there he parts with Ibn Bajja. In truth, he is nearer to the life in life of Ibn Sina, and that, perhaps, explains his constant attacks on the Persian bon vivant.

All his predecessors he joys in correcting, but his especial bête noire is al-Ghazzali. With him it is war on life or death. He has two good causes. One is al-Ghazzali's "Destruction of the Philosophers;" of it, Ibn Rushd, in his turn, writes a "Destruction." This is a clever, incisive criticism, luminous with logical exactitude, yet missing al-Ghazzali's vital earnestness and incapable of reaching his originality. But al-Ghazzali had not only attacked the philosophers; he had also spread the knowledge of their teachings and reasonings, and had said that there was nothing esoteric and impossible of grasp in them for the ordinary mind. He had thus assailed the fundamental principles of the Muwahhid system. Against this, Ibn Rushd wrote the tractates spoken of above. They were evidently addressed to the educated laity; not to the ignorant multitude, but to those who had already read such books as those of al-Ghazzali and been affected by them, yet had not studied philosophy at first hand. That they were not intended for such special students is evident from the elaborate care that is taken in them to conceal, or, if that were not possible, to put a good face upon obnoxious doctrines. Thus, his philosophy left no place in reality for a system of rewards and punishments or even for any individual existence of the soul after death, for a creation of the material world, or for a providence in the direct working of the supreme being on earth. But all these points are involved or glossed over in these tractates.

Further, it is plain that their object was to bring about a reform of religion in itself, and also of the attitude of theologians to students of philosophy. In them he sums up his own position under four heads: First, that philosophy agrees with religion and that religion recommends philosophy. Here, he is fighting for his life. Religion is true, a revelation from God; and philosophy is true, the results reached by the human mind; these two truths cannot contradict each other. Again, men are frequently exhorted in the Qur'an to reflect, to consider, to speculate about things; that means the use of the intelligence, which follows certain laws, long ago traced and worked out by the ancients. We must, therefore, study their works and proceed further on the same course ourselves, i.e., we must study philosophy.

Second, there are two things in religion, literal meaning and interpretation. If we find anything in the Qur'an which seems externally to contradict the results of philosophy, we may be quite sure that there is something under the surface. We must look for some possible interpretation of the passage, some inner meaning; and we shall certainly find it.

[137]

Third, the literal meaning is the duty of the multitude, and interpretation the duty of scholars. Those who are not capable of philosophical reasoning must hold the literal truth of the different statements in the Qur'an. The imagery must be believed by them exactly as it stands, except where it is absolutely evident that we have only an image. On the other hand, philosophers must be given the liberty of interpreting as they choose. If they find it necessary, from some philosophical necessity, to adopt an allegorical interpretation of any passage or to find in it a metaphor, that liberty must be open to them. There must be no laying down of dogmas by the church as to what may be interpreted and what may not. In Ibn Rushd's opinion, the orthodox theologians sometimes interpreted when they should have kept by the letter, and sometimes took literally passages in which they should have found imagery. He did not accuse them of heresy for this, and they should grant him the same liberty.

Fourth, those who know are not to be allowed to communicate interpretations to the multitude. So Ali said, "Speak to the people of that which they understand; would ye that they give the lie to God and His messenger?" Ibn Rushd considered that belief was reached by three different classes of people in three different ways. The many believe because of rhetorical syllogisms (khitabiya), i.e., those whose premises consist of the statements of a religious teacher (maqbulat), or are presumptions (maznunat). Others believe because of controversial syllogisms (jadliya), which are based on principles (mashhurat) or admissions (musallamat). All these premises belong to the class of propositions which are not absolutely certain. The third class, and by far the smaller, consists of the people of demonstration (burhan).

Their belief is based upon syllogisms composed of propositions which are certain. These consist of axioms (awwaliyat) and five other classes of certainties. Each of these three classes of people has to be treated in the way that suits its mental character. It is wrong to put demonstration or controversy before those who can understand only rhetorical reasoning. It destroys their faith and gives them nothing to take its place. The case is similar with those who can only reach controversial reasoning but cannot attain unto demonstration. Thus Ibn Rushd would have the faith of the multitude carefully screened from all contact with the teachings of philosophers. Such books should not be allowed to go into general circulation, and if necessary, the civil authorities should step in to prevent it. If these principles were accepted and followed, a return might be looked for of the golden age of Islam, when there was no theological controversy and men believed sincerely and earnestly.

On this last paragraph it is worth noticing that its threefold distinction is "conveyed" by Ibn Rushd from a little book belonging to al-Ghazzali's later life,

[138]

after he had turned to the study of tradition, Iljam al-Awamm an ilm al-kalam, "The reining in of the commonalty from the science of kalam."

Such was, practically, the end of the Muslim Aristotelians. Some flickers of philosophic study doubt-less remained. So we find a certain Abu-l-Hajjaj ibn Tumlus (d. 620) writing on Aristotle's "Analytics," and the tractates of Ibn Rushd described above were copied at Almeria in 724. But the fate of all Muslim speculation fell, and this school went out in Sufiism. It was not Ibn Rushd that triumphed but Ibn Tufayl, and that side of Ibn Tufayl which was akin to al-Ghazzali. From this point on, the thinkers and Writers of Islam become mystics more and more overwhelmingly. Dogmatic theology itself falls behind, and of philosophical disciplines only formal logic and a metaphysics of the straitest scholastic type are left. Philosophy becomes the handmaid of theology, and a very mechanical handmaid at that. It is only in the schools of the Sufis that we find real development and promise of life. The future lay with them, however dubious it may seem to us that a future in such charge must be.

The greatest Sufi in the Arabic-speaking world was undoubtedly Muhyi ad-Din ibn Arabi. He was born in Murcia in 560, studied hadith, and fiqh at Seville, and in 598 set out to travel in the East. He wandered through the Hijaz, Mesopotamia and Asia Minor, and died at Damascus in 638, leaving behind him an enormous mass of writings, at least 150 of which have come down to us. Why he left Spain is unknown; it is plain that he was under the influence of the Muwahhid movement. He was a Zahirite in law; rejected analogy, opinion, and taqlid, but admitted agreement. His attachment to the opinions of Ibn Hazm especially was very strong. He edited some of that scholar's works, and was only prevented by his objections to taqlid from being a formal Hazmite. But with all that literalness in fiqh, his mysticism in theology was of the most rampant and luxurious description. Between the two sides, it is true, there existed a connection of a kind. He had no need for analogy or opinion or for any of the workings of the vain human intelligence so long as the divine light was flooding his soul and he saw the things of the heavens with plain vision. So his cooks are a strange jumble of theosophy and metaphysical paradoxes, all much like the theosophy of our own day. He evidently took the system of the mutakallims and played with it by means of formal logic and a lively imagination. To what extent he was sincere in his claim of heavenly illuminings and mysterious powers it would be hard to say. The oriental mystic has little difficulty in deceiving himself. His opinions--so far as we can know them--may be briefly sketched as follows: The being of all things is God: there is nothing except Him. All things are an essential unity; every part of the would is the whole world. So man is a unity in essence but a multiplicity in individuals. His anthropology was an advance upon that of al-Ghazzali toward a more unflinching pantheism. He has the same view that the soul of man is a

[139]

spiritual substance different from everything else and proceeding from God. But he obliterates the difference of God and makes souls practically emanations. At death these return into God who sent them forth. All religions to Ibn Arabi were practically indifferent; in them all the divine was working and was worshipped. Yet Islam is the more advantageous and Sufiism is its true philosophy. Further, man has no free-will; he is con-strained by the will of God, which is really all that exists. Nor is there any real difference between good and evil; the essential unity of all things makes such a division impossible.

The last of the Muwahhid circle with whom we need deal--and, perhaps, absolutely the last--is Abd al-Haqq ibn Sa'bin. He was as much a mystic as Ibn Arabi, but was apparently more deeply read in philosophy and did not cast his conceptions in so theological and Qur'anic a mould. He, too, was born. in Murcia about 613, and must very early have founded a school of his own, gathered disciples round him and established a wide reputation. High skill in alchemy, astrology, and magic is ascribed to him, which probably means that he claimed to be a wali, a friend of God, gifted with miraculous powers. He is accused of posing as a prophet, although in orthodox Islam Muhammad is the last and the seal of the prophets But against this, it may be said that he had no need of the actual title, "prophet"; many mystics held--heretically, it is true--that the wali stood higher than the prophet, nabi or rasul. He had evidently besides this a more solid reputation in philosophy, as is shown by his correspondence with Frederick II, the great Hohenstaufen (d. 1250 A.D.). The story is told on the Muslim side only, but has vraisemblance and seems to be tolerably authentic. According to it, Frederick addressed certain questions in philosophy--on the eternity of the world, the nature of the soul, the number and nature of the categories, etc.--to different Muslim princes, begging that they would submit them to their learned men. So the questions came to ar-Rashid, the Muwahhid (reg. 630-640), addressed to Ibn Sa'bin as a scholar whose reputation had reached even the Sicilian court. Ar-Rashid passed them on; Ibn Sa'bin accepted the commission with a smile--this is the Muslim account--and triumphantly and contemptuously expounded the difficulties of the Christian monarch and student. In his replies he certainly displays a very complete and exact knowledge of the Aristotelian and neo-Platonic systems, and is far less a blind follower of Aristotle than is Ibn Rushd. But his schoolmasterly tone is most unpleasant, and we discover in the end that all this is a mere preliminary discipline, leading in itself to agnosticism and a recognition that there is nothing but vanity in this world, and that only in the Vision of the Sufi can certainty and peace be found. So we have again the circle through which al-Ghazzali went. As distinguished from Ibn Rushd, the prophet, with Ibn Sa'bin, takes higher rank than the sage. Beyond the current division of the soul into the vegetative, the animal and the reasonable, he adds two others, derived from the reasonable, the soul of wisdom and the soul of prophecy. The first of these is the soul of the philosopher, and the other of the prophet; and the last is the highest. Of the reasonable soul upward, he predicates immortality.

His position otherwise must have been practically the same as that of Ibn Arabi. Like him he was a Zahirite in law and a mystic in theology. "God is the reality of existing things," he taught, and it is evident that he belonged to the school of pantheism in which God is all, and separate things are emanations from him. In life we have flashes of recognition of the heavenly realities, but only at death-- which is our true birth--do we reach union with the eternal, or, to speak technically, with the Active Intellect.

Apparently it was quite possible for him to hold these views in public so long as the Muwahhids were strong enough to protect him. But their empire was rapidly falling to pieces and the time of freedom had passed. An attack on him at Tunis, where the Hafsids now ruled, drove him to the East about 643, and there he took refuge at--of all places--Mecca. The refuge seems to have been secure. He lived there more than twenty years amid a circle of disciples, among whom was the Sharif himself, and died about 667. There is a poorly authenticated story that he died by suicide. The man himself, with so many of his time and kind, must remain a puzzle to us. For all his haughty pride of learning, it is noted of him that his first disciples were from among the poor. His contemporaries described him as "a Sufi after the manner of the philosophers." The last vestige of the Muwahhid empire passed away in the year of his death.

CHAPTER VI

The rise and spread of darwish Fraternities; the survival and tradition of the Hanbalite doctrine; Abd ar-Razzaq; Ibn Taymiya, his attacks on saint-worship and on the mutakallims; ash-Sha'rani and his times; the modern movements; Wahhabism and the influence of al-Ghazzali; possibilities of the present.

OUR sources now begin to grow more and more scanty, and we must hasten over long intervals of time and pass with little connection from one name to another. Preliminary investigations are also to a great extent lacking, and it is possible that the centuries which we shall merely touch may have witnessed developments only less important than those with which we have already dealt. But that is not probable; for when, after a long silence, the curtain rises again for us in the twelfth Muslim century, we shall find at work only those elements and conditions whose inception and growth we have now set forth.

One name in our rapid flight deserves mention, at least. It is that of Umar ibn al-Farid, the greatest poet that Arabic mysticism has produced. He was born at Cairo in 586, lived for a time at Mecca, and died at Cairo in 632. He led no new movement or advance, but the East still cherishes his memory and his poems.

We have already noticed (p. 177) the beginnings of darwish Fraternities and the founding of monasteries or khanqahs. During the period over which we have just passed, these received a great and enduring impetus. The older ascetics and walis gathered round them groups of personal followers and their pupils carried on their names. But it was long, apparently, before definite corporations were founded of fixed purpose to perpetuate the memory of their masters. One of the earliest of these seems to have been the fraternity of Qadirite darwishes, founded by Abd al-Qadir al-Jilani, who died in 561 at Baghdad, where pilgrimage is still made to his shrine. So, too, the Rifa'ite Fraternity was founded at Baghdad by Ahmad ar-Rifa'a in 576. Another was that of the Shadhilites, named after their founder, ash-Shadhili, who died in 656. Again another is that of the Badawites, whose founder was Ahmad al-Badawi (d. 675); his shrine at Tanta in Lower Egypt is still one of the most popular places of pilgrimage. Again, the order of the Naqshbandite darwishes was founded by Muhammad an-Naqshbandi, who died in 791. Among the Turks by far the most popular religious order is that of the Mawlawites, founded by the great Persian mystical poet, Jalal ad-Din ar-Rumi (d. 672), whose Mesnevi is read over all Islam. These and very many others, especially of later date, are still in existence. Others, once founded, have again become extinct. Thus, Ibn Sa'bin, though he was surrounded by disciples who for a time after his death carried on the order of Sab'inites, does not seem now to have any to do him honor. The same holds of a certain Adi al-Haqqari who founded a cloister near Mawsil and died about 558. It is significant that al-Ghazzali, though he founded a cloister for Sufis at Tus and taught and governed there himself, left no order behind him. Apparently in his time the movement toward continuous corporations had not yet begun. It is true that there are at present in existence darwish Fraternities which claim to be descended from the celebrated ascetics and walis, Ibrahim ibn Adham (d. 161), Sari as-Saqati (d. 257) and Abu Yazid al-Bistami (d. 261), but it may be gravely doubted whether they can show any sound pedigree. The legend of Shaykh Ilwan, who is said to have founded the first order in 49, may be safely rejected. It is significant that the Awlad Ilwan, sons of Ilwan, as his followers are called, form a sect of the Rifa'ites. Further, just as the Sufis have claimed for themselves all the early pious Muslims, and especially the ten to whom Muhammad made specific promise of Paradise (al-ashara al-mubashshara), so these Fraternities are ascribed in their origin to, and put under the guardianship of the first Khalifas, and, in Egypt at least, a direct descendant of Abu Bakr holds authority over all their orders.

In these orders all are darwishes, but only those gifted by God with miraculous powers are walis. Those of them who are begging friars are faqirs. They stand under an elaborate hierarchy grading in dignity and holiness from the Qutb, or Axis, who wanders, often invisible and always unknown to the world, through the lands performing the duties of his office, and who has a favorite station on the roof of the Ka'ba, through his naqibs or assistants, down to the lowest faqir. But the members of these orders are not exclusively faqirs. All classes are enrolled as, in a sense, lay adherents. Certain trades affect certain fraternities; in Egypt, for example, the fishermen are almost all Qadirites and walk in procession on their festival day, carrying colored nets as their banners. Much the same thing held, and holds, of the monastic orders of Europe, but the Muslim does not wait till he is dying to put on the weeds of Ahmad al-Badawi or ash-Shadhili. Finally, reference may be made again to the last and most important of all these orders, the militant Brotherhood of as-Sanusi.

We have now returned to the period of al-Iji and at-Taftazani, when philosophy definitely descended from the throne and became the servant and defender of theology. From this time on, the two independent forces at work are the unveiling of the mystic (kashf) and tradition (naql). The only place for reason (aql) now is to prove the possibility of a given doctrine. That done, its actual truth is proven by tradition. These two then, kashf and naql, hold the field, and the history of Muslim theology from this point to the present day is the history of their conflicts. The mystics are accused of heresy by the traditionalists. The traditionalists are accused by the mystics of formalism, hypocrisy, and, above all, of flat inability to argue logically. Both accusations are certainly true. No fine fence on personality can conceal the fact that Muslim mysticism is simple pantheism of the Plotinian type, the individuals are emanations from the One. On the other hand, the formalism of the traditionalists can hardly be exaggerated. They pass over almost entirely into canon lawyers, meriting richly the fine sarcasm of al-Ghazzali, who asked the faqihs of his day what possible value for the next world could lie in a study of the Qur'anic law of inheritance or the like. Tradition (hadith), in the exact sense of the sayings and doings of Muhammad, falls into the background, and fiqh, the systems built upon it by the generations of lawyers, from the four masters down, takes its place. Again, the accusation of illogical reasoning is also thoroughly sound. The habit of unending subdivision deprived the minds of the canonists of all breadth of scope, and their devotion to the principle of acceptance on authority (taqlid) weakened their feeling for argument. It is true, further, that the mystics, such as they were, had heired all the philosophy left in Islam, and were thus become the representatives of the intellectual life. They had so much of an advantage over their more orthodox opponents. But the intellectual life with them, as with the earlier philosophers, remained of a too subjective character. The

[143]

fatal study of the self, and the self only--that tramping along the high a priori road--and neglect of the objective study of the outside world which ruined their forerunners, was their ruin as well. Outbursts of intellectual energy and revolt we may meet with again and again; there will be few signs of that science which seeks facts patiently in the laboratory, the observatory, and the dissecting-room.

Curiously enough, there fall closely together at this time the death dates of two men of the most opposite schools. The one was Ibn Taymiya, the anthropomorphist free lance, who died in 728, and the other was Abd ar-Razzaq, the pantheistic Sufi, who died in 730. Abd ar-Razzaq of Samarqand and Kashan was a close student and follower of Ibn Arabi. He commented on his books and defended his orthodoxy. In fact, so closely had Ibn Arabi come to be identified with the Sufi position as a whole that a defence of him was a favorite form in which to cast a defence of Sufiism generally. But Abd ar-Razzaq did not follow his master absolutely. On the freedom of the will especially he left him. For Ibn Arabi, the doctrine of the oneness of all things had involved fatalism. Whatever happens is determined by the nature of things, that is, by the nature of God. So the individuals are bound by the whole. Abd ar-Razzaq turned this round. His pantheism was of the same type as that of Ibn Arabi; God, for him, was all. But there is freedom of the divine nature, he went on. It must therefore exist in man also, for he is an emanation from the divine. His every act, it is true, is predetermined, in time, in form, and in place. But his act is brought about by certain causes, themselves predetermined. These are what we would call natural laws in things, natural abilities, aptitudes, etc., in the agent; finally, free choice itself. And that free choice is in man because he is of and from God. Further, it is evident that Abd ar-Razzaq's anxiety is to preserve a basis for morals. Among the predetermining causes he reckons the divine commands, warnings, proofs in the Qur'an. The guidance of religion finds thus its place and the prophets their work. But what of the existence of evil and the necessity of restraint in a world that has emanated from the divine? This problem he faces bravely. Our world must be the best of all possible worlds; otherwise God would have made it better. Difference, then, among men and things belongs to its essence and necessity. Next, justice must consist in accepting these different things and adapting them to their situations. To try to make all things and men alike would be to leave some out of existence altogether. That would be a great injustice. Here, again, religion enters. Its object is to rectify this difference in qualities and gifts. Men are not responsible for these, but they are responsible if they do not labor to correct them. In the hereafter all will be reabsorbed into the divine being and taste such bliss as the rank of each deserves. For those who need it there will be a period of purgatorial chastisement, but that will not be eternal, in sha Allah.

[144]

Like his predecessors, Abd ar-Razzaq divides men into classes according to their insight into divine things. The first is of men of the world, who are ruled by the flesh (nafs) and who live careless of all religion. The second is of men of reason (aql). They through the reason contemplate God, but see only His external attributes. The third is of men of the spirit (ruh) who, in ecstasy, see God face to face in His very essence, which is the substrate of all creation.

In his cosmogony, Abd ar-Razzaq follows, of course, the neo-Platonic model and shows great ingenuity in weaving into it the crude and materialistic phrases and ideas of the Qur'an. Like all Muslim thinkers he displays an anxiety to square with his philosophy the terms dear to the multitude.

To Ibn Taymiya all this was the very abomination of desolation itself. He had no use for mystics, philosophers, Ash'arite theologians, or, in fact, for anyone except himself. A contemporary described him as a man most able and learned in many sciences, but with a screw loose. However it may have been about the last point, there can be no question that he was the reviver for his time and the transmitter to our time of the genuine Hanbalite tradition, and that his work rendered possible the Wahhabites and the Brotherhood of as-Sanusi. He was the champion of the religion of the multitude as opposed to that of the educated few with which we have been dealing so long. This popular theology had been going steadily upon its way and producing its regular riots and disputings. It is related of a certain Ash'arite doctor, Fakhr ad-Din ibn Asakir (d. 620), that, in Damascus, he never dared to pass by a certain way through fear of Hanbalite violence. The same Fakhr ad-Din once gave, as in duty bound, the normal salutation of the Peace to a Hanbalite theologian. The Hanbalite did not return it, which was more than a breach of courtesy, and indicated that he did not regard Fakhr ad-Din as a Muslim. When people remonstrated with him, he turned it as a theological jest and replied, "That man believes in 'Speech in the Mind' (kalam nafsi, hadith fi-n-nafs), so I returned his salutation mentally." The point is a hit at the Ash'arites, who contended that thought was a kind of speech without letters or sounds, and that God's quality of Speech could therefore be without letters or sounds.

But even the simple orthodoxy of the populace had not remained unchanged. It had received a vast accretion of the most multifarious superstitions. The cult of saints, alive and dead, of holy sites, trees, garments, and the observance of all manner of days and seasons had been developing parallel to the advance of Sufiism among the educated. The walis were untiring in the recital of the karamat which God had worked for them, and the populace drank in the wonders greedily. The metaphysical and theological side they left untouched. "This is a holy man," they said, "who can work miracles; we must fear and serve him." And so they would do without much thought whether his morality might not be antinomian and his theology pantheistic. To abate this and other evils and bring back the faith of the fathers was the task which Ibn Taymiya took up.

He was born near Damascus in 661 and educated as a Hanbalite. His family had been Hanbalite for generations, and he himself taught in that school and was reckoned as the greatest Hanbalite of his time. His position, too, was practically that of Ahmad ibn Hanbal, modified by the necessities imposed by new controversaries. Thus he was an anthropomorphist, but of what exact shade is obscure. He was accused of teaching that God was above His throne, could be pointed at, and that He descended from His seat as a man might, i.e., that He was in space. But he certainly distinguished himself from the crasser materialists. He refused to be classed as the adherent of any school or of any system save that of Muhammad and the agreement of the fathers. He claimed for himself the rights of a mujtahid and went back to first sources and principles in everything. His self-confidence was extreme, and he smote down with proud words the Rightly Guided Khalifas, Umar and Ali, themselves. His bases were Qur'an, tradition from the Prophet and from the Companions and analogy. Agreement, in the broad sense of the agreement of the Muslim people, he rejected. If he had accepted it he would have been forced to accept innumerable superstitions, beliefs, and practices--especially the whole doctrine of the walis and their wonders--for their basis was agreement. The agreement of the Companions he did accept, while convicting them right and left of error as individuals.

His life was filled up with persecutions and misfortune. He was a popular idol, and inquiries for his judgment on theological and canonical questions kept pouring in upon him. If there was no inquiry, and he felt that a situation called for an expression of opinion from him, he did not hesitate to send it out with all formality. It is true that it is the duty of every Muslim, so far as he can, to do away or at least to denounce any illegality or unorthodox view or practice which he may observe. This duty evidently weighed heavily on Ibn Taymiya, and there was fear at one time at the Mamluk court lest he might go the way of Ibn Tumart. In one of these utterances he defined the doctrine of God's qualities as Ibn Hazm had done, and joined thereto denunciations of the Ash'arite kalam and of the Qur'anic exegesis of the mutakallims as a whole. They were nothing but the heirs and scholars of philosophers, idolaters, Magians, etc.; and yet they dared to go beyond the Prophet and his heirs and Companions. The consequence of this fatwa or legal opinion was that he was silenced for a time as a teacher. On another occasion he gave out a fatwa on divorce, pronouncing tahlil illegal. Tahlil is a device by which an awkward section in the canon law is evaded. If a man divorces his wife three times, or pronounces a threefold divorce formula, he cannot remarry her until she has been married to another man, has cohabited with him and been divorced by him. Muslim ideas of sexual purity are essentially different from ours, and the

[146]

custom has grown up, when a man has thus divorced his wife in hasty anger, of employing another to marry her on pledge of divorcing her again next day. Sometimes the man so employed refuses to carry out his contract; such refusal is a frequent motif in oriental tales. To avoid this, the husband not infrequently employs one of his slaves and then presents him to his former wife the next day. A slave can legally marry a free woman, but when he becomes her property the marriage is ipso facto annulled, because a slave cannot be the husband of his mistress or a slave woman the wife of her master. It is to Ibn Taymiya's credit that he was one of the few to lift up their voices against this abomination. His independence is shown at its best.

But it was with the Sufis that he had his worst conflicts, and at their hands he suffered most. In many points his career is parallel to that of Ahmad ibn Hanbal, the Sufi movement taking the place that was played by Mu'tazilism in the life of the earlier saint. One great difference, it may be remarked, was that al-Ma'mun urged the persecution of Ibn Hanbal, while an-Nasir, the great Mamluk Sultan (reg. 693, 698-708, 709-741), supported Ibn Taymiya as far as he possibly could. The beginning of the Sufi controversy was characteristic. Ibn Taymiya heard that a certain an-Nasr al-Manbiji (d. 719?), a reputed follower of Ibn Arabi and of Ibn Sa'bin, had reached a position of influence in Cairo. That was enough to make Ibn Taymiya address an epistle to him, intended to turn him from his heresies. It is needless to give in detail the position and content of the epistle. He wrote as a strong monotheist of the old-fashioned type and exposed and assailed unmercifully the doctrine of Unity (ittihad) of the mystics. Al-Manbiji retorted with countercharges of heresy, and; as he had behind him all the Sufis of Egypt-- as great an army as the Christian monks and ascetics or earlier Egypt and much like to them Ibn Taymiya had to pay for his eagerness for a fight with long and painful imprisonment at Cairo, Alexandria and Damascus. Here it is evident that he had lost touch. with the drift of popular, and especially Egyptian, feeling.

But his fearlessness was like that of Ibn Hanbal himself, and in 726 he gave out a fatwa which ran still straighter in the teeth of the beliefs of the people and which sent him to a prison which he never left alive. It had long been a custom in Islam to make pious pilgrimage to the graves of saints and prophets and there to do reverence to their memory and to ask their aid. It was part of that cult of saints which had so overspread and overcome the earlier simplicity of Islam. The most outstanding case in point was, and is, the pilgrimage to the tomb of Muhammad at al-Madina, which has come to be a more or less essential part of the Hajj to the Ka'ba itself. Against all this Ibn Taymiya lifted a voice of emphatic protest. These shrines were in great part false, and when they were genuine the visitation of them was an idolatrous imitation of heathen practices. Equally idolatrous was all invoking of saints or prophets, including Muhammad himself; to God alone

[147]

should prayer be directed. The clamor raised by this fatwa was tremendous. This was no doctrine of the schools which he had touched, but a bit of concrete religiosity which appealed to everyone. His public life practically ended, and the practices which he had denounced abide to this day. It is a bitter satire on his position that when he died in 726 the populace paid to his relics all these signs of superstitious reverence against which he had protested. He became a saint, malgré lui. His work had been to keep alive the Hanbalite doctrine and pass it on unchanged to modern times. He did not destroy philosophy: it was dead of itself before he came. Nor Sufiism: it is still very much alive. Nor kalam: it still continues in the form to which it had crystallized by his time. But he and his disciples made possible the Wahhabites and the monotheistic revival of our day. The faith of Muhammad himself was not to perish entirely from the earth.

It would now be possible to pass at once to the Wahhabite movement in the latter part of the twelfth century of the Hijra. All the elements for the explanation of it and of the modern situation are in our hands. But there is one figure which stands out so clearly in an otherwise most obscure picture and is so significant for the time, that some account must be taken of it. It is that of ash-Sha'rani, theologian, canonist, and mystic. He was a Cairene and died in 973. The rule of Egypt had passed half a century before to the Ottoman Turks, and they governed by means of a Turkish Pasha. The condition of the people, as we find it sketched by ash-Sha'rani, was a most unhappy one. They were bent down, and especially the peasantry, under a load of taxation. The Turks found it advisable, too, to cultivate the friendship of the canon lawyers and professional theologians in order to maintain their hold upon the people. These canonists, in consequence, were rapidly becoming an official class with official privileges. Further, the process, the beginnings of which we have already seen, by which religious science was narrowed to fiqh, had gone still further. Practically, the two classes of theologians left were the canonists and the mystics. And the mystics had fallen far from their pride of power under the Mamluks. They now were of the poor of the laud, a kind of Essenes over against the Pharisees of the schools.

Such, at least, is the picture of his time which ash-Sha'rani gives. How far it is exact must remain uncertain. For, of the many puzzling personalities in Islam, ash-Sha'rani is perhaps for us the most unintelligible. He combined the most abject superstitions of a superstitious ago and country with lofty ethical indignation; social humility of the most extreme with an intellectual pride and arrogance rarely paralleled, a keen and original grasp of the canon law of the four schools with an utter submission of the intellect to the inbreathings of the divine from without; a power of discreet silence as to the inconvenient with an open-mouthed vehemence in other things. He was a devoted follower of Ibn Arabi and defended his memory against the accusation of heresy. Yet his position is

[148]

singularly different from that of Ibn Arabi, and a doubt cannot but rise as to either his knowledge, his intelligence, or his honesty. Practically where he differs from the ordinary Muslim is in his extension of the doctrine of saints. As to the Most Beautiful Names (al-asma al-husna), he follows Ibn Hazm. So, too, as to God's qualities, he follows the older school and would prefer to leave them unconsidered. But he is, otherwise and in general, a sound Ash'arite, e.g., on the doctrine of predestination, and of man's part in his works (iktisab). There is in him no sign of the Plotinian pantheism of Ibn Arabi. The doctrine of God's difference (mukhalafa) he taught, and that He created the world by His will and not by any emanation of energy.

But truth for him is not to be reached by speculation and argument: its only basis is through the unveiling of the inner eye which brings us to the immediate Vision of the Divine. Those who have reached that Vision, guide and teach those who cannot or have not. Upon that Vision all systems are built, and reason can only serve the visionary as a defence against the gainsayer or against his own too wild thoughts. Naturally, with such a starting-point as this the supernatural side of things (al-ghayb) receives strong emphasis. The Jinn and the angels are most intense realities. Ash-Sha'rani met them in familiar converse. He met, too, al-Khadir, the undying pilgrim saint who wanders through the lands, succoring and guiding. The details of these interviews are given with the greatest exactness. A Jinni in the form of a dog ran into his house on such a day by such a door, with a piece of European paper in his mouth--this is a touch of genius--on which certain theological questions were written. The Jinni wished ash-Sha'rani's opinion as to them. Such was the origin of one of his books, and another sprang from a similarly exactly described talk with al-Khadir. Yet he was content also with smaller mercies and reckons as a karama that he was enabled to read through a certain book for some time at the rate of two and a half times daily. To all this it would be possible of course to say flatly that he lied. But such a judgment applied to an oriental is somewhat crude, and the knot of the mystic's mind in any land is not to be so easily cut. Further, the doctrine of the walis is developed by him at length. They possess a certain illumination (ilham), which is, however, different from the inspiration (wahy) of the prophets. So, too, they never reach the grade of the prophets, or a nearness to God where the requirements of a revealed law fall away from them, i.e., they must always walk according to the law of a prophet. They are all guided by God, whatever their particular Rule (tariqa) may be, but the Rule of al-Junayd (p. 176) is the best because it is in most essential agreement with the Law (shari'a) of Islam. Their karamat are true and are a consequence of their devout labors, for these are in agreement with the Qur'an and the Sunna. The order of nature will not be broken for anyone who has not achieved more than is usual in religious knowledge and exercises. All walis stand under a regular hierarchy headed by the Qutb; yet above him in holiness stand the Companions of the Prophet. This marks a very moderate position. Many Sufis had contended that the walis stood higher than even the prophets, not to speak of their Companions.

It will be seen that his position is essentially a mediating one. He wishes to show that the beliefs of the mystics and of the mutakallims are really one although they are reached by different paths. In fiqh he made a similar attempt. The Sufis had always looked down on those theologians who were canonists pure and simple. A study of canon law was a necessity, they thought; but as a propædeutic only. The canonists who went no further never reached religion at all. Especially they held that no Sufi should join himself to any of the four contending schools. Their controversies were upon insignificant details which had nothing to do with the life in God. But could it not be shown that their differences were not actual--one view being true and the other false--but were capable of being reduced to a unity? This was the problem that ash-Sha'rani attacked. These differing opinions, he held, are adapted to different classes of men. Some men of greater gifts and endurance can follow the hardest of these opinions, while the easier are to be recognized as concessions (rukhsa) from God to the weakness of others. Each man may follow freely the view which appeals to him; God has appointed it for him.

Ash-Sha'rani was one of the last original thinkers in Islam; for a thinker he was despite his dealings with the Jinn and al-Khadir. Egypt keeps his memory. A mosque in Cairo bears his name, as does also a division of the Badawite darwishes. In modern times his books have been frequently reprinted, and his influence is one of the ferments in the new Islam.

We must now pass over about two hundred years and come to the latter part of the twelfth century of the Hijra, a period nearly coinciding with the end of the eighteenth of our era. There these two movements come again to light. Wahhabism, the historical origin of which we have already seen (p. 60), is a branch of the school of Ibn Taymiya. Manuscripts of the works of Ibn Taymiya copied by the hand of Ibn Abd al-Wabhab exist in Europe. So the Wahhabites refused to accept as binding the decisions of the four orthodox sects of canon law. Agreement as a source they also reject. The whole People of Muhammad can err and has erred. Only the agreement of the Companions has binding force for them. It is, therefore, the duty and right of every man to draw his own doctrine from the Qur'an and the traditions; the systems of the schools should have no weight with him. Again, they take the authropomorphisms of the Qur'an in their literal sense. God has a hand, God settles Himself on His throne; so it must be held "without inquiring how and without comparison." They profess to be the only true Muslims, applying to themselves the term Muwahhids and calling all others Mushriks, assignees of companions to God. Again, like Ibn Taymiya, they reject

[150]

the intercession of walis with God. It is allowable to ask of God for the sake of a saint but not to pray to the saint. This applies also to Muhammad. Pilgrimage to the tombs of saints, the presenting of offerings there, all acts of reverence, they also forbid. No regard should be paid even to the tomb of the Prophet at al-Madina. All such ceremonies are idolatrous. Whenever possible the Wahhabites destroy and level the shrines of saints.

Over other details, such as the prohibition of the use of tobacco, we need not spend time. Wahhabism as a political force is gone. It has, however, left the Sanusi revolt as its direct descendant and what may be the outcome of that Brotherhood we have no means of guessing. It has also left a general revival and reformation throughout the Church of Islam, much parallel, as has been remarked, to the counter-reformation which followed the Protestant Reformation in Europe.

The second movement is the revival of the influence of al-Ghazzali. That influence never became absolutely extinct and it seems to have remained especially strong in al-Yaman. In that corner of the Muslim world generations of Sufis lived comparatively undisturbed, and it was the Sayyid Murtada, a native of Zabid in Tihama, who by his great commentary on the Ihya of al-Ghazzali practically founded the modern study of that book. There have been two edition of this commentary in ten quarto volumes and many of the Ihya itself and of other works by al-Ghazzali. Whether his readers understand him fully or not, there can be no question of the wide influence which he is now exercising. At Mecca, for example, the orthodox theological teaching is practically Ghazzalian and the controversy throughout all Arabia is whether Ibn Taymiya and al-Ghazzali can be called Shaykhs of Islam. The Wahhabites hold that anyone who thus honors al-Ghazzali is an unbeliever, and the Meccans retort the same of the followers of Ibn Taymiya.

These two tendencies then--that back to the simple monotheism of Muhammad and that to an agnostic mysticism--are the hopeful signs in modern Islam. There are many other drifts in which there is no such hope. Simple materialism under European, mostly French, influence is one. A seeking of salvation in the study of canon law is another. Canon law is still the field to which an enormous proportion of Muslim theologians turn. Again, there are various forms of frankly pantheistic mysticism. That is especially the case among Persians and Turks. For the body of the people, religion is still overburdened, as in Ibn Taymiya's days, with a mass of superstition. Lives of walis containing the wildest and most blasphemous stories abound and are eagerly read. The books of ash-Sha'rani are especially rich in such hagiology. It is difficult for us to realize that stories like the most extravagant in the Thousand and One Nights are the simplest possibilities to the masses of Islam. The canon lawyers, still, in their discussions, take account of the existence of

[151]

Jinn, and no theologian would dare to doubt that Solomon sealed them up in brass bottles. Of philosophy, in the free and large sense, there is no trace. Ibn Rushd's reply to al-Ghazzali's "Destruction of the Philosophers" has been printed, but only as a pendant to that work. In it, too, Ibn Rushd carefully covers his great heresies. His tractates on the study of kalam, spoken of above, have also been reprinted at Cairo from the European edition. But these tractates are arranged to give no clew to his real philosophy. The Arabic Aristotelianism has perished utterly from the Muslim lands. Of the modern Indian Mu'tazilism no account need be taken here. It is derived from Europe and is ordinary Christian Unitarianism, connecting with Muhammad instead of with Jesus.

From the above sketch some necessary conditions are clear, which must be fulfilled if there is to be a chance for a future development in Islam. Education must be widely extended. The proportion of trained minds must be greatly increased and the barrier between them and the commonalty removed. The economy of teaching has failed; it has destroyed the doctrine which it sought to protect. Again, the slavery of the disciple to the master must cease. It must always be possible for the student, in defiance of taqlid, to go back to first principles or to the primary facts and to disregard what the great Imams and Mujtahids have taught. So much of health there was in the Zahirite system.

Third, these primary facts must include the facts of natural science. The student, emancipated from the control of the schools, must turn from the study of himself to an examination of the great world. And that examination must not be cosmological but biological; it must not lose itself in the infinities but find itself in concrete realities. It must experiment and test rather than build lofty hypotheses.

But can the oriental mind thus deny itself? The English educational experiment in Egypt may go far to answer that question.

APPENDICES

I. ILLUSTRATIVE DOCUMENTS TRANSLATED FROM THE ARABIC.

II. SELECTED BIBLIOGRAPHY.

III. CHRONOLOGICAL TABLE.

APPENDIX I

1. ASH-SHAHRASTANI ON THE CLASSIFICATION OF MUSLIM SECTS.

2. TWO TRADITIONS FROM MUHAMMAD ON THE ESSENTIALS OF ISLAM.

3. A SHORT CREED BY AL-ASH'ARI.

4. A SHORT CREED BY AL-GHAZZALI.

5. A SHORT CREED BY AN-NASAFI (MATARIDITE).

6. A SCHOLASTIC EXPOSITION OF THE FUNDAMENTALS OF THEOLOGY.

7. ANALYSIS OF A TREATISE IN CANON LAW.

Notes have been added where such appeared called for, but the index, facilitating reference to the body of the book, renders a full commentary unnecessary. The student should use the index as a vocabulary of technical terms, referring for their explanation to the passages where they occur.

I

ASH-SHAHRASTANI ON THE CLASSIFICATION OF MUSLIM SECTS

Then I applied myself to what of arrangement was easy of attainment and to what of attainment was easy of arrangement, until I had crowded them [the different opinions] into four fundamentals, which are the great principles. The first fundamental concerns the Qualities (sifat) with the Unity (tawhid); it embraces the question of the eternal (azali) Qualities, affirmed by some and denied by others, and of the exposition of the essential Qualities (sifat adh-dhat) and of the active Qualities (sifat al-fi'l) and of what is necessary in God Most High and what is possible for Him and what is impossible; it involves the controversies between the Ash'arites and the Karramites and the Anthropomorphists (mujassims) and the Mu'tazilites. The second fundamental concerns decree (qadar) and justice (adl); it embraces the question of destiny (qada) and decree (qadar); of force (jabr) and acquisition (kasb); of the willing of good and of evil and of the decreed and the known, affirmed by some and denied by others; it involves the controversies between the Qadarites and Najjarites and Jabarites and Ash'arites and Karramites. The third fundamental concerns promise (wa'd) and the decisions (hukms); it embraces the question of faith (iman) and repentance (tawba) and threatening (wa'id) and postponing (irja) and pronouncing anyone an unbeliever (takfir) and leading anyone astray (tadlil), affirmed by some and denied by others; it involves the controversies between the Murji'ites and the Wa'idites and the Mu'tazilites

[153]

and the Ash'arites and the Karramites. The fourth fundamental concerns tradition (sam) and reason (aql) and the prophetic mission (risala) and the imamate; it embraces the questions of the determination of actions as good (tahsin) or vile (taqbih); of the advantageous (salah) and most advantageous (aslah); of benignity (lutf); of the prophets being guarded against sin (isma); of the condition of the imamate, by statute (nass) according to some and by agreement (ijma) according to others, and how it is transferred on the view of those who say it is by statute, and how it is fixed on the view of those who say it is by agreement; it involves the controversies between the Shi'ites and the Kharijites and the Mu'tazilites and the Karramites and the Ash'arites.--Translated from Cureton's Arabic text, p. 4.

II

THE PROPHET IN A TRADITION

"Islam is built upon five things; testimony that there is no god but God and that Muhammad is the Apostle of God. Prayer (salat), the Poor-rate (zakat), Pilgrimage (hajj) and Fast (sawm) in Ramadan."

A TRADITION OF THE PROPHET

Jibril came in the form of an Arab of the desert and sat down so that his knees touched the knees of the Prophet and said, "O Apostle of God, what is Islam?" He said, "That thou should bear witness that there is no god save God and that I am the Apostle of God; that thou shouldest perform the prayers (salat) and bring the poor-rate (zakat) and fast in the month of Ramadan and pilgrimage to the House if the way is possible for thee." He said, "Thou hast spoken truly." Then he said, "What is Faith (iman)?" The Prophet said, "That thou should believe in God and His angels and His cooks and His messengers and in the Last Day, and that thou should believe in the decreeing (qadar) both of good and of evil." He said, "Thou hast spoken truly." Then he said, "What is right doing (ihsan)?" The Prophet said, "That thou should serve God as though thou sawest Him; for though thou seest Him not, He sees thee." He said, "Thou hast spoken truly." Then he said, "When shall be the Last Day (as-sa'a)?" The Prophet said, "The questioned knoweth not more of that than the questioner." Then he arose and went out. And the Prophet said, "That was Jibril; he came to you to teach you your religion (din)."-- Translated from Cureton's text of ash-Shahrastani, p. 27.

III

A SHORT CREED BY AL-ASH'ARI

Our doctrine which we teach and our religion (diyana) which we follow consists in clinging fast to the Book of God and the Usage (sunna) of His Prophet and to that which is handed down from the Companions, their immediate followers (tabi's) and from the leaders (imams) in tradition--with that we take refuge; and we teach that which Ahmad ibn Hanbal--may God illumine his face, exalt his rank and make great his reward--followed; and we shun that which is opposed to his doctrine. For he is the excellent leader, the perfect chief, through whom God made plain the truth, when error was made manifest, and showed the path and smote down the innovations of the innovators, the deviations of the deviators and the doubts of the doubters. So, the mercy of God be upon him for an appointed leader and an instructed chief, and upon all the leaders of the Muslims.

The sum of our doctrine is this, that we believe in God, His Angels, His Books, His Apostles, in all that has come from God, and what trustworthy men (thiqat) have reported from the Apostles of God; we oppose nothing thereof. That God is One God, Single, One, Eternal; beside Him no God exists; He has taken to Himself no wife (sahiba), nor child (walad); and that Muhammad is His Servant (abd) and His Apostle. That Paradise and Hell are Verity and that the Hour (as-sa'a) will come without doubt, and God will arouse those that are in the graves. That God has settled Himself (istawa) upon His throne, as He has said, (Qur. 20, 4); "the Rahman has settled Himself upon His throne." That God has a countenance, as He has said, (Qur. 55, 27); "and the countenance of thy Lord will abide, full of majesty and glory;" and two hands, as He has said, (Qur. 5, 69); "much more! both His hands are spread out," and (Qur. 38, 75); "that which I have created with both My hands;" and two eyes, without asking how (bila kayfa), as He has said, (Qur. 54, 14'); "which swims forth under Our eyes." That whoever thinks that God's name is other than He, is in error. That God has Knowledge (ilm), as He has said, (Qur. 35, 12); "Not one woman becomes pregnant and brings forth, except by His knowledge." We maintain that God has Power (qudra), as He has said, (Qur. 41, 14); "and have they not seen that God who created them is stronger than they?" We maintain that God has Hearing (sam) and Seeing (basar) and do not deny it, as do the Mu'tazilites, Jahmites and Kharijites. We teach that God's Word (kalam) is uncreated, and that He has never created anything except by saying to it, "Be!" and it forthwith became, as He has said, (Qur, 16, 42); "Our speech to anything when We willed it was, 'Be' and it was." Nothing exists upon earth, be it good or bad, but that which, God wills; but all things are by God's Will (mashya). No one is able to do anything before God does it, neither is anyone independent of God, nor can he withdraw himself from God's Knowledge. There is no Creator but God. The works (amals) of creatures are created and predestined by God, as He said, (Qur. 37, 94); "and God has created you and what ye do." Man is able to create nothing; but they are created, as He

[155]

has said, (Qur. 35, 31); "Is there any Creator except God?" and (Qur. 16, 17) "and is He who created like him who created not?" and (Qur. 52, 35); "were they created out of nothing, or are they the creators?" and such passages are many in the Qur'an. And God maintains the believers in obedience to Him, is gracious unto them, cares for them, reforms them, and guides them aright; but the unbelievers He leads astray, guides them not aright, vouchsafes them not Faith (iman), by His Grace, as the People of error and pride maintain. For should He be gracious unto them and help them aright, then would they be pious, and should He guide them aright, then would they allow themselves to be guided aright, as He has said, (Qur. 7, 177); "whom God guideth aright, he allows himself to be guided aright, and whom He leads astray, they are he losers." God is able to help the unbelieving aright and to be gracious unto thorn, so that they shall become believing, but He wills that they shall be unbelieving as is known. For He has made them impervious to all help and sealed their hearts. Good and Evil happen according to the Destiny (qada) and Decree (qadar) of God for good and. evil, for the sweet and the bitter. We know that the misfortune that befalls us is not in order that we may go astray, and that the good fortune which befalls us is not in order that we may go aright. We have no control over that which is good or hurtful to us, except so far as God wills. We flee from our anxieties to God and commit at all times our distress and poverty to Him. We teach that the Qur'an is God's Word, and that it is uncreated, and that whosoever says that it is created is an unbeliever (kafir). We believe that God at the Day of Resurrection (yawm al-qiyama) will be visible to the eyes, as the moon is seen upon the night of the full moon; the believers will see Him, according to traditions which have come down from the Prophet. We teach that while the believers will see Him, the unbelievers will be separated from Him by a wall of division, as God has said, (Qur. 83, 15); "Surely not! They will be separated from their Lord, upon that Day." We teach that Moses besought God that he might see Him in this world; then God revealed Himself to the mountain and turned it into dust and taught Moses thereby that he could not see Him in this world (Qur. 7, 139). We are of the opinion that we may not accuse anyone of unbelief (kufr), who prays towards Mecca, on account of sin committed by him, such as unchastity, theft, wine drinking, as the Kharijites believe, who judge that these thereby become unbelievers. We teach that whoever commits a great sin (kabira), or anything like it, holding it to be allowed, is an unbeliever, since he does not believe in its prohibition. We teach that Islam is a wider idea than Faith (iman), so that not every Islam is Faith. We believe that God turns the hearts upside down, and holds them between two of His fingers, that He lays the heavens upon a finger and the earth upon a finger, according to the tradition from the Prophet. We believe that God will not leave in Hell any of those who confess His Unity (muwahhid) and hold fast to the Faith, and that there is no Hell for him whom the Prophet has by his witness appointed to Paradise. We hope for Paradise for sinners and fear on their account, that they will be punished in Hell. We teach that God will release a few out of Hell, on account of Muhammad's intercession (shafa'a) after they have been scorched there. We believe in the punishment of the grave. We believe that the Tank (hawd) and the Balance are Verities: that the Bridge as-Sirat is a Verity; that the Arousing (ba'th) after death is a Verity; that God will set up His creatures in a place (mawqif) and will hold a reckoning with the Believers. 1 We believe that Faith (iman) consists in word (qawl) and in work (amal) and that it increases and diminishes. We trust in the sound Traditions handed down from the Apostle of God, which trustworthy people (thiqat), just man from just man, up to the Apostle, have transmitted. We hold by the love of the early Believers (salaf), whom God chose to be Companions to the Prophet, and we praise them with the praise with which God praised them, and we carry on their succession. We assert that the Imam succeeding the Apostle of God was Abu Bakr; that God through him made the Religion (din) mighty, and caused him to conquer the Apostates (murtadds). The Muslims made him their Imam, just as Muhammad had made him Imam at prayers. Then followed [as legal Imam] Umar ibn al-Khattab; then Uthman ibn Affan; his murderers killed him out of wickedness and enmity; then Ali ibn Abi Talib. These are the Imams after the Apostle, and their Khalifate is that of the Prophetic office [i.e., they are, though not prophets, successors of the Prophet]. We bear witness of Paradise for the Ten (al-asharatu-l-mubashshara), to whom the Apostle bore witness of it, and we carry on the succession of the other Companions of the Prophet and hold ourselves far from that which was in dispute between them. We hold that the four Imams were in the true way, were rightly guided and excellent, so that no one equals them in excellence. We hold as true the traditions which the People of Tradition (naql) have established, concerning the descent of God to the lowest heaven (sama ad-dunya), and that the Lord will say, "Is there a supplicant? Is there a seeker for forgiveness?" and the rest of that which they have handed down and established, contrary to that which the mistaken and misled opine. We ground ourselves in our opposition on the Qur'an, the Sunna of the Prophet, the agreement of the Muslims and what is in accordance therewith, but put forth no novelty (bid'a) not sanctioned by God, and opine of God nothing that we have not been taught. We teach that God will come on the Day of Resurrection, as He has said, (Qur. 89, 23); "When the earth shall be turned to dust, and the Lord shall appear and the angels, rank on rank," and that God is near to His servants, in what way (kayfa) He wills, as He has said, (Qur. 50, 15); "and We are nearer to him than the artery in his neck;" and (Qur. 53, 8); "Then He approached and came near and was two bows' length distant or even nearer." To our Religion (din) belongs further, that we on Fridays and on festival days pray behind every person, pious and profane--so are the conditions for congregational prayers, as it is handed down from Abd Allah ibn Umar that he

[157]

prayed behind al-Hajjaj. To our Religion belongs the wiping (mash) of the inner boots (khuffs) upon a journey and at home, in contradiction to the deniers of this. 1 We uphold the prayer for peace for the Imams of the Muslims, submission to their office, and maintain the error of those who hold it right to rise against them whenever there may be apparent in them a falling away from right. We are against armed rebellion against them and civil war.

We believe in the appearance of anti-Christ (ad-Dajjal) according to the tradition handed down from the Prophet; in the punishment of the grave, and in Munkar and Nakir and in their questions to the buried in their graves. We hold the tradition of the journey to heaven (mi'raj, Qur. 17) of Muhammad as true, and declare many of the visions in sleep to be true, and we say that there is an explanation for them. We uphold the alms for the dead of the Muslims and prayer for them, and believe that God will help them therewith. We hold as true that there are enchanters in the world, and that enchantment is and exists. We hold as a religious duty the prayer which is held over the dead of those who have prayed toward Mecca, whether they have been believers or godless; we uphold also their right of testation. We acknowledge that Paradise and Hell are created, and that whoever dies or is killed, dies or is killed at his appointed time (ajal); that the articles of sustenance (rizq) from God, with which He sustains His creatures, are permitted (halal) and forbidden (haram); 2 that Satan makes evil suggestions to men, and puts them in doubt, and causes them to be possessed, contrary to that which the Mu'tazilites and the Jahmites maintain, as God said, (Qur. 2, 276); "Those who take usury will [at the Resurrection] stand there like one whom Satan causes to be possessed by madness," and (Qur. 114, 4 ff.); "I take my refuge in God, from the evil suggestion, from the stealthy one who makes suggestions in the hearts of men, by means of men and Jinn." We affirm that God may distinguish the pious by signs which He manifests through them. Our teaching concerning the little children of the polytheists (mushriqs) is this, that God will kindle a fire in the other world for them, and will say, "Run in there;"--as the tradition says. 1 We believe that God knows what men do and what they will to do, what happens and how that which does not happen, if it should happen, would happen. We believe in the obedience of the Imams and in their counsel of the Muslims. We consider right the separation from every inciter to innovation (bid'a) and the turning aside from the People of wandering desires (ahl al-ahwa).-- Translated from the Arabic text in Spitta's Zur Geschichte al-As'ari's, pp. 133 ff.

Footnotes

296:1 For Muslim eschatology reference may still he made to Sale's introduction to the Qur'an, § 4. The punishment of the grave is what, in the case of unbelievers, follows the inquisition by the two angels Munkar and Nakir; see on them Lane's Modern Egyptians, chap. xxviii; on the whole subject, see translations by Gautier and Wolff and tractate by Rüling (Bibliography, p. 367)

298:1 This, one of the dividing questions between Sunnites and Shi'ites, belongs to theology as well as law. See p. 314 and Goldziher, Zur Literaturgeschichte der Si'a, p. 87.

298:2 The Mu'tazilites held that articles of sustenance of a forbidden nature, such as pork or wine, could not be called rizq in this technical sense; that God could not so use them. The orthodox retorted p. 299 that a man might live his life out on forbidden things; had he then been independent of God as to his sustenance? The Mu'tazilites defined rizq as "a possession which its possessor eats" and as "that from which one is not hindered from profiting"; the orthodox, as a name for that which God sends to man and the other animals and they eat it and profit by it.

299:1 Some will run into the fire and find themselves immediately in Paradise; these would have been believers. Others will refuse, and will be treated as their parents.

A SHORT CREED BY AL-GHAZZALI

An exposition of the Creed of the People of the Sunna on the two Words of Witnessing (kalimatan ash-shahada) which form one of the Foundations of Islam.

[Intended to be committed to memory by children. It forms the first section of the second book of his Ihya, vol. ii, pp. 17-42 of edit. of Cairo with commentary of the Sayyid Murtadà.]

We say--and in God is our trust--Praise belongeth unto God, the Beginner, the Bringer back, the Doer of what He willeth, the Lord of the Glorious Throne and of Mighty Grasp, the Guider of His chosen creatures to the right path and to the true way, the Granter of benefits to them after the witness to the Unity (tawhid) by guarding their articles of belief from obscurities of doubt and opposition, He that bringeth them to follow His Apostle, the Chosen one (al-Mustafa), and to imitate the traces of his Companions, the most honored, through His aid and right guidance revealed to them in His essence and His works by His beautiful qualities which none perceives, save he who inclines his ear. He is the witness who maketh known to them that He in His essence is One without any partner (sharik). Single without any similar, Eternal without any opposite, Separate without any like. He is One, Prior (qadim) with nothing before Him, from eternity (azali) without any beginning, abiding in existence with none after Him, to eternity (abadi) without any end, subsisting without ending, abiding without termination. He hath not ceased and He will not cease to be described with glorious epithets; finishing and ending, through the cutting off of the ages and .the terminating of allotted times, have no rule over Him, but He is the First and Last, the External and the Internal, and He knoweth everything.

We witness that He is not a body possessing form, nor a substance possessing bounds and limits: He does not resemble bodies, either in limitation or in accepting division. He is not a substance and substances do not exist in Him; and He is not an accident and accidents do not exist in Him, nay He does not resemble an entity, and no entity resembles Him; nothing is like Him and He is not like anything; measure does not bound Him and boundaries do not contain Him; the directions do not surround Him and neither the earth nor the heavens are on different sides of Him. Lo, He is seated firmly upon His Throne (arsh), after the manner which He has said, and in the sense in which He willed a being seated firmly (istiwa), which is far removed from contact and fixity of location and being established and being enveloped and being removed. The Throne does not carry Him, but the Throne and those that carry it are carried by the grace of His power and mastered by His grasp. He is above the Throne and the Heavens and above everything unto the limit of the Pleiades, with an aboveness which does not bring Him nearer to the Throne and the Heavens, just as it does not make Him further from the earth and the Pleiades. Nay, He is exalted by degrees from the Throne and the Heavens, just as He is exalted by degrees from the earth and the Pleiades; and He, in spite of that, is near to every entity and is "nearer to a creature than the artery of his neck" (Qur. 50, 15), and He witnesseth everything, since His nearness does not resemble the nearness of bodies, just as His essence does not resemble the essence of bodies. He does not exist in anything, just as nothing exists in Him: He has exalted Himself far therefrom that a place should contain Him, just as He has sanctified Himself far therefrom that time should limit Him. Nay, He was before He had created Time and Place and He is now above that which He was above, and distinct from His creatures through His qualities. There is not in His essence His equal, nor in His equal His essence. He is far removed from change of state or of place. Events have no place in Him, and mishaps do not befall him. Nay, He does not cease, through His glorious epithets, to be far removed from changing, and through His perfect qualities to be independent of perfecting increase. The existence of His essence is known by reason; His essence is seen with the eyes, a benefit from Him and a grace to the pious, in the Abiding Abode and a completion in beatitude from Him, through gazing upon His gracious face.

We witness that He is living, powerful, commanding, conquering; inadequacy and weakness befall Him not; slumber seizes Him not, nor sleep. Passing away does not happen to Him, nor death. He is Lord of the Worlds, the Visible and the Invisible, that of Force and that of Might; He possesses Rule and Conquest and Creation and Command; the heavens are rolled in His right hand and the created things are overcome in His grasp; He is separate in creating and inventing; He is one in bringing into existence and innovating; He created the creation and their works and decreed their sustenance and their terms of life; not a decreed thing escapes His grasp and the mutations of things are not distant from His power; the things which He hath decreed cannot be reckoned and the things which He knoweth have no end.

We witness that He knoweth all the things that can be known, comprehending that which happeneth from the bounds of the earths unto the topmost heavens; no grain in the earth or the heavens is distant from His knowledge. Yea, He knows the creeping of the black ant upon the rugged rock in a dark night, and He perceives the movement of the mote in the midst of the air; He knows the secret and the concealed and has knowledge of the suggestions of the minds and the movements of the thoughts and the concealed things of the inmost parts, by a knowledge which is prior from eternity; He has not ceased to be describable by it, from the ages of the ages, not by a knowledge which renews itself and arises in His essence by arrival and removal.

We witness that He is a Willer of the things that are, a Director of the things that happen; there does not come about in the world, seen or unseen, little or much, small or great, good or evil, advantage or disadvantage,. faith or unbelief, knowledge or ignorance, success or loss, increase or diminution, obedience or rebellion, except by His will. What He wills is, and what He wills not is not. Not a glance of one who looks, or a slip of one who thinks is outside of His will: He is the Creator, the Bringer back, the Doer of that which He wills. There is no opponent of His command and no repeater of His destiny and no refuge for a creature from disobeying Him, except by His help and His mercy, and no strength to a creature to obey Him except by His will. Even though mankind and the Jinn and the Angels and the Shaytans were to unite to remove a single grain in the world or to bring it to rest without His will, they would be too weak for that. His will subsists in His essence as one of His qualities; He hath not ceased to be described through it as a Willer, in His infinity, of the existence of things at their appointed times which He hath decreed. So they come into existence at their appointed times even as He has willed in His infinity without precedence or sequence. They happen according to the agreement of His knowledge and His will, without exchange or change in planning of things, nor with arranging of

[161]

thoughts or awaiting of time, and therefore one thing does not distract Him from another.

And we witness that He is a Hearer and a Seer. He hears and sees, and no audible thing is distant from His hearing, and no visible thing is far from His seeing, however fine it may be. Distance does not curtain off His hearing and darkness does not dull His seeing; He sees without eyeball or eyelid, and hears without earholes or ears, just as He knows without a brain and seizes without a limb and creates without an instrument, since His qualities do not resemble the qualities of created things, just as His essence does not resemble the essences of created things.

And we witness that He speaks, commanding, forbidding, praising, threatening, with a speech from all eternity, prior, subsisting in His essence not resembling the speech of created things. It is not a sound which originates through the slipping out of air, or striking of bodies; nor is it a letter which is separated off by closing down a lip or moving a tongue. And the Qur'an and the Tawrat [the Law of Moses] and the Injil [the Gospel] and the Zabbur [the Psalms] are His book revealed to His Apostles. And the Qur'an is repeated by tongues, written in copies, preserved in hearts: yet it, in spite of that, is prior, subsisting in the essence of God, not subject to division and separation through being transferred to hearts and leaves. And Musa heard the speech of God without a sound and without a letter, just as the pious see the essence of God, in the other world, without a substance or an attribute.

And since He has those qualities, He is Living, Knowing, Powerful, a Willer, a Hearer, a Seer, a Speaker, through Life, Power, Knowledge, Will, Hearing, Seeing, Speech, not by a thing separated from His essence.

We witness that there is no entity besides Him, except what is originated from His action and proceeds from His justice, after the most beautiful and perfect and complete and just of ways. He is wise in His actions, just in His determinations; there is no analogy between His justice and the justice of creatures, since tyranny is conceivable in the case of a creature, when he deals with the property of some other than himself, but tyranny is not conceivable in the case of God. For He never encounters any property in another besides Himself, so that His dealing with it might he tyranny. Everything besides Him, consisting of men and Jinn and Angels and Shaytans and the heavens and the earth and animals and plants and inanimate things and substance and attribute and things perceived and things felt, is an originated thing, which He created by His power, before any other had created it, after it had not existed, and which He invented after that it had not been a thing, since He in eternity was an entity by Him-self, and there was not along

[162]

with Him any other than He. So He originated the creation thereafter, by way of manifestation of His power, and verification of that which had preceded of His Will, and of that which existed in eternity of His Word; not because He had any lack of it or need of it. And He is gracious in creating and in making for the first times and in imposing of duty--not of necessity--and He is generous in benefiting; and well-doing and gracious helping belong to Him, since He is able to bring upon His creatures different kinds of punishment and to test them with different varieties of pains and ailments. And if He did that, it would be justice on His part, and would not be a vile action or tyranny in Him. He rewardeth His believing creatures for their acts of obedience by a decision which is of generosity and of promise and not of right and of obligation, since no particular action toward anyone is incumbent upon Him, and tyranny is inconceivable in Him, and no one possesses a right against Him. And His right to acts of obedience is binding upon the creatures because He has made it binding through the tongues of His prophets, not by reason alone. But f e sent apostles and manifested their truth by plain miracles, and they brought His commands and forbiddings and promisings and threatenings. So, belief in them as to what they have brought is incumbent upon the creation.

THE SECOND WORD OF WITNESSING is witnessing that the apostolate belongs to the apostle, and that God sent the unlettered Qurayshite prophet, Muhammad, with his apostolate to the totality of Arabs and foreigners and Jinn and men. And He abrogated by his law the other laws, except so much of them as He confirmed; and made him excellent over the rest of the prophets and made him the Lord of Mankind and declared incomplete the Faith that consists in witnessing the Unity, which is saying, "There is no god except God," so long as there is not joined to that a witnessing to the Apostle, which is saying, "Muhammad is the Apostle of God." And He made obligatory upon the creation belief in him, as to all which he narrated concerning the things of this world and the next. And that He would not accept the faith of a creature, so long as he did not believe in that which the Prophet narrated concerning things after death. The first of that is the question of Munkar and Nakir; these are two awful and terrible beings who will cause the creature to sit up in his grave, complete, both soul and body; and they will ask him, "Who is thy Lord, and what is thy religion (din), and who is thy Prophet?" They are the two testers in the grave and their questioning is the first testing after death. And that he should believe in the punishment of the grave--that it is a Verity and that its judgment upon the body and the soul is just, according to what God wills. And that he should believe in the Balance--it with the two scales and the tongue, the magnitude of which is like unto the stages of the heavens and the earth. In it, deeds are weighed by the power of God Most High; and its weights in that day will be of the weight of motes and mustard seeds, to show the exactitude of its justice. The leaves of the good deeds will be placed in a beautiful form in the scale of light; and then the Balance will be weighed down by them according to the measure of their degree with God, by the grace of God. And the leaves of the deeds will be cast in a vile form into the scale of darkness, and the Balance will be light with them, through the justice of God. And that he should believe that the Bridge (as-sirat) is a Verity; it is a bridge stretched over the back of Hell (jahannam), sharper than a sword and finer than a hair. The feet of the unbelievers slip upon it, by the decree of God, and fall with them into the Fire. But the feet of believers stand firm upon it, by the grace of God, and so they pass into the Abiding Abode. And that he should believe in the Tank (hawd), to which the people shall go down, the Tank of Muhammad from which the believers shall drink before entering the Garden and after passing the Bridge. Whoever drinks of it a single draught will never thirst again thereafter. Its breadth is a journey of a month; its water is whiter than milk and sweeter than honey; around it are ewers in numbers like the stars of heaven; into it flow two canals from al-Kawthar (Qur. 108). And that he should believe in the Reckoning and in the distinctions between men in it, him with whom it will go hard in the Reckoning and him to whom compassion will be shown therein, and him who enters the Garden without any reckoning,--these are the honored (muqarrab). God Most High will ask whomsoever He will of the prophets, concerning the carrying of His message, and whomsoever He will of the unbelievers, concerning the rejection of the messengers; and He will ask the innovators (mubtadi's) concerning the Sunna; and the Muslims concerning works. And that he should believe that the attestors of God's Unity (muwahhids) will be brought forth from the Fire, after vengeance has been taken on them, so that there will not remain in Hell an attestor of God's Unity. And that he should believe in the intercession (shafa'a) of the prophets, next of the learned (ulama), next of the martyrs, next of the rest of the believers-- each according to his dignity and rank with God Most High. And he who remains of the believers, and has no intercessor, shall be brought forth of the grace of God, whose are Might and Majesty. So there shall not abide eternally in the Fire a single believer, but whoever has in his heart the weight of a single grain of faith shall be brought forth therefrom. And that he should confess the excellence of the Companions--May God be well pleased with them!--and their rank; and that the most excellent of mankind, after the Prophet, is Abu Bakr, next Umar, next Uthman, next Ali--May God be well pleased with them! And that he should think well of all the Companions and should praise them like as he praises God, whose are Might and Majesty, and His Apostles. All this is of that which has been handed down in traditions from the Prophet and in narratives from the followers. He who confesses all this, relying upon it, is of the People of the Truth and the Company of the Sunna, and hath separated himself from the band of error and the sect of innovation (bid'a). So we ask from God perfection of certainty and firm

[164]

standing in the Faith (din) for us and for all Muslims through His compassion.--lo! He is the Most Compassionate!--and may the blessing of God be upon our Lord Muhammad and upon every chosen creature.

V

ARTICLES OF BELIEF OF NAJM AD-DIN ABU HAFS AN-NASAFI

[A Mataridite who d. A.H. 537. This creed is still used as a text-book in schools. It is translated from Cureton's edition (London, 1843) with the assistance of at-Taftazani's commentary (Constantinople, A.H. 1310). The asterisks mark the points on which al-Mataridi differed from al-Ash'ari.]

In the name of God, the merciful Compassionator.

The Shaykh, the Imam, Najm ad-Din Abu Hafs Umar ibn Muhammad ibn Ahmad an-Nasafi--may God have mercy upon him!--said;--The People of Verity, contradicting the Sceptics [Sufistiqiya, i.e., Sophists] say that the real natures of things are validly established and that the science of them is certain.

Further, that the sources of knowledge for mankind are three: the sound Senses, true Narration (khabar), and Reason (aql). As for the Senses, they are five: Hearing, Sight, Smell, Taste and Touch, and by each sense you are informed concerning that for which it is appointed. True Narration, again, is of two kinds. The one is Narration handed down along a large number of lines of tradition (mutawatir); that is, it is established by the tongues of a number of people of whom we cannot imagine that they would agree in a lie. It compels a knowledge which is of necessity (daruri), such as the knowledge of departed kings in past times and of distant countries. And the second is Narration by the Apostle (rasul) aided by miracle [i.e., Muhammad], and it compels deduced knowledge (istidlali), and the knowledge established by it resembles in certainty and fixity the knowledge established by necessity.

Then as for Reason, it is a cause of knowledge also; and whatever is established by intuition (badaha) is of necessity, as the knowledge that everything is greater than its parts; and whatever is established by inference is acquired knowledge (iktisabi), as the existence of fire from the appearance of smoke. And the Inner Light (ilham) with the People of Verity is not one of the causes of knowledge as to the soundness of anything. 1

Further, the world in the totality of its parts is a thing originated (muhdath), in that it consists of Substances (ayns) and Attributes (arads). The Substances are what

[165]

exist in themselves, and a substance is either a compound, that is a body (jism), or not compounded like an essence (jawhar), namely a division that is not further divided. And the attributes are what do not exist in themselves but have a dependent existence in bodies or essences, such as colors, tastes, conditions (kawns), odors.

The Originator (Muhdith) of the world is God Most High, the One, the Eternal, the Decreeing, the Knowing, the Hearing, the Seeing, the Willing. He is not an attribute, nor a body, nor an essence, nor a thing formed, nor a thing bounded, nor a thing numbered, nor a thing divided, nor a thing compounded, nor a thing limited; and He is not described by quiddity (mahiya), nor by modality (kayfiya), and He does not exist in place or time, and there is nothing that resembles Him and nothing that is outwith His knowledge and power.

He has qualities (sifat) from all eternity (azali) existing in His essence. They are not He nor are they any other than He. They are Knowledge and Power and Life and Strength and Hearing and Seeing and Doing and Creating and Sustaining and Speech (kalam).

And He, whose Majesty is majestic, speaks with a Word (kalam). This Word is a quality from all eternity, not belonging to the genus of letters and sounds, a quality that is incompatible with coming to silence and that has no weakness.

God Most High speaks with this Word, commanding and prohibiting and narrating. And the Qur'an is the untreated Word of God, repeated by our tongues, heard by our ears, written in our copies, preserved in our hearts, yet not simply a transient state (hal) in these [i.e., the tongues, ears, etc.]. And Creating (takwin) is a quality of God Most High from all eternity, and it is the Creating of the world and of every one of its parts at the time of its becoming existent, and this quality of Creating is not the thing created, according to our opinion.* And Willing is a quality of God Most High from all eternity, existing in His essence.

And that there is a Vision (ru'ya) of God Most High is allowed by reason and certified by tradition (naql). A proof on authority has come down with the affirmation that believers have a Vision of God Most High in Paradise and that He is seen, not in a place or in a direction or by facing or the joining of glances or the placing of a distance between him who sees and God Most High.

And God Most High is the Creator of all actions of His creatures, whether of unbelief or belief, of obedience or of rebellion; all of them are by the will of God and His sentence and His conclusion and His decreeing.

[166]

And to His creatures belong actions of choice (ikhtiyar),* for which they are rewarded or punished, and the good in these is by the good pleasure of God (rida) and the vile in them is not by His good pleasure.*

And the ability to do the action (istita'a) goes along with the action and is the essence of the power (qudra) by which the action takes place, and this word "ability" means the soundness of the causes and instruments and limbs. And the validity of the imposition of the task (taklif) is based upon this ability,* and the creature has not a task imposed upon him that is not in his power.

And the pain which is found in one who is beaten as a consequence of being beaten by any man, and the state of being broken in glass as a consequence of its being broken by any man, and such things, all that is created by God Most High, and the creature has no part in its creation and a slain man is dead because his appointed time (ajal) has come; and death exists in a slain man and is created by God Most High, and the appointed time is one. 1

And that which is forbidden (haram) is still Sustenance (rizq), and each one receives his own Sustenance whether it consists of permitted or of forbidden things; and let no one imagine that a man shall not eat his Sustenance or that another than he shall eat his Sustenance.

And God leadeth astray whom He wills and guideth aright whom He wills, and it is not incumbent upon God Most High to do that which may be best (aslah) for the creature.

The punishment of the grave for unbelievers and for some rebellious ones of the believers, and the bliss of the obedient in the grave, and the questioning by Munkar and Nakir are established by proofs of authority. And the Quickening of the Dead (ba'th) is a Verity, and the Weighing is a Verity, and the Book is a Verity and the Tank (hawd) is a Verity, and the Bridge, as-Sirat, is a Verity, and the Garden is a Verity, and the Fire is a Verity, and they are both created, existing, continuing; they shall not pass away and their people shall not pass away.

A great sin (kabira) does not exclude the creature who believes from the Belief (iman) and does not make him an unbeliever. And God does not forgive him who joins another with Himself, but He forgives anything beneath that to whom He wills, of sins small (saghira) or great.

And there may be punishment for a small and pardon for a great one, if it be not of the nature of considering lawful what is forbidden, for that is unbelief (kufr).

[167]

And the intercession (shafa'a) of the Apostles and of the excellent on behalf of those who commit great sins is established.

And those believers who commit great sins do not remain eternally in the Fire although they die without repentance.

Belief (iman) is assent (tasdiq) to that which comes from God and confession (iqrar) of it. Then, as for Works (amal), they are acts of obedience and gradually increase of themselves, but Belief does not increase and does not diminish. And Belief and al-Islam are one.* And whenever assent and confession are found in a creature, it is right that he should say, "I am a believer in truth." And it is not fitting that he should say, "I am a believer if God will." *

The happy one sometimes becomes miserable and the miserable one sometimes becomes happy,* and the changing is in happiness and misery, and not in making happy and making miserable: for those are both qualities of God Most High, and there is no changing in Him nor in His qualities.

And in the sending of Apostles (rasuls) is an advantage and God has sent Apostles of flesh unto flesh with good tidings, warning and explaining to men the things of the world and of faith, of which they have need. And He has aided them with miracles (mu'jizat) which break the order of nature. The first of the Prophets (nabis) was Adam and the last is Muhammad, Upon both of them be Peace! A statement of their number has been handed down in several traditions, but the more fitting course is that there should be no limiting to a number in naming them; God Most High has said, "Of them are those concerning whom We have recited to thee, and of them are those concerning whom We have not recited to thee." And there is no security in a statement of number against there being entered among them some that are not of them, or of there being excluded from them some that are of them. They all give intelligence concerning God Most High, are veracious and sincere, and the most excellent of the Prophets is Muhammad--Upon him be Peace!

The Angels are servants of God and work according to His commands. They are not described as masculine or feminine.

And God has books which He has revealed to His Prophets, and in them are His commands and His promises.

The Night Journey (mi'raj) of the Apostle of God--Upon whom be Blessing and Peace! while awake, in the body, to Heaven, then to what place God Most High willed of the Exalted Regions, is a Verity.

[168]

The Wonders (karamat) of the Saints (walis) are a Verity. And a Wonder on the part of a Saint appears by way of a contradiction of the ordinary course of nature, such as passing over a great distance in a short time, and the appearing of meat and drink and clothing at a time of need, and walking upon the water and in the air, and the speech of stones and of beasts, and the warding off of an evil that is approaching, and the guarding of him who is anxious from enemies, and other things of the same kind. And such a thing is to be reckoned as an evidentiary miracle (mu'jiza) on behalf of the Apostle followed by the Saint on whose part the wonder appears. For it is evident by it that he is a Saint and he could never be a Saint unless he were right in his religion and worship and in abiding by the message committed to his Apostle.

The most excellent of mankind after the Prophets are Abu Bakr, the Very Veracious (as-Siddiq), then Umar, the Divider (al-Faruq), then Uthman, he of the Two Lights (Dhu-n-Nurayn), then Ali--The good-will of God be upon them! Their Khalifates were in this order, and the Khalifate extended to thirty years; then, thereafter, came kings and princes.

The Muslims cannot do without a leader (Imam) who shall occupy himself with the enforcing of their decisions, and in maintaining their boundaries and guarding their frontiers, and equipping their armies, and receiving their alms, and putting down robberies and thieving and highwaymen, and maintaining the Friday services and the Festivals, and removing quarrels that fall between creatures, and receiving evidence bearing on legal claims, and marrying minors, male and female, and those who have no guardians, and dividing booty. And it is necessary that the leader should be visible, not hidden and expected to appear (muntazar), and that he should be of the tribe of Quraysh and not of any other. And he is not assigned exclusively to the sons of Hashim nor to the children of Ali. And it is not a condition that he should be protected by God from sin (isma), nor that he should be the most excellent of the people of his time, but it is a condition that he should have administrative ability, should be a good governor and be able to carry out decrees and to guard the restrictive ordinances (hadds) of Islam and to protect the wronged against him who wrongs him. And he is not to be deposed from the leadership on account of immorality or tyranny.

Prayer is allowable behind anyone whether pure or a sinner. And we give the salutation of Peace to the pure and to the sinner.

And we abstain from the mention of the Companions (sahibs) of the Prophet except with good.

[169]

And we bear witness that Paradise is for the ten to whom the Prophet--God bless him and give him Peace!--gave good tidings of Paradise (al-asharatu-l-mubashshara).

And we approve the wiping (mash) of the inner-shoes (khuffs) both at home and when on a journey.

And we do not regard nabidh as forbidden.

And the Saint does not reach the level of the Prophets. And the creature does not come to a point where commands and prohibitions and the details of the statutes in their out-ward sense (zahir) fall away from him; and the turning aside from these to the views which the People of the Inner Meaning (batin) assert is a deviation (ilhad) through unbelief.

And feeling safe from God is unbelief. And despairing of God is unbelief. And rejection of the statutes and contempt for the law is unbelief. And believing a diviner (kahin) in what he tells of the Unseen (ghayb) is unbelief. And what does not exist (ma'dum) is known of God Most High just as what exists (mawjud) is known of Him and it [i.e., what does not exist] is neither a thing (shay) nor an object of vision (mar'an).

And in prayer of the living for the dead, and in alms offered for them there is an advantage to them. And God Most High answers prayers and supplies needs.

And what the Prophet has reported of the conditions of the last day (as-sa'a), of the appearance of ad-Dajjal and of the beast of the earth [cf. Revelations xiii, 11 ff.] and of Yajuj and Majuj and the descent of Isa from heaven and the rising of the sun in the west, that is verity.

And the Mujtahids sometimes err and sometimes hit the mark. And the Apostles of mankind are more excellent than the Apostles of the angels; and the Apostles of the angels are more excellent than the generality of mankind; and the generality of mankind of the true believers is more excellent than the generality of the angels.

Footnotes

309:1 This is not the normal doctrine of Islam and the commentators have to explain this passage away. Consult in the chapters on theology, the whole Sufi development and especially the views of al-Ghazzali. Al-Mataridi was greatly

[170]

influenced by Abu Hanifa, who was hostile to mystics. Notice, too, the philosophical basis and beginning of this creed.

311:1 A sect of the Mu'tazilites held that a man could have two ajals, one his end by a natural death appointed by God, the other his end by a violent death, not so appointed. The "Philosophers" are said to have held that one ajal would be when the mechanism of the body ceased to work through the failing of its essential moisture and heat, and another ajal might come through sicknesses and accident generally.

VI

THE CREED CALLED THE SUFFICIENCY OF THE COMMONALTY IN THE SCIENCE OF SCHOLASTIC THEOLOGY, BY MUHAMMAD AL-FUDALI [D. FIRST HALF OF THE THIRTEENTH CENTURY OF THE HIJRA]

[Translated from the Arabic text of Cairo, A.H. 1315, with the commentary of al-Bayjuri.]

In the name of God, the merciful Compassionator. Praise belongeth unto God who alone bringeth into existence, and blessing and peace be upon our Lord Muhammad, his family and companions, possessors of beauty and guidance.

To proceed: The creature who stands in need of the mercy of his exalted Lord, Muhammad ibn ash-Shafi'i al-Fudali says: One of the brethren asked me that I should compose a tractate on the divine unity (tawhid), and I agreed to that, following the example of the most learned Shaykh, as-Sanusi, [d. 895,] in the establishing of proofs, except that I adduced each proof (dalil) in connection with the doctrine that was to be proved, and added to it an exposition on account of my knowledge of the limitations of that student. So, in the ascription of praise to God Most High, it became a tractate, useful and excellent for the establishing of that which is in it. And I called it, THE SUFFICIENCY OF THE PEOPLE IN THAT WHICH IS NECESSARY TO THEM OF THE SCIENCE OF SCHOLASTIC THEOLOGY (kalam). And I pray God Most High that He will make it useful, for He is my sufficiency, and excellent is the Guardian.

Know that it is incumbent upon every Muslim that he should know fifty articles of belief (aqidas), and for each article that he should know a proof, general (ijmali) or detailed (tafsili). Some say that it is required that he should know a detailed proof, but the common opinion is that a general proof suffices for each article of the fifty. An example of a detailed proof is when someone says, "What is the

[171]

proof of the existence (wujud) of God?" that the answer should be, "These created things." That the asker should then say, "Do the created things prove the existence of God on the side of their possibility or on the side of their existence after non-existence (adam)?" and that his question should be answered. And if the further question is not answered, but the only answer is, "These created things," and the answerer does not know whether it is on the side of their possibility or of their existence after non-existence, then the proof is said to be general; but it is sufficient according to the common position. And with regard to taqlid (blind acceptance), which is that fifty articles are known but no proof of then is known, either general or detailed, the learned differ. Some say that it does not suffice, and that the mukallad (blind accepter) is an unbeliever (kafir). Ibn al-Arabi [d. 543] held this and as-Sanusi, and the latter gave in his commentary on his kubra a lengthy refutation of those who hold that taqlid is sufficient. Yet there is a report that he retired from this position, and acknowledged the sufficiency of taqlid; but I have never seen in his books anything but the opinion that it does not suffice.

INTRODUCTION

Know that an understanding of the fifty following articles must be based upon three things--the necessary (wajib), the impossible (mustahil), and the possible (ja'iz). The necessary is that the non-existence of which cannot be apprehended by the intellect (aql), that is, the intellect cannot affirm its non-existence, as boundary to a body (jirm), i.e., its taking up a certain measure of space (faragh). An example of a body is a tree or a stone. Then, whenever a person says to you, that a tree, for example, does not take up room (mahall) in the earth, your intellect cannot affirm that, for its taking up room is a necessary thing, the absence of which your intellect cannot affirm. The impossible is that the existence of which cannot be apprehended; that is, the intellect cannot affirm its existence. Then, whenever anyone says that such a body is bare of motion and rest at the same time, your intellect cannot affirm that, because being bare of motion and rest at the same time is an impossibility, the occurrence and existence of which the intellect cannot affirm, and whenever it is said that weakness (ajz) is impossible in God, the meaning is that the occurrence or existence of weakness in God is unthinkable. So, too, with the other impossibilities. And the possible is that the existence of which at one time, and the non-existence at another, the intellect can affirm, as the existence of a child of Zayd's. When, then, someone says that Zayd has a child, your intellect acknowledges the possibility of the truth of that; and whenever he says that Zayd has no child, your intellect acknowledges the possibility of the truth of that. So the existence and the non-existence of a child of Zayd is possible; the intellect can believe in its existence or in its non-existence. And whenever it is said that God's sustaining Zayd with a dinar is a possibility,

[172]

the meaning is that the intellect assents to the existence of that sustaining (rizq) at one time and to its non-existence at another.

On these three distinctions, then, is based the science of the articles of belief; and these three are necessary for every mukallaf [one who has a task imposed upon him; in this case of religious duty], male and female, for that upon which the necessary is based is necessary. The Imam al-Haramayn (d. 478) even held that an understanding of these three constituted reason itself and that he who did not know the meaning of necessary, impossible and possible, was not a reasoning being. So, whenever it is said here that Power is necessary] (wajib) in God, the meaning is that the intellect cannot affirm its non-existence, because the necessary is that the non-existence of which the intellect cannot affirm, as has preceded. But necessary (wajib, incumbent) in the sense of that the not doing of which is punished, is an idea which does not enter into the science of the divine Unity. So, do not let the matter be confused for you. It is true that if one says that belief in the Power of God is incumbent (wajib) on the mukallaf, the meaning is that he is rewarded for that and punished for omitting that. Thus there is a distinction between saying that belief in such and such is incumbent and that the knowledge, for example, is necessary. For when it is said that knowledge is necessary in God, the meaning is that the intellect cannot affirm the non-existence of knowledge in God. But when it is said that belief in that knowledge is incumbent, the meaning is that belief in it is rewarded and lack of belief punished. So, apply thyself to the distinction between the two and be not of those who regard taqlid in the articles of Religion as right, that so your faith (iman) should differ from the truth and you should abide in the Fire, according to those who hold that taqlid does not suffice. As-Sanusi said, "A person is not a Believer when he says, 'I hold by the Articles and will not abandon them though I be cut in pieces;' nay, he is not a Believer until he knows each Article of the fifty, along with its proof." And this science of theology must be studied first of all sciences, as may be gathered from the commentary [by at-Taftazani, d. 791] on as-Sanusi's Articles; for he made this science a foundation on which other things are built. So a judgment as to anyone's ceremonial ablution (wudu) or prayer is not valid unless the person in question knows these articles or, on the other hand, holds them without proof.

Now, let us state to you the fifty articles shortly, before stating them in detail. Know, then, that twenty qualities are necessary in God Most High, that twenty are impossible in Him and that one is possible. This makes up forty-one. And in the case of the Apostles, four qualities are necessary, four impossible and one possible. This makes up the fifty. And there shall come an accurate account of doctrines along with the statement of them, if it be the will of God Most High.

[173]

The first of the qualities necessary in God is existence (wujud); and there is a difference of opinion as to its meaning. All except the Imam al-Ash'ari and his followers hold that existence is the state (hal) necessary to the essence so long as the essence abides; and this state has no cause (illa). And the meaning of it being a state is that it does not attain to the degree of an entity (mawjud) and does not fall to the degree of a non-entity (ma'dum), so that it should be non-existence pure, but is half way between an entity and a non-entity. So the existence of Zayd, for example, is a state necessary to his essence; that is, it cannot be separated from his essence. And when it is said that it has no cause, the meaning is that it does not originate in anything, as opposed to Zayd's potentiality (qadir, powerful), for example, which originates in his power (qudra). So Zayd's potentiality and his existence are two states which subsist in his essence, un-perceived by any of the five senses; only, the first has a cause in which it originates, and it is power, and the second has no cause. This is the description of a personal state (hal nafsi) and every state subsisting in an essence, without a cause, is a personal quality (sifa nafsiya). It is that without which the essence is unthinkable; that is, the essence cannot be apprehended by the intellect and comprehended except through its personal quality, like limitation for a body. For, if you apprehend and comprehend a body, you have comprehended that it is limited. So, according to this doctrine-- that existence is a state--the essence of God is not His existence and the essences of the created things are not their existences. But al-Ash'ari and his followers hold that existence is the self (ayn) of an entity, and according to their view the existence of God is the self of His essence and not an addition to it externally, and the existence of a created thing is the self of its essence. And, on this view, it is not clear how existence can be reckoned as a quality, because existence is the self of the essence, and a quality, on the other hand, as we have seen already, is something else than the essence. But if he makes existence a quality, then the thing is plain and the meaning that existence is necessary in God, according to the first view, is that the personal quality is a state established in God; and its meaning, on the second view, is that the essence of God is an entity with external reality, so that if the veil were removed from us we would see it. The essence of God, then, is a reality; only, its existence is something else than it, on the one view, and is it, on the other.

And the proof of the existence of God is the origin (huduth) of the world; that is, its existence after non-existence. The world consists of bodies (jirms) like essences; and accidents (arads) like motion, and rest and colors. And the origin of the world is a proof of the existence of God only because it is not sound reasoning that it should originate through itself without someone bringing it into existence. Before it existed, its existence equalled its non-existence; then, when it entered existence and its non-existence ceased, we know that its existence overbalanced its non-existence. But this existence had previously equalled the non-existence; and it is not sound reasoning that it could overbalance the non-existence through itself; so that it is clear that there must have been one who caused the overbalancing, other than itself, and it is He that brought it into existence; for it is impossible that one of two equal things could overbalance the other without an overbalancer. For example, before Zayd exists it is possible that he may come into existence in such and such a year and also that he may remain in non-existence. So, his existence is equal to his non-existence. So, then, when he exists and his non-existence ceases, in the time in which he exists, we know that his existence is by a bringer-into-existence and not through himself. The proof, in short, is that you say:--The world, consisting of bodies and accidents, is a thing originated (hadith), i.e., an entity after non-existence. And every originated thing cannot help but have an originator (muhdith). Therefore, the world must have had an originator.

This is what can be gained by an intellectual proof. But as for the Originator being named by the Glorious and Lofty Expression [i.e., Allah, God] or the other Names (asma), knowledge of that is to be gained from the Prophets only. So note this point carefully and also the proof which has preceded, that the originating of the world is a proof of the existence of Him Most High.

But as for the proof that the world has had an origin, know that the world consists of bodies and accidents only, as has preceded. And the accidents, like motion and rest, are originated, because you observe their changing from existence to non-existence and from non-existence to existence. You see it is so in the motion of Zayd. His motion is lacking if he is at rest; and his rest is lacking if he is in motion. Then his rest, which comes after his motion, exists after that it has been lacking through motion; and his motion, which comes after his rest, exists after that it has been lacking through his rest. And existence after non-existence means having an origin. And bodies are inseparable from attributes, because they are never free from either motion or rest. And whatever is inseparable from a thing having origin must have origin; i.e., must be an entity after non-existence. So, the bodies are originated also, like the attributes. The proof, in short, is that you say: Bodies are inseparable from attributes and these have an origin; everything that is inseparable from that which has an origin, itself has an origin; therefore, bodies have an origin. And the origin of the two things--bodies and attributes--that is their existence after non-existence, is a proof of the existence of Him Most High, because everything having an origin must have an originator, and there is no originator of the world save God Most High alone, who has no partner (sharik) as shall be shown in the proof of His Unity. This, then, is the general proof, a knowledge of which is incumbent upon every mukallaf, male and female, according to the opinion of Ibn al-Arabi and as-Sanusi, who hold those who do not know it to be unbelievers. So, beware lest there be a contradiction in your faith.

The second Quality necessary in God is Priority (qidam); its meaning is lack of beginning. And the meaning of God's being Prior (qadim) is that there was no beginning to His existence, as opposed to Zayd, for example. Zayd's existence had a beginning and it was the creation from the drop from which he was created. And there is a difference of opinion whether Prior and Azali (eternal with respect to past time) mean the same or not. Those who hold that they mean the same, define them as that which has no beginning, and explain "that which" by thing (shay). That is, prior and azali are the thing which has no beginning; so the essence of God and His qualities are included. And those who hold that their meaning is different define prior as the entity which had no beginning and azali as that which had no beginning, covering thus both entity and nonentity, So azali is broader than prior, but they both come together in the essence of God and His existential qualities. The essence of God is azali and His Power (qudra) is azali. But only azali is said of the states (hals) like God's being powerful, in accordance with the doctrine of the states. For God's being powerful is called azali, in accordance with that doctrine, and is not called prior, because in prior there must be existence, and "being powerful" does not rise to the level of existence [to being an entity], but is only a state (hal).

And the proof of God's Priority is that if He were not Prior He would be a thing originated (hadith), because there is no medium between the prior and the thing originated; to everything of which priority is denied, origin belongs. But if God were a thing originated, He would need an originator, and His originator would need an originator, and so on. Then, if the originators did not coincide, there would be the Endless Chain (tasalsul), that is a sequence of things, one after another to infinity; and the Endless Chain is impossible. And if the series of originators comes to an end by it being said that the originator of God was originated by Him, then we have the Circle (dawr) and it is that one thing depends on another thing which again depends on the first. For if God had an originator, He would depend on this originator; but the hypothesis is that God originated this originator and so the originator depends on Him. But the Circle is impossible; that is, its existence is unthinkable. And that which leads to the Circle and to the Chain, both being impossible, involves the originating of God. So, the originating of God is impossible; for what involves an impossibility is impossible. The proof, in short, is that you say, "If God were other than Prior, through being a thing originated, He would have need of an originator. Then the Circle or the Chain would be unavoidable; but they are both impossible. So, the originating of God is impossible and His Priority is established; and that is what has been sought." This is the general proof of the Priority of God, and by it the mukallaf escapes from the

[176]

noose of taqlid, the remainer in which will abide eternally in the Fire, according to the opinion of Ibn al-Arabi and as-Sanusi, as has proceeded.

The third Quality necessary in God is Continuance (baqa). The meaning of it is lack of termination of the existence; and the meaning of God's being continuing is that there is no end to His existence. And the proof of God's continuance is that if it were possible that any lack could be joined to Him, then He would be a thing originated and would need an originator and then the Circle or the Chain would necessarily follow. A definition of each one of these two has preceded in the proof of Priority and in the explanation that to a thing with which non-existence is possible, priority must be denied. For the existence of everyone to whom non-existence is joined is possible, and everything whose existence is possible is a thing originated, and everything originated requires an originator. But Priority has been established for God by the preceding proof, and non-existence is impossible for everything for which Priority has been established. So the proof of Continuance in God is the same as the proof of Priority. That proof, in short, is that you say, "If Continuance is not necessary in Him, then Priority must be negated of Him. But Priority cannot be negated on account of the preceding proof." This is the general proof of Continuance, a knowledge of which is incumbent on every individual. And similarly a knowledge of every article is necessary and of its general proof. Then, if some of the articles are known with their proofs, and the rest are not known with their proofs, that is not sufficient according to the opinion of those who do not regard taqlid as sufficient.

The fourth Quality necessary in God is difference (mukhalafa) from originated things. That is, from created things (makhluqat), for God is different from every created thing, men, Jinn, angels and the rest; and it is not good that He should be described with the descriptions which apply to created things, as walking, sitting, having members of the body, for He is far removed (munazzah) from members of the body, as mouth, eye, ear and the like. Then, from everything that is in your mind of length and breadth and shortness and fatness, God is different; He has removed Himself far from all descriptions which apply to the creation. And the proof of the necessity of this difference in God is that if any originated thing resembled Him, that is, if it were laid down that God could be described with any of the things with which an originated thing is described, then He would be an originated thing. And if God were an originated thing, then He would need an originator, and His originator, another originator, and so we would come necessarily to the circle or the chain, and both of these are impossible. This proof, in short, is that you say, "If God resembles a created thing in anything, He is an originated thing, because what is possible in one of two things resembling each other, is possible in the other. But that God should be originated is impossible, for priority is necessary in Him. And when being originated is denied in Him, His

[177]

difference from created things stands fast and there is absolutely no resemblance between Him and the originated things. This is the general proof, the knowledge of which is necessary, as has preceded.

The fifth Quality necessary in God is self-subsistence (qiyam bin-nafs). That is in the essence; and its meaning is that there is independence of a locus (mahall, subject) and a specifier (mukhassis). The locus is the essence and the specifier is the bringer-into-existence (mujid); then the meaning of God's subsisting in Himself is that He is independent of an essence in which He may subsist, or of a bringer-into-existence; for He is the bringer-into-existence of all things. The proof that He subsists in Himself is that you say, "If God had need of a locus, that is an essence, in which He might subsist, as whiteness has need of an essence in which it may subsist, He would be a quality, as whiteness, for example, is a quality. But it is not sound to say of Him that He is a quality, for He is described by qualities, and a quality is not described by qualities, so He is not a quality. And if He had need of a bringer-into-existence, He would be an originated thing, and His originator would be an originated thing also, and the Circle or the Chain would necessarily follow. Then it stands fast that He is the absolutely independent, that is, He is independent of everything. But the created thing that is independent is independent in a limited sense only; that is, of one thing in place of another. And may God rule thy guidance.

The sixth Quality in God is Unity (wihdaniya). It is unity in essence and qualities and acts in the sense of absence of multiplicity. And the meaning of God's being one in His essence is that His essence is not compounded of parts, and this compounding is called internal quantity (kamm muttasil). And in the sense that there is not in existence or in possibility an essence which resembles the essence of God, this impossibility of resemblance is called external quantity (kamm munfasil). The unity, then, in the essence denies both quantities, external and internal. And the meaning of God's Oneness in qualities is that He has not two qualities agreeing in name and meaning, like two Powers, or two Knowledges or two Wills--for He has only one Power and one Will and one Knowledge, in opposition to Abu Sahl, who held that He had knowledges to the number of the things known. And this, I mean multiplicity in qualities, is called internal quantity in qualities. Or the sense is, that no one has a quality resembling a quality of God. And this, I mean anyone possessing a quality, etc., is called external quantity in qualities. Oneness, then, in qualities, negates quantity in them, internal and external. And the meaning of God's Oneness in acts is that no created thing possesses an act, for God is the creator of the acts of created things, prophets, angels and the rest. And as for what happens when an individual dies or falls into pain on opposing himself to a saint (wali), that is by the creation of God, who creates it when the saint is angry with the man who opposes him. Do not then

[178]

explain Oneness in acts by saying that no other than God has an act like God's act, for that involves that some other than God has an act, but that it is not like the act of God. That is false. God it is who is the creator of all acts. What comes from you by way of movement of the hand, when you strike Zayd, for example, is by the creation of God. He has said (Qur. 37, 99), "God created you, and what do ye do?" And another than God being possessor of an act is called external quantity in acts.

So the unity necessary in God denies the five impossible quantities. Internal quantity in the essence makes the essence a compound of parts; external quantity means that there is an essence which resembles it. Internal quantity in the qualities is that God has two Powers, for example; external quantity in them means that someone else has a quality which resembles one of His qualities. External quantity in acts means that some other than God possesses an act. These five quantities deny the unity necessary in God. The meaning of quantity is number (adad).

The proof that Unity is necessary in God is the existence of the world. If God had a partner (sharik) in divinity (uluhiya), the case could not be in doubt. Either they would agree on the existence of the world, in that one of them would say, "I will cause the world to exist," and the other would say, "I will cause it to exist along with thee, that we may help one another in it." Or they would disagree, and one of them would say, "I will cause the world to exist by my power," and the other, "I will that the existence be lacking." Then, if they agreed upon the existence of the world in that both of them together caused it to exist, and it existed through their action, that would necessarily involve the coincidence of two impressors upon one impression, which is impossible. And if they disagreed, it is plain that the will of one either would be carried out or it would not be carried out. If the will of one, rather than the other, is carried out, then the other whose will is not carried out must be weaker. But our hypothesis was that he was equal in divinity to the one whose will was carried out. So whenever weakness is established in the case of the one, it is established in the case of the other, for he is like the other. And if the wills of both are not carried out, they are both weak. And upon every alternative, that they agree or differ, the existence of a single thing of the world is impossible; because if they agree on its existence, there necessarily follows the coincidence of two impressers upon one impression if their will is carried out, and that is impossible. So the carrying out of their will is not affected, and it is not possible that a single thing of the world should come into existence then. And if they disagree and the will of one of them is carried out, the other is weak. But he is his like. So it is not possible that there should come into existence a single thing of this world, for he is weak. So the God is not except one. And if they differ and their will is not carried out, they are weak and not able to cause the existence of a thing of the world. But the world exists, by common witness (mushahada). So it stands fast that the God is one; and that was what was sought. So the existence of the world is proof of the Unity of God and that He has no partner in any act, and no second cause in an action. He is the independent (al-Ghani), the absolutely independent.

And from this proof it may be known that there is no impression, by fire or a knife or eating, upon anything, consisting of burning or cutting or satiety, but God makes the being burnt in a thing which fire touches, when it touches it, and being cut in a thing with which a knife is brought into contact, when it is brought into contact with it, and satiety at eating and satisfaction at drinking. And he who holds that fire burns by its nature (tab), and water satisfies by its nature, and so on, is an unbeliever (kafir) by agreement (ijma). And he who holds that it burns by a power (quwa) created in it by God, is ignorant and corrupt, because he knows not the true nature (haqiqa) of Unity.

This is the general proof a knowledge of which is incumbent upon every individual, male and female: and he who knows it not is an unbeliever, according to as-Sanusi and al-Arabi. And may God rule thy guidance.

And Priority and Continuance and Difference from originated things and Self-Subsistence and Unity are negative qualities (sifat salabiya), that is, their meaning is negation and exclusion, for each of them excludes from God what does not be-seem Him.

The seventh Quality necessary in God is Power (qudra). It is a quality which makes an impression on a thing that is capable of existence or non-existence. So it comes into connection (ta'allaqa) with a non-entity and makes it an entity, as it came into connection with you before you existed. And it comes into connection with an entity and reduces it to a non-entity, as it comes into contact with a body which God desires should become a non-entity, that is, a not-thing (la shay). This connection is called accomplished (tanjizi) in the sense that it is actual (bil-fi'l), and this accomplished connection is a thing that takes place (hadith). But this quality has also an eternal, potential connection (saluhi qadim), and it is its potentiality from eternity of bringing into existence. It is potential in eternity to make Zayd tall or short or broad, or give him knowledge; but its accomplished connection is conditioned by the state in which Zayd is. So it has two connections; one eternal, potential, which has been described, and one accomplished, happening. The last is its connection with a non-entity, when it makes it an entity; and with an entity, when it makes it a non-entity. And this, I mean its connection with an entity or a non-entity, is a real (haqiqi) connection. But it has also a figurative (majazi) connection. That is, its connection with an

[180]

entity after it has become so and before it has become a non-entity, as it is connected with us after we have come to exist and before we have ceased to exist. It is called the connection of grasping (ta'alluqu-l-qabdati) in the sense that the entity is in the grasp (qabda) of the Power of God. If God will, He makes it remain an entity; and if He will, He reduces it to non-entity. And its connection with the non-entity before that God wills its existence is like its connection with Zayd at the time of the Flood (tufan), for example; it also is a connection of grasping in the sense that the non-entity is in the grasp of the Power of God. If God wills, He makes it remain in non-existence, and if He wills, He brings it out into existence. And similar is its connection with us after our death and before the resurrection (ba'th). It, too, is called a connection of grasping in the sense of what has preceded. So the quality of Power has seven connections: (1) eternal, (2) connection of grasping (that is, its connection with us before God wills our existence), (3) actual connection (that is, God's bringing the thing into existence), (4) connection of grasping (that is, connection with a thing after existence and before God has willed non-existence), (5) actual connection (that is, God's making a thing a non-entity), (6) connection of grasping after non-existence and before the resurrection, (7) actual connection (that is, God's making us exist on the day of resurrection).

But the real connections of these are two; God's bringing into existence and bringing into non-existence. This is a detailed statement; and a general statement would be that God's Power has two connections--as is commonly accepted--a potential and an accomplished; but the accomplished is limited to actual bringing into existence and non-existence. And the connection of grasping is not to be described as accomplished, nor as eternal. And what has preceded about this quality connecting with existence and non-existence is the opinion of the multitude on the subject. But some hold that it does not connect with non-existence; that whenever God desires the non-existence of an individual, He takes away from him the aids (imdadat) which are the cause of his continuance.

The eighth Quality necessary in God is Will (irada). It is the quality which specifies the possible with one of the things possible to it. For example, tallness and shortness are possible to Zayd; then Will specifies him with one,--tallness, say. Power brings tallness out of non-existence into existence. So Will specifies and Power brings out. And the possibilities (mumkinat) with which Power and Will connect are six: (1) existence, (2) non-existence, (3) qualities, like tallness and shortness, (4) times, (5) places, (6) directions.

And the possibilities are called "the mutual opposers" (mutaqabilat), existence opposes non-existence and tallness opposes shortness and direction upward opposes direction downward, and one place, like Egypt, opposes another place, like Syria. And this, in short, means that it is possible in the case of Zayd, for example, that he should remain in non-existence and also that he should enter existence at this time. Then, whenever he enters existence, Will has specified existence instead of non-existence, and Power has brought out existence. And it would have been possible that he might have entered existence at the time of the Flood (tufan) or at some other time; so that which specifies his existence at this time instead of any other is Will. And it is possible that he should be tall or short; then that which specifies his tallness instead of shortness is Will. And it is possible that he should be in the direction upward, then that which specifies him in the direction downward is Will. And Power and Will are two qualities subsisting in God's essence--two entities; if the veil were removed from us we could see them. They have connection with the possible only; but none with the impossible, such as a partner for God. He is far removed from that! Nor with the necessary, like the essence of God and His qualities. Ignorance is the saying of those who hold that God has power to take a son (walad); for Power has no connection with the impossible and taking a son is impossible. But it should not be said that because He has no power to take a son, He is therefore weak. We say that weakness would follow only if the impossible were of that which is allotted to Power. But Power has not been connected with that, seeing that nothing is allotted to it except the possible. And Will has two connections, one eternally potential, and it is its potentiality to specify from all eternity. So, in the case of the tall or the short Zayd, it is possible that he might be otherwise than what he is, so far as relationship to the potentiality of Will is concerned. For Will is potential that Zayd should be a Sultan or a scavenger, so far as the potential connection is concerned. And Will has also an eternal accomplished connection, and it is the specifying by God of a thing with a quality which it possesses. So God specified Zayd from all eternity by His Will with the knowledge that he possesses. And his being specified with knowledge, for example, is eternal and is called an eternal accomplished connection. And the potentiality of Will to specify him with knowledge, etc., in relationship to the essence of Will, cutting off all consideration of actual specifying, is called an eternal potential connection. And some say that Will has also a temporal, accomplished connection. It is, for example, the specifying of Zayd with tallness, when he is actually brought into existence. According to this view, Will has three connections; but the truth is that this third is not a connection but is the making manifest of the eternal, accomplished connection.

And the connection of Power and Will is common to every possible thing to the extent that the affections of the mind (khatarat) which arise in the mind of an individual are specified by the Will of God and created by His Power as the Shaykh al-Malawi [Ahmad al-Malawi, d. 1181] has said in some of his books. But

[182]

know that the attributing of specifying to Will and of bringing out into existence to Power is only metaphorical; for the true specifier is God by His Will and the true producer and bringer-into-existence is God by His Power. Then, in the case of the saying of the common people that Power does such and such to so and so, if it is meant that the doing belongs to Power actually, or to it and to the essence of God, that is unbelief (kufr). Rather, the doing belongs to the essence of God by His Power.

The ninth Quality necessary in God is Knowledge (ilm). It is an eternal quality subsisting in the essence of God, an entity by which what is known is revealed with a revealing of the nature of complete comprehension (ihata), without any concealment having preceded. It is connected with the necessary, the possible and the impossible. He knows His own essence and qualities by His Knowledge. And He knows impossibilities in the sense that He knows that a partner is impossible to Him and that, if one existed, corruption would accrue from it. And Knowledge has an eternal, accomplished connection only. For God knows these things that have been mentioned from all eternity with a complete knowledge that is not by way of opinion (zann) or doubt (shakk); because opinion and doubt are impossibilities in God. And the meaning of the saying, "without any concealment having preceded," is that He knows things eternally; He is not first ignorant of them and then knowing them. But an originated being (hadith) is ignorant of a thing and then knows it. And God's Knowledge has no potential connection in the sense that there is a potentiality that such and such should be revealed by it, because that involves that the thing in question has not been actually revealed, and lack of actual revealing of it is ignorance.

The tenth Quality necessary in God is Life (hayah). It is a quality which in him in whom it subsists validates perception, as knowledge and hearing and seeing: that is, it is valid that he should be described therewith. But being characterized by actual perception does not necessarily follow from possessing the quality, Life. And it is not connected with anything, entity or non-entity.

The proof that Knowledge and Power and Will and Life are necessary is the existence of the created things. Because, if any one of these four is denied, why does the created world exist? So, since the created things exist, we know that God is to be described by these qualities. And the reason of the existence of the created things depending on these four is this. He who makes a thing does not make it except when he knows the thing. Then he wills the thing which he would make and, after his willing, he busies himself with making it by his power. Further, it is known that the maker cannot but be living. And Knowledge and Will and Power are called qualities of impression (sifat at-ta'thir), for making an impression depends upon them. Because he who wills a thing must have knowledge of it

[183]

before he aims at it; then, after he has aimed at it, he busies himself with doing it. For example, when there is something in your house and you wish to take it, your knowledge precedes your wish to take it, and after your wish to take it, you take it actually. The connection of these qualities, then, is in a certain order, in the case of an originated being; first comes the knowledge of the thing, then the aiming at it, then the doing. But in the case of God, on the other hand, there is no sequence in His qualities, except in our comprehension; in that, Knowledge comes first, then Will, then Power. But as for the making of an impression externally, there is no sequence in the qualities of God. It is not said that Knowledge comes into actual connection, then Will, then Power; because all that belongs to originated beings. Order is only according to our comprehensions.

The eleventh and twelfth Qualities of God are Hearing (sam) and Seeing (basar). These are two qualities subsisting in the essence of God and connected with every entity; that is, by them is revealed every entity, necessary or possible. And Hearing and Seeing are connected with the essence of God and His qualities.; that is, His essence and qualities are revealed to Him by His Seeing and Hearing, besides the revealing of His Knowledge. And God hears the essences of Zayd and Amr and a wall and He sees them. And He hears the sound of the possessor of a sound and He sees it, that is the sound. Then, if you say, "Hearing a sound is plain, but hearing the essence of Zayd and the essence of a wall is not plain; so, too, the connection of seeing with sounds, for sounds are heard only," we reply, "Belief in this is incumbent upon us because these two qualities are connected with every entity; but the how (kayfiya) of the connection is unknown to us. God hears the essence of Zayd, but we do not know how hearing is connected with that essence. And it is not meant that He hears the walking of the essence of Zayd, for the hearing of his walking enters into the hearing of all the sounds (sawt), but what is meant is that He hears the essence of Zayd and his body (juththa), besides hearing his walking. But we do not know how the hearing of God is connected with the person (nafs) of the essence. This is what is binding upon every individual, male and female--Our trust is in God!

The proof of Hearing and Seeing is the saying of God that He is a Hearer and Seer. And know that the connection of Hearing and Seeing in relation to originated things is an eternal, potential connection before the existence of these, and after their existence it is a temporal, accomplished connection. That is, after their existence, they are revealed to God by His Hearing and Seeing besides the revealing of His Knowledge. So they have two connections. And in relation to God and His qualities, the connection is eternal, accomplished, in the sense that His essence and His qualities are revealed to Him from all eternity through His Hearing and Seeing. So, God hears His essence and all His existential qualities [all except the states and the negative qualities], Power, Hearing, and all the rest;

[184]

but we do not know how the connection is, and He sees His essence and His qualities of existence, Power, Seeing and the rest, but again we do not know how the connection is. The preceding statement that Hearing and Seeing are connected with every entity is the opinion of as-Sanusi and those who follow him; it is the preponderating one. But it is said, also, that Hearing is only connected with sounds and Seeing with objects of vision. And God's Hearing is not with ear or ear-hole, and His Seeing is not with eyeball or eyelid.

The thirteenth Quality of God is Speech (kalam). It is an eternal quality, subsisting in God's essence, not a word or sound, and far removed from order of preceding and following, from inflection and structure, opposed to the speech of originated beings. And by the Speech that is necessary to God is not meant the Glorious Expressions (lafz) revealed to the Prophet, because these are originated and the quality that subsists in the essence of God is eternal. And these embrace preceding and following, inflection and chapters and verses; but the eternal quality is bare of all these things. It has no verses or chapters or inflections, because such belong to the speech which embraces letters and sounds, and the eternal quality is far removed from letters and sounds, as has preceded. And those Glorious Expressions are not a guide to the eternal quality in the sense that the eternal quality can be understood from them. What is understood from these expressions equals what would be understood from the eternal quality if the veil were removed from us and we could hear it. In short, these expressions are a guide to its meaning, and this meaning equals what would be understood from the eternal Speech which subsists in the essence of God. So meditate this distinction, for many have erred in it. And both the Glorious Expressions and the eternal quality are called Qur'an and the Word (kalam) of God. But the Glorious Expressions are created and written on the Preserved Tablet (al-lawh-al-mahfuz); Jibril brought them down [i.e., revealed them] to the Prophet after that they had been brought down in the Night of Decree (laylatu-l-qadr; Qur. 97, 1) to the Mighty House (baytu-l-izza), a place in the Heaven nearest to the earth; it was written in books (sahifas) and placed in the Mighty House. It is said that it was brought down to the Mighty House all at once and then brought down to the Prophet in twenty years, and some say, in twenty-five. And it is also said that it was brought down to the Mighty House only to the amount that was to be revealed each year and not all at once.

And that which was brought down to the Prophet was expression and meaning. And it is said also that only the meaning was brought down to him. There is a conflict of opinion on this; some say that the Prophet clothed the meaning with expressions of his own, and others, that he who so clothed the meaning, was Jibril. But the truth is that it was sent down in expressions and meaning. In short, the quality subsisting in the essence of God is not a letter nor a sound. And the

Mu'tazilites called in doubt the existence of a kind of Speech without letters. But the People of the Sunna answered that because thoughts in the mind (hadith an-nafs), a kind of speech with which an individual speaks to himself, are without letter or sound, there exists a kind of speech without letters or words. By this the People of the Sunna do not wish to institute a comparison between the Speech of God and thoughts in the mind; for the Speech of God is eternal and thoughts in the mind are originated. They wished to disprove the contention of the Mu'tazilites when they urged that speech cannot exist without letter or sound.

The proof of the necessity of Speech in God is His saving (Qur. 4, 162); "and God spoke to Moses." So He has established Speech for Himself. And Speech connects with that with which Knowledge connects, of necessary and possible and impossible. But the connection of Knowledge with these is a connection of revealing, in the sense that they are revealed to God by His Knowledge; and the connection of Speech with them is a connection of proof, in the sense that if the veil were taken away from us and we heard the eternal Speech we would understand these things from it.

The fourteenth Quality subsisting in God is Being Powerful (kawn qadir). It is a Quality subsisting in His essence, not an entity and not a non-entity. It is not Power, but between it and Power is a reciprocal inseparability. When Power exists in an essence, the quality called "Being Powerful" exists in that essence, equally whether that essence is eternal or originated. So, God creates in the essence of Zayd Power actual, and He creates also in it the quality called Zayd's Being Powerful. This quality is called a state (hal) and Power is a cause (illa) in it in the case of created things. But in the case of God, Power is not said to be a cause in His Being Powerful; it is only said that between Power and God's Being Powerful there is a reciprocal inseparability. The Mu'tazilites hold also the reciprocal inseparability between the Power of an originated being and its Being Powerful. But they do not say that the second quality is by the creation of God, only that when God creates Power in an originated being, there proceeds from the Power a quality called Being Powerful, without creation.

The Fifteenth Quality necessary in God is Being a Willer (kawn murid). It is a quality subsisting in His essence, not an entity and not a non-entity. It is called a state (hal) and it is not Will, equally whether the essence is eternal or created. So, God creates in the essence of Zayd Will actual, and He creates in it the quality called Zayd's Being a Willer. And what is said above, about the disagreement between the Mu'tazilites and the People of the Sunna on Being Powerful, applies also to Being a Willer.

[The same thing applies exactly to Qualities Sixteen, Seventeen, Eighteen, Nineteen and Twenty,--Being a Knower (alim), a Living One (hayy), a Hearer (sami), a Seer (basir), a Speaker (mutakallim).]

NOTICE. The Qualities, Power, Will, Knowledge, Life, Hearing, Seeing, Speech, which have preceded, are called, "Qualities consisting of ideas" (sifat al-ma'ani, thought-qualities as opposed to active qualities; see below); on account of the connection of the general with the particular (idafatu-l-amm lil-khass), or the explanatory connection (al-idafatu-l-bayaniya). And those which follow these, God's Being Powerful, etc., are called "Qualities derived from ideas" (sifat ma' nawiya), by way of derivation (nisba) from the "Qualities consisting of ideas," because they are inseparable from them in a thing eternal and proceed from them in a thing originated, according to what has preceded.

And the Mataridites added to the "Qualities consisting of Ideas," an Eighth Quality and called it, Making to Be (takwin). It is a quality and an entity like the rest of the "Qualities consisting of Ideas"; if the veil were removed from us we would see it, just as we would see the other "Qualities consisting of Ideas" if the veil were removed from us. But the Ash'arites opposed them and urged that there was no advantage in having a quality, Making to Be, besides Power, because the Mataridites said that God brought into existence and out of existence by the quality of Making to Be. Then these replied that Power prepared the possibility for existence, that is, made it ready to receive existence after it had not been ready; that thereafter Making to Be brought it into existence actually. The Ash'arites replied that the possible was ready for existence without anything further. And on account of their having added this quality, they said that the active qualities (sifat al-af'al), such as Creating (khalq), Bringing to Life (ihya), Sustaining (razq), Bringing to Death (imata), were eternal, because these expressions are names of the quality Making to Be, which is a quality and an entity, according to them. But it is eternal; therefore these active qualities are eternal. But according to the Ash'arites, the active qualities are originated, because they are only names of the connections of Power. So Bringing to Life is a name for the connection of Power with Life, and Sustaining is a name for the connection of Power with the creature to be sustained, and Creating is a name for its connection with the thing to be created, and Bringing to Death, a name for its connection with death. And the connections of Power, according to them, are originated.

And among the Fifty Articles are twenty which express the opposites of the twenty above. They are Non-existence, the opposite to Existence.

The Second, Origin (huduth), is the opposite of Priority.

[187]

The Third, Transitoriness (fana), is the opposite of Continuance.

The Fourth, Resemblance (mumathala), is the opposite of Difference. It is impossible that God should resemble originated things in any of those things with which they are described; time has no effect upon Him and He has not a place or movement or rest; and He is not described with colors or with a direction; it is not said with regard to Him that He is above such a body, or on the right of such a body. And He is no direction from Him. So it is not said, "I am under God." And the saying of the commonalty, "I am under our Lord," and "My Lord is over me," is to be disapproved. Unbelief is to be feared on the part of him who holds the use of it to be an article of his faith.

The Fifth is having need of a locus (ihtiyaz ila mahall), that is, an essence in which He may subsist, or a Specifier, that is a bringer-into-existence. This is the opposite of Self-subsistence.

The Sixth is Multiplicity (ta'addud), in the sense of combination in the essence or the qualities, or the existence of a being similar in essence or qualities or acts. This is the opposite of Unity.

The Seventh is Weakness (ajz) and it is the opposite of Power. So, being unequal to any possibility is impossible in God.

The Eighth is Unwillingness (karaha, lit. dislike). It is the opposite of Will, and it is impossible in God that He should bring into existence anything of the world, along with Unwillingness toward it, that is, lack of Will. Entities are possibilities which God brought into existence by His Will and Choice (ikhtiyar). And it is derived from the necessity of Will in God, that the existence of created things is not through causation (ta'lil), or by way of nature (tab). Amt the difference between the two is that the entity which exists through causation is whatever exists whenever its cause exists, without dependence on another thing. The movement of the finger is the cause of the movement of the ring; when the one exists, the second exists, without dependence on anything else. And the entity which exists, by way of nature, depends upon a condition and upon the nullifying of a hindrance. So, fire does not burn except on the condition of contact with wood and the nullifying of moistness which is the hindrance of its burning. For fire burns by its nature according to those who hold the doctrine of nature--Whom may God curse!--But the truth is, that God creates the being burned in the wood when it is in contact with the fire, just as He creates the movement of the ring when movement of the finger exists. And there is no such thing as existence through causation or nature. So it is an impossibility in God that there should be a cause in the world which proceeds from Him without His choice, or that there should be a course of nature and that the world should exist thereby.

The Ninth is Ignorance (jahl). Ignorance of any possible thing is impossible in God, equally whether it is simple, that is, lack of knowledge of a thing; or compound, that is, perception of a thing as different from what it really is. And Inattention (ghafala) and Neglect (dhuhul) are impossible in God. This is the opposite of Knowledge.

The Tenth is Death (mawt). It is the opposite of Life.

The Eleventh is Deafness (samam). It is the opposite of Hearing.

The Twelfth is Blindness (ama). It is the opposite of Seeing.

The Thirteenth is Dumbness (kharas). In it is the idea of Silence (bakam) and it is the opposite of Speech.

The Fourteenth is God's Being Weak (kawn ajiz). It is the opposite of His Being Powerful.

The Fifteenth is His Being an Unwilling One (kawn karih). It is the opposite of His Being a Willer.

The Sixteenth is His Being an Ignorant One (kawn jahil). It is the opposite of His Being a Knower.

The Seventeenth is His Being a Dead One (kawn mayyit). It is the opposite of His Being a Living One.

The Eighteenth is His Being Deaf (asamm). It is the opposite of His Being a Hearer.

The Nineteenth is His Being Blind (a'ma). It is the opposite of His Being a Seer.

The Twentieth is His Being Silent (abkam). In it is the idea of Dumbness (kharas) and it is the opposite of His Being a Speaker.

All those twenty are impossible in God. And know that the proof of each one of the twenty qualities necessary in God establishes the existence of that quality in Him and denies to Him its opposite And the proofs of the seven thought-qualities are proofs of the seven derived from these. Thus, there are Forty Articles; twenty of them are necessary in God; twenty are denied in Him; and there are twenty general proofs, each proof establishing a quality and annulling its opposite.

NOTICE. Some say that things are four, entities, non-entities, states and relations (i'tibarat). The entities are like the essence of Zayd which we see; the non-entities are like your child before it is created; the states are like Being Powerful; and so, too, the relations, like the establishing of standing in Zayd. This--I mean that things are four--is the view which as-Sanusi follows in his Sughra, for he asserts in it the existence of states and makes the necessary qualities to be twenty. But elsewhere, he follows the opinion which denies states, and that is the right view.

According to that view, the Qualities are thirteen in number, because the seven derived qualities--God's Being Powerful, etc., drop out. God has no quality called Being Powerful, because the right view is denial that states are things. According to this, then, things are three:--entities, non-entities and relations. Then when the seven derived qualities drop out from the twenty necessary qualities, seven drop also from the opposites, and there is no quality called, Being Weak, etc., and there is no need to number these among the impossibilities. So, the impossibilities are thirteen also; at least, if existence is reckoned as a quality. That it should be is the opinion of all except al-Ash'ari. But the opinion of al-Ash'ari was that Existence is the self (ayn) of an entity. So, the existence of God is the self of His essence and not a quality. The necessary qualities, on that view, are twelve. Priority and Continuance and Difference and Self-subsistence --expressed also as Absolute Independence--and Unity and Power and Will and Knowledge and Life and Hearing and Seeing and Speech; and the derived qualities drop out, because their existence is based upon the view that there are things called states; but the right view is the opposite.

And if you wish to instruct the commonalty in the qualities of God, then state them as names (asma) derived from the qualities just mentioned. So it is said that God is an Entity, Prior, Different from originated things, Independent of everything, One, Powerful, a Willer, a Knower, Living, a Hearer, a Seer, a Speaker. And they should knew their opposites.

And know that some of the Shaykhs distinguish between states and relationships and say of both that they are not entities and also not non-entities. But each has a reality in itself, except that a state has a connection with and a subsistence in an essence, and a relation has no connection with an essence. And it is said that a relation has a reality outside of the mind. But to this it is opposed. that a relation is a quality, and if it has no connection with an essence and has a reality outside of the mind, where is the thing qualified by it? A quality does not subsist in itself, but must needs have a thing which it qualifies. So the truth is that relations have

[190]

no reality except in the mind. And they are of two kinds; the invented relation (i'tibara ikhtira'i), it is that which has no ground in existence, as your making a generous man niggardly; and second, the apprehended relation (intiza'i, claiming), it is that which has ground outside of your mind, as asserting the subsistence of Zayd, for that may be claimed from your saying, "Zayd subsists"; so the describing of Zayd as subsisting is existent outside of your mind.

The forty-first Article is Possibility in the case of God. It is incumbent upon every mukallaf that he should believe that it is possible for God to create good and evil, to create Islam in Zayd and unbelief in Amr, knowledge in one of them and ignorance in the other. And another of the things, belief in which is incumbent upon every mukallaf, is that the good and the bad of things is by Destiny (qada) and Decree (qadar). And there is a difference of opinion as to the meaning of destiny and decree. It is said that destiny is the will of God and the eternal (azali) connection of that will; and decree is God's bringing into existence the thing in agreement with the will. So the Will of God which is connected eternally with your becoming a learned man or a Sultan is destiny; and the bringing knowledge into existence in you, after your existence, or the Sultanship, in agreement with the Will, is decree. And it is said that destiny is God's eternal knowledge and its connection with the thing known; and decree is God's bringing things into existence in agreement with His knowledge. So, God's knowing that which is connected eternally with a person's becoming a learned man after he enters existence is destiny, and the bringing knowledge into existence in that man after he enters existence is decree. And according to each of those two views, destiny is prior (qadim), because it is one of the qualities of God, whether Will or Knowledge; and decree is originated, because it is bringing into existence, and bringing into existence is one of the connections of Power, and the connections of Power are originated.

And the proof that possibly things are possible in the case of God is that there is general agreement on their possibility. If the doing of any possible thing were incumbent upon God, the possible would be turned into a necessary thing. And if the doing of a possible thing were hindered from Him, the possible would be turned into an impossible. But the turning of the possible into a necessary or an impossible is false. By this, you may know that there is nothing incumbent upon God, against the doctrine of the Mu'tazilites, who say that it is incumbent upon God to do that which is best (salah) for the creature. So, it would be incumbent upon Him that He should sustain the creature, but this is falsehood against Him and a lie from which He is far removed. He creates faith in Zayd, for example, and gives him knowledge out of His free grace, without there being any necessity upon Him. And one of the arguments which may be brought against the Mu'tazilites is that afflictions come upon little children, such as ailments and diseases. And in this there is not that which is best for them. So, if doing that which is best is incumbent upon Him, why do afflictions descend upon little children? For they say that God could not abandon that which is incumbent upon Him, for abandoning it would be defect, and God is far removed from defect, by Agreement. And God's rewarding the obedient is a grace from Him, and His punishing the rebellious is justice from Him. For obedience does not advantage Him, nor rebellion injure Him; He is the Advantager and the Injurer. And these acts of obedience or rebellion are only signs of God's rewarding or punishing those described by them. Then him whom He wills to draw near to Himself, He helps to obedience: and in him whose abandoning and rejection He wills, He creates rebellion. And all acts of good and bad are by the creation of God, for He creates the creature and that which the creature does, as He has said (Qur. 37, 94), "and God hath created you and that which ye do."

And the belief is also incumbent that God may be seen in the Other World by believers, for He has joined the seeing (ru'ya) of Him with the standing fast of the mountain in His saying (Qur. 7, 139), "And if it standeth fast in its place, thou wilt see Me." And the standing fast of the mountain was possible: then, that which is connected with it of seeing must also have been possible; because what is connected with the possible is possible. But our seeing God must be without inquiring how (bila kayfa); it is not like our seeing one another. God is not seen in a direction, nor in a color, nor in a body; He is far removed from that. And the Mu'tazilites--may God make them vile!--deny the seeing of God. That is one of their perverse and false articles of belief. And another of their corrupt articles is their saying that the creature creates his own actions. For this, they are called Qadarites, because they say that the actions of the creature are by his own qudra (power), just as the sect which holds that the creature is forced to the action he does, is called Jabrite, derived from their holding a being forced (jabr) on the part of the creature, and a being compelled. It, too, is a perverse article. And the truth is that the creature does not create his own actions and is not forced, lull. that God creates the actions which issue from the creature, along with the creature's having a free choice (ikhtiyar) in them. As-Sa'd [Sa'd ad-Din at-Taftazani, see above] said, in his commentary on the Articles, "It is not possible to render this free choice by any expression, but the creature finds a difference between the movement of his baud when he moves it himself and when the wind moves it against his will."

And to that which is possible in God belongs also the sending of a number of Apostles (rasuls). And God's sending them is by His grace, and by way of necessity, as has preceded.

[192]

And it is necessary to confess that the most excellent of created beings, absolutely, is our Prophet [Muhammad], and there follow him in excellency the rest of the Endowed with Earnestness and Patience (ulu-l-azm; see Qur. 46, 34); they are our Lord Ibrahim, our Lord Musa, our Lord Isa, and our Lord Nuh; and this is their order in excellency. And that they are five along with our Prophet, and four after him is the correct view. And it is said. too, that the Endowed with Earnestness and Patience are more numerous. And there follow them in excellency the rest of the Apostles. Then, the rest of the Prophets (nabis), then the Angels.

And it is necessary to confess that God has aided them with miracles (mu'jizat) and that He has distinguished our Prophet in that he is the seal of the Apostles, and that leis law (shar) will not be abrogated till time is fulfilled. And Isa, after his descent, will judge according to the law of our Prophet. It is said that he will take it from the Qur'an and the Sunna. It is said also that he will go to the Glorious Tomb [of Muhammad] and learn from him. And know that he will abrogate one part of the law of our Prophet with a later part, just as the waiting period of a woman after the death of her husband was changed from a year to four months and ten days. And in this there is no defect.

And it is necessary also that every mukallaf, male and female, should know in detail the Apostles who are mentioned in the Qur'an, and should believe in them in detail. As for the other Prophets, belief is necessary in them as a whole. As-Sa'd handed down an authority in his commentary on the Maqasid that belief in all the Prophets as a whole suffices, but he was not followed.

And someone put them into verse as follows:

"There is imposed upon every mukallaf a knowledge
Of Prophets in detail, who have been named
In that document of ours [i.e., the Qur'an]. Of them are eight
After ten [i.e., eighteen]. And there remain seven who are
Idris, Hud, Shu'ayb, Salih, and similarly,
Dhu-l-Kifl, Adam, with the Chosen One [Muhammad] they close."

And it is necessary to confess that the Companions (sahibs) of the Prophet are the most excellent of the generations. Then their followers (tabi's); then the followers of their followers. And the most excellent of the Companions is Abu Bakr, then Umar, then Uthman, then Ali--in this order. But al-Alqami said that our Lady Fatima and her brother, our Lord Ibrahim, were absolutely more excellent than the Companions, including the Four [Khalifas]. And our Lord Malik [ibn Anas] was wont to say, "There is none more excellent than the children of the Prophet." This

[193]

is that the confession of which is incumbent; and we will meet God confessing it, if it is His Will.

And of that the confession of which is also necessary, is that the Prophet was born in Mecca and died in al-Madina. It is incumbent on fathers that they teach that to their children. Al-Ajhuri said, "It is incumbent on the individual that he know the genealogy of the Prophet on his father's side and on his mother's." A statement of it will come in our Conclusion, if God will. The learned have said, "Every individual ought to know the number of the children of the Prophet and the order in which they were born, for an individual ought to know his Lords, and they are the Lords of the People." But they do not explain, in what I have seen, whether that is required (mawjub) or desired (mandub); the analogy (qiyas) of things similar to it would say it was required. His children were seven, three male and four female, according to the right view. Their order of birth was: al-Qasim, he was the first of his children, then Zaynab, then Ruqayya, then Fatima, then Umm Kulthum, then Abd Allah, he had the to-names (laqab) at-Tayyib and at-Tahir, which are to-names of Abd Allah, not names of two other different persons. These were all children of our Lady Khadija. And the seventh was our Lord Ibrahim, born of Mariya, the Copt. So it stands. Let us now return to the conclusion of the Articles.

The Forty-second is the Veracity (sidq) of the Apostles in all their sayings.

The Forty-third is their trustworthiness (amana), that is, their being preserved (isma) from falling into things forbidden (muharram) or disliked (makruh).

The Forty-fourth is their Conveying (tabligh) to the creatures that which they were commanded to convey. The Forty-fifth is intelligence (fatana). These four things are necessary in the Apostles in the sense that the lack of them is unthinkable. And Faith depends on the knowledge of these, according to the controversy between as-Sanusi and his opponents.

The opposites of these four are impossible in the Apostles, that is, Lying (kidhb), Unfaithfulness (khiyana) in a thing forbidden or disliked, Concealment (kitman) of a thing they have been commanded to convey, and Stupidity (balada). These four are impossible in them, in the sense that the existence of them is unthinkable. And Faith depends upon the knowledge of these, as has preceded.

These are Nine and Forty Articles and the Fiftieth is the possibility of the occurrence of such fleshly accidents in them as do not lead to defect in their lofty rank.

[194]

And the proof of the existence of Veracity in them is that if they were to lie, then information from God would be a lie, for He has guaranteed the claim of the Apostles by the manifestation of miracles at their hands. For the miracle is revealed in place of an utterance from God, "My servant is truthful in all that he brings from Me." That is, whenever an Apostle comes to his people and says, "I am an Apostle to you from God," and they say to him, "What is the proof of your apostolate?" then he shall say, "The splitting of this mountain," for example. And when they say to him, "Bring what you say," God will split that mountain at their saying, as a guarantee of the claim of the Apostle to the apostolate. So, God's splitting the mountain is sent down in place of an utterance from God, "My servant is truthful in all which he brings to you from Me." And if the Apostle were lying, this information would be lying. But lying is impossible in the case of God, so lying on the part of the Apostles is impossible. And whenever lying is denied in them, Veracity is established.

And as for the proof of the Trustworthiness, that is, their being preserved internally and externally from forbidden and disliked things; if they were unfaithful in committing such things, we would be commanded to do the like. But it is impossible that we could be commanded to do a forbidden or disliked thing, "for God does not command a vile thing" (Qur. 7, 27). And it is evident that they did nothing except obedience, whether required or desired, and "permitted" (mubah) things entered among their actions only to show, whenever they did a "permitted" thing, that it was allowable (ja'iz.)

And as for the proof of Intelligence, if it were failing in them, how would they be able to establish an argument against an adversary? But the Qur'an indicates in more than one place, that they must establish arguments against adversaries. And such establishing of arguments is only possible with intelligence.

And the proof that fleshly accidents do befall them is that they do not cease to ascend in their lofty rank; for the occurrence of such accidents is in them for increase in their lofty rank, for example, and that others may be consoled, and that the thoughtful may know that the world is not a place of recompense for the lovers of God; since if it were, why should aught of the defilements of the world befall the Apostles? The Blessing of God be upon them and upon their Mighty Head, our Lord Muhammad, and upon his family and companions and descendants, all!

The Fifty Articles are completed with their Glorious Proofs.

Let us mention to you now somewhat of that which must be held of the things whose proofs are authority (sam'i): Know that it must be believed that our

[195]

Prophet has a Tank (hawd); and ignorance as to whether it is on one side or the other of the Bridge (as-sirat) does not hurt. On the Day of Resurrection (yawm al-qiyama) the creatures will go down to drink of it. It is different from al-Kawther, which is a River in the Garden.

And it must also be believed that he will make intercession (shafa'a) on the Day of Resurrection in the midst of the Judgment, when we shall stand and long to depart, even though it be into the Fire. Then he shall intercede that they may depart from the Station (mawqif); and this intercession belongs to him only.

And it mast also be believed that falling into great sins (kabiras), other than Unbelief (kufr), does not involve Unbelief, but repentance (tawba) from the sin is necessary at once; and if the sin be a small one (saghira) repentance is necessary to him who is liable to fall into it. And repentance is not injured by returning to sin; but for the new sin a new repentance is necessary.

And it is incumbent upon the individual that he set aside arrogance (kibr) and jealousy (hasad) and slander (ghiba) on account of what the Prophet has said, "The gates of the Heavens have curtains which reject the works of the people of arrogance, jealousy and slander." That is, they prevent them from rising, and so they are not received. Jealousy is a desiring that the well-being of another should pass away, equally whether it is desired that it should come to the jealous one or not. And arrogance is considering the truth to be falsehood and rejecting it, and despising God's creation. And it is incumbent also upon him that he should not spread malicious slanders among the people, for a tradition has come down, "A slanderer (qattat) shall not enter the Garden." And jealousy is forbidden, as is said above, when the well-being does not lead its possessor to transgression, and if it does, then desire that the well-being should pass away is allowable.

It is necessary also to hold that some of those who commit great sins will be punished, though it is only one of them.

CONCLUSION. Faith (iman), in the usage of the language, is acknowledgment that something is true (tasdiq), in general. In that way it is used by God, when he reports the words of the sons of Ya'qub (Qur. 12, 17). "But thou dost not believe us [art not a believer (mu'min) in us]." Legally, it is belief in all that the Prophet has brought. But there is a difference of opinion as to the meaning of belief, when used in this way. Some say that it means knowledge (ma'rifa) and that everyone who knows what the Prophet has brought is a believer (mu'min). But this interpretation is opposed by the fact that the unbeliever (kafir) knows, but is not a believer. Nor does this interpretation agree with the common saying, that the muqallad is a believer, although he does not know. And the right view as to the

[196]

interpretation of belief is that it is a mental utterance (hadith an-nafs) following conviction, equally whether it is conviction on account of proof, which is called knowledge, or on account of acceptance on authority (taqlid). This excludes the unbeliever because he does not possess the mental utterance, the idea of which is that you say, "I am well pleased with what the Prophet has brought." The mind of the unbeliever does not say this. And it includes the muqallad; for he possesses the mental utterance following conviction, though the conviction is not based on a proof.

And of that which must be believed is the genealogy of the Prophet, both on his father's side and on his mother's. On his father's side he is our Lord, Muhammad, son of Abd Allah, son of Abd al-Muttalib, son of Hashim, son of Abd Manaf, son of Qusay, son of Kilab, son of Murra, son of Ka'b, son of Lu'ay, or Luway, son of Ghalib, son of Fihr, son of Malik, son of Nadr, son of Kinana, son of Khuzayma, son of Mudrika, son of Alyas, son of Mudar, son of Nizar, son of Ma'add, son of Adnan. And the Agreement (ijma) unites upon this genealogy up to Adnan. But after him to Adam there is no sure path in that which has been handed down. And as to his genealogy on his mother's side, she is Amina, daughter of Wahb, son of Abd Manaf, son of Zuhra--this Abd Manaf is not the same as his ancestor on the other line--son of Kilab, who is already one of his ancestors. So the two lines of descent join in Kilab.

And it is necessary also to know that he was of mixed white and red complexion, according to what some of them have said.

This is the last of that which God has made easy by His grace. His Blessing be upon our Lord Muhammad and upon his family and his Companions and his descendants, so long as the mindful are mindful of him and the heedless are heedless of the thought of him. And Praise belongeth unto God, the Lord of the Worl

VII

ANALYSIS OF THE Taqrib OF ABU SHUJA AL-ISPAHANI 1

Book I. Of Ceremonial Purity (Tahara)

1. The water which may be used for ceremonial ablutions.

2. Legal materials for utensils; what can be purified and what cannot.

3. The use of the toothpick.

[197]

4. Description of the different stages of a ceremonial ablution (wudu).

5. On cleansing from excrement and its ritual generally.

6. The five things which require a fresh wudu.

7. The six things which require a complete ablution of the whole body (ghusl) and its ritual.

8. The seventeen occasions on which a ghusl is prescribed.

9. When it is allowable to wash the inner shoes (khuffs) instead of the feet.

10. The conditions and ritual for the use of sand (tayammum) instead of water.

11. On uncleannesses (najasat) and how and how far they can be removed.

12. On ailments of women; duration of pregnancy and their conditions.

Book II. Of Prayer

1. The times of prayer (salat).

2. Upon whom prayer is incumbent, and

3. On what occasions.

4. The antecedent requirements of prayer.

5. The eighteen essential parts of prayer.

6. The four things in which the prayer of a woman differs from that of a man.

7. The eleven things which nullify prayer.

8. A reckoning of the occurrences of certain frequently repeated elements in prayer.

9. On omissions in prayer.

10. The five occasions on which prayer is not allowable.

11. The duty and ritual of congregational prayer.

1. The conditions for the fast (siyam); its description; what breaks it.

2. What is meritorious in fasting; when and for whom it is forbidden; how breaking the fast must be expiated.

3. The conditions and nature of religious retreat (i'tikaf).

Book V. Of the Pilgrimage

1. The conditions of pilgrimaging (hajj); its essentials and other elements.

2. The ten things forbidden on pilgrimage.

3. The five sacrifices of the pilgrimage.

Book VI. Of Barter and Other Business Transactions

1. Conditions and kinds of barter (bay); what may be bartered and what not.

2. Description and conditions of the bargain with payment in advance (salam).

3. Of pledging (rahn).

4. Of those who are not to be permitted to administer their own property (hajar as-safih).

5. Of bankruptcy and composition and common rights in a highway (sulh).

6. The conditions for the transfer of debts and credits (hawala).

7. Of security for debts (daman).

8. Of personal security for debts (kafala).

9. Of partnership (shirka).

10. Of agency (wakala).

11. Of confession (iqrar).

12. Of loans (i'ara).

13. Of illegal seizure and use of property; indemnity for it and its damage (ghasb).

[200]

[201]

5. On the wedding feast (walima).

6. On the equality of the rights of the wives and the authority of the husband.

7. On divorce for incompatibility (khul).

8. The forms of divorce (talaq).

9. On taking a wife back and the three-fold divorce.

10. The oath not to cohabit (ila).

11. The temporary separation by the formula, zihar Qur. 58.

12. The form of accusation of adultery and the defence (li'an).

13. The period during which a previously married woman cannot remarry (idda).

14. Of relations with female slaves.

15. The support and behavior of a woman, divorced or a widow; mourning.

16. Law of relationship through suckling (irda).

17. The support (nafaqa) due to a wife.

18. The support due to children and parents, slaves and domestic animals.

19. Of the custody of children (hidana).

Book IX. Of Crimes of Violence to the Person (jinaya)

1. On murder, homicide and chance medley.

2. The lax talionis (qisas) for murder, and

3. For wounds and mutilations.

4. The blood-wit (diya).

5. Use of weak evidence in case of murder.

6. Personal penance for homicide.

Book X. Of Restrictive Ordinances of God (hadd)

1. Of fornication (zina) of one who. has been or is married (muhsan), and of one who has not been or is not married.

2. Of accusing of fornication.

3. Of drinking wine or any intoxicating drink.

4. Of theft.

5. Of highway robbery.

6. Of killing in defence.

7. Of rebelling against a just government.

8. Of apostasy.

9. Of abandoning the usage of prayer.

Book XI. Of the Holy War (jihad)

1. The general law of jihad.

2. The distribution of booty taken in the field (ghanima).

3. The law of the tax on unbelievers (fay).

4. The law of the poll-tax on unbelievers (jizya).

Book XII. Of Hunting and the Slaughter of Animals

1. How an animal may be killed in the chase or otherwise.

2. What flesh may be eaten.

3. The ritual of sacrifice (udhiya).

4. The ritual of sacrifice for a child (aqiqa).

Book XIII. Of Racing and Shooting with the Bow

Book XIV. Of Oaths and Vows (yamin, nadhr)

[203]

1. What oaths are allowable and binding; how expiated.

2. Lawful and unlawful vows.

Book XV. Of Judgments and Evidence (qada, shahada)

1. Of the judge (qadi) and court usage.

2. The division (qasm) of property held in common.

3. Of evidence and oaths.

4. The conditions of being a legal witness (adil).

5. The difference of claims (haqq), on the part. of God, and on the part of man, and their legal treatment.

Book XVI. Of Manumission of Slaves

1. General conditions of manumission (itq).

2. The clientship which follows (wala).

3. Of freeing at death (tadbir).

4. Of the slave buying his freedom (kitaba).

5. Of the slave (umm walad) that has borne a child to her master or to another and of her children.

Footnotes

351:1 See in bibliography, S. Keijzer, Précis, etc. Much help as to details of religious ritual and law will be found in Hughes's Dictionary of Islam, Sachau's Muhammedanisches Recht, Lane's Modern Egyptians, and commentary to his translation of the Arabian Nights, Burton's Pilgrimage, and Sell's Faith of Islam.

APPENDIX II

I. BOOKS AND ARTICLES, GENERAL AND FUNDAMENTAL, FOR THE STUDY OF ISLAM.

II. ON MUSLIM HISTORY AND ON PRESENT CONDITION OF MUSLIM WORLD.

III. ON MUSLIM TRADITIONS AND LAW.

IV. ON MUSLIM THEOLOGY, PHILOSOPHY AND MYSTICISM.

I

BOOKS AND ARTICLES, GENERAL AND FUNDAMENTAL, FOR THE STUDY OF ISLAM

The non-Arabist will gain much insight into Muslim life and thought by reading such translations as that of Ibn Khallikan by De Slane (Paris-London; 1843-71), the Persian Tabari, by Zotenberg (Paris; 1867-74), Ibn Batuta by Defrémery and Sanguinetti (Paris; 1853-58), Mas'udi by C. Barbier de Meynard and Pavet de Courteille (Paris; 1861-77), Ibd Khaldun's Prolégomènes by De Slane (Paris; 1862-68), ad-Dimishqi by Mehren (Copenhagen; 1874), al-Beruni's Chronology by Sachau (London; 1879).

The translations and notes in De Sacy's Chrestomathie arabe (Paris; 1826) can also be used to advantage.

Very many valuable articles will be found scattered through the Zeitschrift of the German Oriental Society (hereafter ZDMG), the Journal asiatique (hereafter JA), the Journal of the Royal Asiatic Society (hereafter JRAS) and the Vienna Zeitschrift für die Kunde des Morgenlandes (hereafter WZ).

It is always worth while to consult the Encyclopædia Britannica.

The best translations of the Qur'an into English are those by E. H. Palmer (2 vols., Oxford; 1880) and J. M. Rodwell (London; 1871). The first more perfectly represents the spirit and tone, and the second more exactly the letter. The commentary added by Sale to his version and his introduction are still useful.

The Thousand and One Nights should be read in its entirety in Arabic or in a translation by every student of Islam. English translation by Lane (incomplete but accurate and with very valuable commentary); Burton (last edition almost

[205]

complete; 12 vols., London: 1894). Payne's translation is complete, as is also Burton's privately printed edition; but, while exceedingly readable, Payne hardly represents the tone of the original. There is an almost complete and very cheap German version by Henning published by Reclaim, Leipzig); Mardrus' French version is inaccurate and free to such an extent as to make it useless. Galland's version is a work of genius; but it belongs to French and not to Arabic literature.

R. P. A. Dozy: Essai sur l'histoire de l'islamisme. Leyden, 1879. A readable introduction.

A. MÜLLER: Der Islam im Morgen-und-Abendland. 2 vols. Berlin, 1885, 1887. The best general history of Islam.

STANLEY LANE-POOLE: The Mohammedan Dynasties; chronological and genealogical tables with historical introductions. Westminster, 1894. An indispensable book for any student of Muslim history.

C. BROCKELMANN: Geschichte der arabischen Litteratur. 2 vols. Weimar, 1898, 1899. Indispensable for names, dates, and books, but not a history in any true sense.

T. B. HUGHES: A Dictionary of Islam. London, 1896. Very full of information, but to be used with caution. Based on Persian sources largely.

E. W. LANE: An Account of the Manners and Customs of the Modern Egyptians. First edition, London, 1836; third, 1842. Many others. Indispensable.

C. M. DOUGHTY. Travels in Arabia Deserta 2 vols. Cambridge, 1888. By far the best book on nomad life in Arabia. Gives the fullest and clearest idea of the nature and workings of the Arab mind.

J. L. BURCKHARDT: Notes on the Bedouins and Wahabys. 2 vols. London, 1831.

T L. BURCKHARDT: Travels in Arabia. 2 vols. London, 1829.

R. F. BURTON: Personal Narrative of a Pilgrimage to al-Madinah and Meccah. 2 vols. Last edition, London, 1898. On the Hajj and Muslim life, thought and studies generally in the middle of the nineteenth century. Readable and accurate to a degree.

C. SNOUCK HURGRONJE: Mekka. 2 vols. and portfolio of plates. Haag, 1888, 1889. Is somewhat dull beside Burton, but very full and accurate.

W. ROBERTSON SMITH Lectures on the Religion of the Semites. First Series. New edition, London, 1894. Kinship and Marriage in Early Arabia. Cambridge, 1885.

IGNAZ GOLDZIHER: Muhammedanische Studien. I, Halle a. S., 1889. II, 1890. Epoch-marking books; as are all Goldziher's contributions to the history of Muslim civilization.

ALFRED VON KREMER Geschichte der herrschenden Ideen des Islams. Leipzig, 1868.

ALFRED VON KREMER Culturgeschichte des Orients enter den Chalifen. 2 vols. Wien, 1875-77. Culturgeschichtliche Streifzüge. Leipzig, 1873.

EDWARD G. BROWNE: A Year Among the Persians. London, 1893. A most valuable account of modern Persian life, philosophy, and theology, and especially of Sufiism and Babism.

EDWARD G. BROWNE: A Literary History of Persia. New York, 1902. Really political and religious prolegomena to such a history.

G. A. HERKLOTS: Qanoon-e-Islam, or the Customs of the Moosulmans of India. London, 1832.

II

ON MUSLIM HISTORY AND ON PRESENT CONDITION OF MUSLIM WORLD

AUGUST MÜLLER: Die Beherrscher der Gläubigen. Berlin, 1882. A very brightly written sketch based on thorough knowledge.

GUSTAV WEIL: Geschichte der Chalifen. 3 vols. Mannheim, 1846-1851.

SIR WILLIAM MUIR: The Caliphate, its Rise, Decline and Fall. London, 1891.

THEODOR NÖLDEKE: Zur tendentiösen Gestaltung der Urgeschichte des Islâms. ZDMG, lii, pp. 16 ff. All Nöldeke's papers on the early history of Islam are worthy of the most careful study.

G. VON VLOTEN: Zur Abbasiden Geschichte. ZDMG, lii, pp. 213 ff. On the early Abbasids.

R. E. BRÜNNOW: De Charidschiten unter den ersten Omayyaden. Leyden, 1884.

EDUARD SACHAU: Über eine Arabische Chronik aus Zanzibar. Mitth. a.d. Sem. f. Orient. Sprachen. Berlin, 1898. On Ibadites.

GEORGE PERCY BADGER: History of the Imams and Seyyids of Oman, by Salîl-ibn-Razîk. London: Hakluyt Society, 1871. Valuable for Ibadite history, law and theology.

M. J. DE GOEJE: Mémoire sur les Carmathes du Bahraïn et les Fatimides. Leyden, 1886.

JOHN NICHOLSON: An Account of the Establishment of the Fatemite Dynasty in Africa. Tübingen and Bristol, 1840.

QUATREMÈRE: Mémoires historiques sur la dynastie des Khalifes Fatimites. JA, 3, ii.

SYLVESTRE DE SACY: Exposé de la religion des Druzes et la vie du Khalife Hakem-biamr-allah. 2 vols. Paris, 1838.

F. WÜSTENFELD: Geschichte der Fatimiden-Khalifen. Göttingen, 1881.

STANLEY LANE-POOLE: A History of Egypt in the Middle Ages. New York, 1901. For the origin and founding of the Fatimid Dynasty, the Khalifa al-Hakim, etc.

H. L. FLEISCHER: Briefwechsel zwischen den Anführern der Wahhabiten und dem Pasha von Damaskus. Kleinere Schriften, iii, pp. 341 ff. First published in ZDMG for year 1857.

E. REHATSEK; The History of the Wahhabys in Arabia and In India. Journal of Asiatic Society of Bengal. No. xxxviii (read January, 1880).

Turkey in Europe, by "Odysseus." London, 1900. The present situation, with its historical antecedents in European Turkey and the Balkans generally.

H. O. DWIGHT: Constantinople and its Problems. New York, 1901.

A. S. WHITE: The Expansion of Egypt. London, 1899. The present situation in Egypt and its historical antecedents.

W. W. HUNTER: Our Indian Mussulmans. London, 1871.

SIR LEWIS PELLY: The Miracle Play of Hasan and Husain. London, 1879.

W. S. BLUNT: The Future of Islam. London, 1880.

III

ON MUSLIM TRADITIONS AND LAW

The Mishkat, translated by Matthews. Calcutta, 1809. (A collection of traditions.)

The Hidaya, translated by C. Hamilton. II edition. London, 1870.

N. B. E. BAILLIE: A Digest of Muhammadan Law. Hanifi Code. London, 1865.

The same. Imameea Code. London, 1869. The first volume deals with Sunnite, the second with Shi'ite law.

S. KEIJZER: Précis de Jurisprudence Musulmane selon le rite Châfeite par Abu Chodja; texte arabe avec traduction et annotations. Leyden, 1859. To be used with caution.

EDUARD SACHAU: Muhammadanisches Recht nach Schafiitischer Lehre. Stuttgart & Berlin, 1897. Based largely on al-Bajuri's commentary to Abu Shuja; covers rather less than half the material of a corpus of canon law and is the best general introduction to the subject.

IGNAZ GOLDZIHER: Die Zâhiriten, ihr Lehrsystem und ihre Geschichte. Leipzig, 1884.

IGNAZ GOLDZIHER: Neue Materialien zur Litteratur des Ueberlieferungswesen bei den Muhammedanem. ZDMG, I, pp. 465 ff. Deals with Musnad of Ahmad ibn Hanbal.

IGNAZ GOLDZIHER: Zur Litteratur des Ichtilâf al-madhâhíb. ZDMG, xxxviii, pp. 669 ff. Contains a notice of ash-Sha'rani.

IGNAZ GOLDZIHER; Uber eine Formel in der judischen Responsen-litteratur. ZDMG, liii, pp. 645 ff. On fatwas and ijtihad.

IGNAZ GOLDZIHER: Das Princip des Istishab in muham. Gesetzwissenschaft. WZ, i, pp. 228 ff.

EDUARD SACHAU: Muhammedanisches Erbrecht nach, der Lehre der Ibaditischen Araber von Zanzibar und Ostafrika. Sitzungsberichte der kön. preuss. Akad., 1894.

EDUARD SACHAU: Zur ältesten Geschichte des muhammedanischen Rechts. Wien. Akad., 1870.

SNOUCK HURGRONJE: Le droit musulman. Revue de l'histoire des religions, xxxvii, pp. 1 ff, and 174 ff.

SNOUCK HURGRONJE: Muhammedanisches Recht nach schafiitischer Lehre von Eduard Sachau; Anzeige, ZDMG, liii, pp. 125 ff.

S. K. KEUN DE HOOGERWOERD: Studien zur Einführung in das Recht des Islam. Erlangen, 1901. Contains introduction and part of section on law of marriage. Gives a good but miscellaneous bibliography and is written from a Persian point of view; transliteration is peculiarly eccentric and Arabic scholarship is unsound.

J. WELLHAUSEN: Medina vor dem Islam. Muhammad's Gemeindeordnung von Medina. In "Skizzen und Vorarbeiten," Viertes Heft. Berlin, 1889.

HUART: Les Zindîqs en droit musulman. Eleventh Congress of Orientalists, part iii, pp. 69 ff.

D. B. MACDONALD: The Emancipation of Slaves under Muslim Law. American Monthly Review of Reviews, March, 1900.

IV

ON MUSLIM THEOLOGY, PHILOSOPHY AND MYSTICISM

THEODOR HAARBRÜCKER: Asch-Schahrastâni's Religionsparteien und Philosophenschulen übersetzt und erklärt, 2 vols. Halle, 1850-51. The Arabic text, without which Haarbrücker's German is sometimes hardly intelligible, was published by Cureton, London, 1846.

T. J. DE BOER: Geschichte der Philosophie im Islam. Stuttgart, 1901. Unsatisfactory but the best that there is. It is only a sketch and takes hardly sufficient account of theology and mysticism.

STANLEY LANE-POOLE: Studies in a Mosque. II edition. London, 1893. Miscellaneous essays, lightly written but trustworthy.

KREHL: Beiträge zur Characteristik der Lehre vom Glauben in Islam. Leipzig, 1877.

G. VON VLOTEN: Les Hachwia et Nabita. Eleventh Congress of Orientalists, part iii, pp. 99 ff. On early religious sects.

G. VON VLOTEN: Irdja. ZDMG, xiv, pp. 181 ff. On the Murji'ites.

EDUARD SACHAU: Uber de religiosen Anschauungen der ibaditischen Muhammedaner in Oman und Ostafrica. Mitth. a. d. Sem. f. Orient. Sprachen. Berlin, 1899.

H. STEINER: Die Mu'taziliten oder die Freidenker im Islam. Leipzig, 1865.

WILHELM SPITTA: Zur Geschichte Abu l-Hasan al-Ash'ari's. Leipzig, 1876. The best as yet on al-Ash'ari, but to be used with caution, especially in the translations of theological texts.

MARTIN SCHREINER: Zur Geschichte des Ash'aritenthums. In Actes du huitième Congress International des Orientalistes, I, i, pp. 77 ff. Leiden, 1891.

M. A. F. MEHREN: Exposé de la réforme de l'Islamisme commencée au troisième siècle de l'Hégire par Abou-l-Hasan Ali el-Ash'ari et continuée par son école. Third International Congress of Orientalists, vol. ii.

G. FLÜGEL: Al-Kindi genannt "der Philosoph der Araber." Ein Vorbild seiner Zeit und seines Volkes. Leipzig, 1857.

SIR WILLIAM MUIR: The Apology of al-Kindy, written at the court of al-Mâmûn. London, 1882.

E. SELL: The Faith of Islam. London, 1896. II edition. A valuable book, but from the point of view of an Indian missionary. Hence the tone is polemic and the technicalities are Persian rather than Arabic.

WALTER M. PATTEN: Ahmad ibn Hanbal and the Mihna. Leyden, 1897. There is a valuable review by Goldziher in ZDMG. lii, pp. 155 ff. It traces connection of Hanbalites with Ibn Taymiya and Wahhabites.

HEINRICH RITTER: Ueber unsere Kenntniss der Arabischen Philosophie. Göttingen, 1844.

FRIEDRICH DIETERICI: Alfarabi's phitosophische Abhandlungen herausgegeben. Leiden, 1890. Aus den arabischen übersetzt. Leiden, 1892.

AL-FARABI: Der Musterstaat. Herausgegeben und Übersetzt von Frdr. Dieterici. Leiden, 1900.

G. FLÜGEL: Ueber Inhalt und Verfasser der arabisehen Encyclopädie der Ikhwan as-Safa. ZDMG, xiii, pp. 1 ff. See, too, an excellent article by August Müller in Ersch und Gruber, ii, 42, pp. 272 ff., and Stanley Lane-Poole in his Studies in a Mosque.

FRIEDRICH DIETERICI: Die Philosophie der Araber im X. Jahrhundert n. Chr. aus der Schriften der lauteren Brüder herausgegeben. Berlin and Leipzig, 1861-1879.

IGNAZ GOLDZIHER: Materialien zur Entwickelungs-geschichte des Sufismus. WZ, xiii, pp. 35 ff.

THEODOR NÖLDEKE: Sufi. ZDMG, xlviii, pp. 45 ff. On the derivation and early usage of the name Sufi.

ADELBERT MERX: Idee und Grundlinien einer allgemeinen Geschichte der Mystik. Heidelberg, 1893.

JOHN P. BROWN: The Derwishes or Oriental Spiritualism. London, 1868. A valuable but uncritical description of modern Turkish and Persian Darwishes.

SIR JAMES REDHOUSE: The Mesnevi of Jelal eddin ar-rumi translated into English. Book I. London, 1881. See, too, a translation by Whinfield, London, 1887, and an edition of selected ghazels from the Diwan with translation and valuable introduction by R. A. Nicholson, Cambridge University Press, 1898.

E. J. W. GIBB: A History of Ottoman Poetry. Vol. i. London, 1900. A valuable statement of the later Persian and Turkish mysticism and metaphysic on pp. 13-70.

E. H. PALMER: Oriental Mysticism. Cambridge, 1867.

CARRA DE VAUX: Avicenne. Paris, 1900. Contains an introductory sketch of philosophy and theology up to the time of Ibn Sina. Algazali. Paris, 1902. A continuation of the first.

A. VON KREMER: Uber die philosophischen Gedichte des Abul Ala Ma'arry. Wien, 1888.

A. VON KREMER: Gedichte des Abu-i-Ala Ma'arri. ZDMG, xxix, 304; xxx, 40; xxxi, pp. 471 ff.; xxxviii, 499 ff.

ABU-L-ALA AL-MA'ARRI: Letters Arabic and English, with notes, etc., edited by D. S. Margoliouth. Oxford, 1898. See, too, papers by R. A. Nicholson in JRAS, October, 1900, ff.; and by Margoliouth, for April, 1902.

E. FITZGERALD: The Ruba'iyat of Omar Khayyam. With a commentary by H. M. Batson and a biographical Introduction by

E. D. Ross. New York, 1900. The biography by Ross is the only at all adequate treatment of the life and times of Umar which yet exists. Of the Ruba'iyat themselves there are several adequate translations, e.g. by Whinfield, Payne and Mrs. Cadell.

MARTIN SCHREINER: Zur Geschichte der Polemik zwischen Juden und Muhammedanem. ZDMG, xlii, pp. 591 ff. Deals with Ibn Hazm and Fakhr ad-Din ar-Razi.

MARTIN SCHREINER: Beiträge zur Geschichte der theologischen Bewegungen in Islam. ZDMG, lii, pp 463 ff.; 513 ff.; liii, pp. 51 ff. A most valuable collection of materials with considerable gaps and imperfect digestion.

D. B. MACDONALD: The Life of al-Ghazzali. In the Journal of the American Oriental Society, vol. xx, pp. 71-132.

D. B. MACDONALD: Emotional Religion in Islam as affected by Music and Singing. Being a translation of a book of the Ihya of al-Ghazzali. In JRAS for April and October, 1901, and January, 1902.

MIGUEL ASIN PALACIOS: Algazel, dogmatica, moral, ascetica. Zaragoza, 1901.

C. BARBIER DE MEYNARD: Traduction nouvelle du Traité de Ghazzali, intitulé Le Preservatif de l'Erreur. In JA, vii, 9, pp. 5 ff.

T. J. DE BOER: Die Widersprüche der Philosophie nach al-Ghazzali und ihr Ausgleich durch Ibn. Roshd. Strassburg, 1894.

A translation of al-Ghazzali's Tahafut has been begun by Carra de Vaux in Le Muséon, xxviii, p. 143 (June, 1899).

IGNAZ GOLDZIHER: Materialien zur Kenntniss des Almohadenbewegung in Nordafrika. ZDMG, xli, pp. 30 ff.

IGNAZ GOLDZIHER: Die Bekenntnissformeln der Almohaden. ZDMG, xliv, pp. 168 ff.

ROBERT FLINT: Historical Philosophy in France and French Belgium and Switzerland. New York, 1894. Contains an excellent estimate of Ibn Khaldun as a philosophical historian.

A. VON KREMER: Ibn Chaldun and seine Culturgeschichte der islamischen Reiche. Wien, 1879.

ERNEST RENAN: Averroes et l'Averroisme. III edition. Paris, 1861. Reviewed by Dozy in JA, 5, ii, pp. 93 ff. This review contains a curious description of a Parliament of Religions at Baghdad about A.D. 1000.

Philosophie end Theologie von Averroes. Aus dem Arabischen übersetzt von M.J. Müller. München, 1875. The Arabic text was published by Müller in 1859.

LEON GAUTHIER: Ibn Thofail-Hayy ben Yaqdhan, roman philosophique. Texte arabe . . . et traduction française. Alger, 1900. There is an earlier edition of Ibn Tufayl's romance by the younger Pocock with a Latin version. Oxford, 1671.

M. A. F. MEHREN: Correspondance du Philosophe Soufi Ibn Sa'bin Abd oul-Haqq avec l'Empereur Frédéric II. de Hohenstaufen. In JA, vii, 14, pp. 341 ff.

S. GUYARD: Abd ar-Razzaq et son traité de la Prédestination et du libre arbitre. In JA, vii, 1, pp. 125 ff.

A. DE KREMER: Notice sur Sha'rany. In JA, vi, 11, pp. 253 ff.

G. FLUGEL: Scha'rani und sein Werk uber die muhammadanische Glaubenslehre. ZDMG, xx, p. 1 ff.

IGNAZ GOLDZIHER: Beiträge zur Litteraturgeschichte der Shi'a. Wien, 1874.

JAMES L. MERRICK: The Life and Religion of Mohammed, as contained in the Sheeah Traditions of the Ifyat-ul-Kuloob. Boston, 1850.

J. B. RULING: Beiträge zur Eschatologie des Islam. Leipzig, 1895.

L. GAUTHIER: Ad-dourra al-fakhira; la perle précieuse de Ghazali. Genève, 1878. In Arabic and French; a valuable account of Muslim eschatology.

M. WOLFF: Muhammedanische Eschatologie. Leipzig, 1872. In Arabic and German; an account of popular Muslim eschatology.

DEPONT ET CAPPOLANI: Les Confréries religieuses Musulmanes. Alger, 1897.

SNOUCK HURGRONJE: Les Confréries religieuses, la Mecque et le Panislamisme, in Revue de l'histoire des religions, xliv, pp. 262 ff.

APPENDIX III

For typographical reasons the smooth guttural Ha, the palatals Sad, Dad, Ta, Za, and the long vowels are indicated by italic. The same system is followed in the index.

CHRONOLOGICAL TABLE

A.H.

11	M.d.; Abu Bakr Kh.
13	'Umar Kh.
14	Battle of al-Qadisiya; fall of Jerusalem; al-Basra founded; fall of Damascus.
17	Al-Kufa founded; Syria and Mesopotamia conquered.
20	Conquest of Egypt.
21	Battle of Nahawand; Persia conquered.

23   'Uthman Kh.

30   Final redaction of the Qur'an.

35   'Ali Kh.

36   Battle of Carmel.

40   'Ali d.

41   Mu'awiya I. Kh.; Herat.

49   'Al-Hasan d.

56   Samarqand.

60   Schism of Ibadites from Kharijites.

61   Karbala & d. of al-Husayn.

73   Storm of Mecca & d. of 'Abd Allah b. Az-Zubayr.

74   Carthage.

80   Ma'bad executed.

81   M. b. al-Hanafiya d.

93   Toledo.

99-101 'Umar II. Kh.

110   Hasan al-Basri d.

114   Charles the Hammer at Tours (A. D. 732).

121 Zayd b. Zayn al-'Abidin d.

124 Az-Zuhri d.

127-132 Marwan II. Kh.

130 Jahm b. Safwan killed?

131 Wasil b. 'Ata d.

132 Fall of Umayyads; as-Saffah first 'Abbasid Kh.

134 First Ibadite Imam.

135 Rabi'a d.

136-158 Al-Mansur Kh.

138-422 Umayyads of Cordova.

140 Ibn al-Muqaffa' killed.

143 Halley's comet.

144 'Amr b. 'Ubayd d.?

145 Baghdad founded; 'A'isha d. of Ja'far as-Sadiq d.

147 Homage to al-Mahdi as successor in Kh.

148 Ja'far as-Sadiq d.

150 Abu Hanifa d.; trace of Sufi monastery in Damascus.

157 Al-Awza'i d.

158-169 Al-Mahdi Kh.; John of Damascus d.?

161   Sufyan ath-Thawri d.; Ibrahim b. Adham d.

165   Da'ud b. Nusayr d.

167   Bashshar b. Burd killed.

170-193 Harun ar-Rashid Kh.

172-375 Idrisids.

179   Malik b. Anas d. 68

A.H.

182   The Qadi Abu Yusuf d.

187   Fall of Barmecides; al-Fudayl b. 'Iyad d.

189   M. b. al-Hasan d.

198-218 Al-Ma'mun Kh.

200   Ma'ruf of al-Karkh d.; trace of Sufi monastery in Khurasan.

204   Ash-Shafi'i d.

208   Abu 'Ubayda d.; the Lady Nafisa d.

211   Theodorus Abucara d.

212   Decree that the Qur'an is created.

[218]

213   Thumama b. Ashras d.

215   Abu Sulayman of Damascus d.; 2nd decree.

218-234 The Mihna; Al-Mu'tasim Kh.

220   Ma'mar b. 'Abbad.

223   Fatima of Naysabur d.

226   Abu Hudhayl M. al-'Allaf d.

227   Bishr al-Hafi d.; al-Wathiq Kh.

231   An-Nazzam d.

232   Al-Mutawakkil Kh.

234   Decree that Qur'an is uncreated; Scotus Erigena transl. pseudo-Dionysius, A. D. 850.

240   Ibn Abi Duwad d.

241   Ahmad b. Hanbal d.

243   Al-Harith al-Muhasibi d.

245   Dhu-n-Nun d.; al-Karabisi d.

250-316 'Alids of Zaydite branch in north Persia.

255   Al-Jahiz d.

256   Ibn Karram d.

257   Al-Bukhari d.; Sari as-Saqati d.

260   Al-Kindi d.? M. b. al-Hasan al-Mutazar vanished.

261   Muslim d.; Abu Yazid al-Bistami d.

270   Da'ud az-Zahiri d.

273   Ibn Maja d.

275   Abu Da'ud as-Sijistani d.

277   Qarmatians hold fortress in Arab 'Iraq.

279   At-Tirmidhi d.

280   Zaydite Imams at as-Sa'da and San'a.

289   'Ubayd Allah al-Mahdi in North Africa.

295-320 Al-Muqtadir 'Abbasid Kh.

297   First Fatimid Kh.; al-Junayd d.

300   Return of al-Ash'ari.

303   An-Nasa'i d.; Al-Jubba'i d.

309   Al-Hallaj executed.

317   Umayyads of Cordova take title of Commander of the Faithful; Qarmatians in Mecca.

320-447 Buwayhids; al-Ash'ari d.?

322   Ibn ash-Shalmaghani.

331   At-Tahawi d.

332   Al-Mataridi d.

333-356 Sayf ad-Dawla.

334   Buwayhids in Baghdad; ash-Shibli d.

339   Return of Black Stone by Qarmatians; al-Farabi d.

356   Fatimids conquer Egypt; Cairo founded.

360   Ikhwan as-Safa fl.

362   Ibn Hani d.

381-422 Al-Qadir Kh.

386   Abu Talib al-Makki d.

388-421 Mahmud of Ghazna.

403   Al-Baqilani d.

408   Persecution of Mu'tazilites under al-Qadir.

         p. 370

A.H.

411   Al-Hakim Fatimid Kh. vanished; Firdawsi d.

428   Ibn Sina d.

434   Abu Dharr d.

440   Al-Beruni d.

447   Tughril Beg, the Saljuq, in Baghdad.

449   Abu-l-'Ala al-Ma'arri d.

450   Persecution of Ash'arites.

455   Alp-Arslan; Nizam al-Mulk Wazir; end of persecution of Ash'arites.

456   Ibn Hazm az-Zahiri d.

465   Al-Qushayri d.

478   Imam al-Haramayn d.

481   Nasir b. Khusraw d.

483   Hasan b. as-Sabbah seizes Alamut.

485   Nizam al-Mulk assass.

488   Al-Ghazzali leaves Baghdad.

505   Al-Ghazzali d.

515   'Umar al-Khayyam d.

516   Al-Baghawi d.

524   Ibn Tumart al-Mahdi d.

524-558 'Abd al-Mu'min.

524-667 The Muwahhids.

533   Abu Bakr b. Bajja d.

537   Abu Hafs an-Nassfi d.

538   Az-Zamakhshari d.

540   Yehuda Halevi d. = A.D. 1145.

546   Abu Bakr b. al-'Arabi d.

548   Ash-Shahrastani d.

558   'Abd al-Mu'min the Muwahhid d.

558   'Adi al-Hakkari d.

558-580 Abu Ya'qub the Muwahhid.

561   'Abd al-Qadir al-Jilani, founder of order of darwishes, d.

567   Conquest of Egypt by Saladin and end of Fatimids.

576   Order of Rifa'ites founded.

580   Abu Ya'qub d.

580-596 Abu Yusuf al-Mansur.

581   Ibn Tufayl d.

587   As-Suhrawardi executed.

589   Saladin d.

590   Abu Shuja' d.?

595   Ibn Rushd d.; Abu Yusuf al-Mansur the Muwahhid d.

601   Maimonides d. = A.D. 1204.

606   Fakhr ad-Din ar-Razi d.

620   Abu-l-Hajjaj b. Tumlus d.; Fakhr ad-Din b. 'Asakir d.; St. Francis of
        Assisi d. = A. D. 1226.

625-941 Hafsids at Tunis.

630-640 Ar-Rashid the Muwahhid.

632   'Umar b. al-Farid.

638   Ibn 'Arabi d.

648   Frederick II. d. = A.D. 1250.

654   End of Assassins by Mongols; Ash-Shadhili, founder of order of
        darwishes, d.

667   Ibn Sab'in d.; end of Muwahhids.

672   Jalal ad-Din ar-Rumi d.

675   Ahmad al-Badawi, founder of order of darwishes, d.

681   Ibn Khallikan d.

685   Al-Baydawi d.

693,   Muhammad An-Nasir, Mamluk Sultan, reg.

698-
708,
709-741

719   An-Nasr al-Manbiji d.?

724   Ibn Rushd is still studied at Almeria.

728   Ibn Taymiya d.; Meister Eckhart d. = A.D. 1328.

730   'Abd ar-Razzaq d.

756   Al-'Iji d; Heinrich Suso d.

791   At-Taftazani d.; an-Naqshbandi, founder of order of darwishes, d.

A.H.

808   Ibn Khaldun d.

857   Capture of Constantinople by Ottomans and office of Shaykh al-Islam created = A.D. 1453. Thomas á Kempis d. = A. D. 1471.

895   M. b. Yusuf as-Sanusi d.

907   Accession of Safawids.

922   Conquest of Egypt by Ottoman Turks.

945   Death of al-Mutawakkil, last 'Abbasid.

951   Beginning of Sharifs of Morocco.

973   Ash-Sha'rani d.

1201   'Abd al-Wahhab d. = A. D. 1787.

1205   Sayyid Murtada d.; al-Fudali fl. circ. 1220.

1252   Foundation of Brotherhood of as-Sanusi = A.D, 1837.

1260   Ibrahim al-Bajuri d.; Decree of Porte that apostate Muslims should not be put to death.

1275   Death of founder of Brotherhood of as-Sanusi = A.D. 1859.

CPSIA information can be obtained
at www.ICGtesting.com
Printed in the USA
LVHW100803280821
696342LV00011B/702